Complex Peace Operation
Civil–Military Relations

This book explores the impact of different civil–military structures on operational effectiveness in complex peace operations. Recent operations in Iraq, Afghanistan and Somalia are examples of grand failures to enforce peace and to promote democracy and development through international interventions. A missing variable in analyses of these conflicts hitherto has been the nature of the civil–military interface and its impact.

The principal argument of this book is that the civil–military interface should, ideally, be integrated within the interagency arena as well as within the defence ministry. Such integration has the potential to provide joint civil–military planning and comprehensive approaches to operations. It also creates mutual trust and understanding among officers and civil servants from different departments, agencies and units, and thereby, a co-operative interagency culture. For the civil–military interface to function effectively within the chain of command during operations, a co-operative culture of trust is essential. Crucially, structurally and culturally integrated civil–military structures are likely to provide a more balanced view of the functional imperative of the armed forces. The results are armed forces fit for whatever purpose the political leadership decides for them – including complex peace support operations. Empirically, the book applies the theoretical framework to a comparative study of US and British patterns of civil–military relations, their strategic cultures and their operations in Iraq.

This book will be of much interest to students of peace operations, civil–military relations, humanitarian intervention and security studies/IR in general.

Robert Egnell is a lecturer in War Studies at the Swedish National Defence College and a senior researcher at the Swedish Defence Research Agency. He was awarded the 2008 Kenneth N. Waltz Dissertation Prize for the best thesis in the field of international security.

Routledge military studies

Complex Peace Operations and Civil–Military Relations

Winning the peace

Robert Egnell

Routledge
Taylor & Francis Group

LONDON AND NEW YORK

First published 2009
by Routledge
2 Park Square, Milton Park, Abingdon, Oxon, OX14 4RN

Simultaneously published in the USA and Canada
by Routledge
711 Third Avenue, New York, NY 10017

Routledge is an imprint of the Taylor & Francis Group, an informa business

First issued in paperback 2011

Typeset in Times by Wearset Ltd, Boldon, Tyne and Wear

British Library Cataloguing in Publication Data
A catalogue record for this book is available from the British Library

Library of Congress Cataloging in Publication Data
Egnell, Robert.
Complex peace operations and civil-military relations : winning the
peace / Robert Egnell.
    p. cm.
Includes bibliographical references and index.
1. Civil-military relations–United States–History–21st century.
2. Civil-military relations–Great Britain–History–21st century.
3. United States–Military policy. 4. Great Britain–Military policy.
5. Iraq War, 2003– 6. Iraq–Strategic aspects. I. Title.
JK330.E46 2009
355.4'9–dc22   2008052258

ISBN10: 0-415-49023-5 (hbk)
ISBN10: 0-415-66509-4 (pbk)
ISBN10: 0-203-87623-7 (ebk)

ISBN13: 978-0-415-49023-8 (hbk)
ISBN13: 978-0-415-66509-4 (pbk)
ISBN13: 978-0-203-87623-7 (ebk)

For my family

Contents

PART IV
Comparative analysis   149

Acknowledgements

Writing this book has in many ways been a labour of love. However, it would have been an impossible task without the essential support from a number of individuals and institutions. My greatest intellectual debt is to Professor Christopher Dandeker, whose multidisciplinary and uniquely rich approach to military studies has been a constant inspiration since I first arrived at King's College London as a Masters student in 2002. Not only did Professor Dandeker encourage me to take on the challenge of doctoral studies. By always encouraging, being thought-provoking, and prepared to give up his time, he was also an exemplary supervisor. He is a true source of inspiration for my own academic ambitions, and I am truly grateful that our relationship has continued and grown despite the loss of formal ties. There are a number of people who have provided important and very helpful feedback at different stages of the process. I would, therefore, like to express my sincere gratitude to Mats Berdal, Christopher Coker, Pascal Vennesson, John Mackinlay, Barrie Paskins, and last, but not least, my anonymous reviewers.

I would also like to gratefully acknowledge the financial support of the School of Social Science and Public Policy, King's College London, which funded my research with a generous scholarship and additional travel grants. Without the generous financial support and encouragement from Helge Ax:son Johnson's Foundation, the Foundation for the Memory of Lars Hierta, Erik and Johan Ennerfeldt's Fund and the Swedish Defence Forces, the necessary research trips would not have been possible. Finally, special thanks go to my employer during the final process, the Swedish Defence Research Agency (FOI), which has been kind enough to allow me to revise the manuscript during work hours.

I would also like to thank the Department of Political Science and Public Administration at the University of Dar es Salaam, Tanzania, as well as the Department of War Studies at the Swedish National Defence College for providing the necessary institutional homes during my years away from London. Without the friendly and stimulating environments of these institutions, my work would have been tremendously more difficult.

I have, of course, learnt a great deal from countless conversations with colleagues and friends, but I am particularly indebted to Adam Grissom, Martin Kimani, Jeff Michaels, Jan Ångström and Peter Haldén for infinite discussions on much more than our research topics. I can only hope we can find the time to continue these discussions in the future. Adam and Jeff also deserve special thanks for helping to arrange a research trip to Washington DC. I am also deeply grateful to my family who have been incredibly supportive throughout this long process. My wife Ditte has not only been an intellectual sounding board, but has, more importantly, managed the task of keeping me on track towards the completion of the book. This book is, therefore, dedicated to my parents, my wife and our two wonderful boys.

Part I
Setting the scene

1 Introduction

Effectiveness in complex peace operations

Despite a massive effort, stability in Iraq remains elusive and the situation is deteriorating. The Iraqi government cannot now govern, sustain, and defend itself without the support of the United States.... The ability of the United States to shape outcomes is diminishing. Time is running out.

The Iraq Study Group, December 2006

The conclusion of *The Iraq Study Group Report* was published almost four years after the invasion of Iraq. Despite the enormous efforts by the US and her main coalition partner, the UK, at that time, the campaign in Iraq had constituted nothing less than a failure. Since then, the situation has clearly improved, but despite military successes during the surge of 2007 that stabilized Iraq to an extent not seen since the invasion in 2003, the political breakthroughs and reconciliation processes that were the aims of the surge have not been realized. Successes at the tactical level are not translated into the strategic aims. The campaign in Iraq is by no means an exception. The post-Cold War era has presented the world's remaining great powers with a large number of internal and regional conflicts, failing states, massive human rights violations and global terrorism. The results of the responses to these challenges have been mixed at best, and it is clear that the failures in Somalia and Rwanda have made the more powerful and lasting impressions. In the new millennium, the trend towards interventions in complex emergencies has continued, and the security environment of the post-Cold War and post-9/11 context makes complex peace operations, as currently witnessed in Afghanistan and Iraq, the most likely and the most important military tasks. Therefore, understanding why the intervening powers have failed to achieve the strategic aims in these types of operations is of great importance. This book makes a significant contribution in this quest by introducing the variable of civil–military relations to explain operational effectiveness.

While a large number of factors can be mustered to explain the conduct and effectiveness of armed forces in military operations – the political nature of the state, strategic doctrine, military culture and history, the nature of the enemy, geography, training and equipment – this book studies the effect of the often overlooked factor of civil–military relations. Importantly, the patterns of civil–military relations in a state, although not the most obvious causal variable when explaining operational conduct, are more or less related to the majority of the factors mentioned above. Operating at an overarching level in the causal chain, this single variable, therefore, has the potential to relate and co-ordinate a large number of factors into a more comprehensive narrative, explaining effectiveness in complex operations. Thus, understanding the patterns of civil–military relations in states significantly helps increase the understanding of what causes military organizations to operate the way they do. Coupled with the nature of the contemporary strategic context, as well as strategic and tactical lessons learned from different forms of complex peace operations, the civil–military variable also helps explain the reasons why seemingly superior Western military organizations have struggled and even lost against guerrilla type asymmetric opponents.

The aim of this book is, therefore, to increase the understanding of the civil–military dimension of operational conduct and effectiveness in the context of complex peace operations. How do the patterns of civil–military relations affect the conduct and effectiveness of operations in the context of complex peace operations, and how can civil–military structures be improved for increased effectiveness during operations?

The principal argument of the book is that the nature of civil–military relations within a particular state has an important impact on the effectiveness of its armed forces within the contemporary strategic context of complex and irregular peace operations. More specifically, an integrated approach to civil–military relations that provides an extensive interagency system as well as integrated civil–military structures within the ministry of defence, is more likely to produce armed forces that are 'fit for purpose', and, consequently, effective during operations. There are two main reasons why integrated civil–military structures at the strategic level provide better results in complex peace operations. First, integrated structures provide more accurate and up-to-date interpretations and adjustment to the functional imperative of the armed forces. This means that the instruments of national power, not least the military, are better suited to deal with the particular challenges of the contemporary strategic context. Second, integrated structures provide more inclusive command and control structures at the strategic level of the operational chain of command, which means that all relevant actors in complex operations are co-ordinated through integrated assessment, planning and execution of operations – providing what is often referred to as a comprehensive approach to operations.

The policy implications are significant as they contradict the bureaucratic cultures of departmental stove-piping that are prevalent in most political systems. The multitude of tasks and the complexity of the political aims in contemporary peace operations mean that the different instruments of national power must be involved and co-ordinated during strategic assessment and planning for effective conduct in operations. This requires well-functioning interagency structures and a co-operative working culture of trust and mutual understanding. It also requires extensive civil–military integration within the defence ministries for multifunctional planning with the political objectives in mind. In short, multifunctional operations require integrated multifunctional bureaucracies – something that contradicts the traditional policy advice to separate political and military leaders and thereby achieve purity of both political and military affairs for maximized military effectiveness.

The implications for theory are equally significant. Strategic theory and analysis of military effectiveness must include the civil–military dimension as it is an essential variable. It can even be asked as to what extent it is relevant to speak of military operational effectiveness, or 'fighting power', in a context where operations are inherently multidimensional, involving diplomatic, military and economic aspects. A comprehensive view of operational effectiveness is more useful and the question should be whether a country's entire security apparatus is 'fit for purpose' and effective. The field of civil–military relations must also be expanded to include what this book calls the direct impact on effectiveness – the impact of the civil–military interface as an important level in the chain of command during operations. Another implication is that the normative Huntingtonian argument regarding the benefits of objective civilian control through a divide between the military and civilian leaderships is once more refuted.

The number of studies on civil–military relations in different countries, especially the US, is vast. Despite theoretical problems and limited applicability in the contemporary strategic context, the most important contributions to this literature remain Samuel Huntington's *The Soldier and the State* (1957) and Morris Janowitz's *The Professional Soldier* (1960). More recently, we should add Peter Feaver's important work *Armed Servants* (2003) to that list. Of course, the studies of military effectiveness in terms of strategy and operational conduct in Iraq from 2003 and other complex operations, such as Vietnam, Malaya, Kosovo and Bosnia, are equally plentiful. The contribution of this book lies in the marriage of these two fields of enquiry. By explaining effectiveness and operational conduct using the patterns of civil–military relations as the explanatory variable, this book increases the understanding of both fields. The field of civil–military relations has a weakness in the analytical overemphasis on civilian democratic control at the expense of military effectiveness (Nielsen 2005; Strachan 2006). Moreover, the impact of different patterns of civil–military relations during operations has not been explored. This is a serious gap in the literature on civil–military relations as well as in the field of strategic studies. Until important recent studies that have sought to explain why the seemingly more powerful actors sometimes lose against weaker enemies, the literature on strategy and military effectiveness has traditionally overemphasized the military and physical factors (Biddle 2004; Brooks 2003).

This book develops a new theoretical framework for analysis of how civil–military relations affect the conduct of operations in complex peace operations. In short, this framework argues that the organization of the civil–military interface affects the conduct of operations in two important ways: *directly*, by providing the highest levels in the chain of command – the level where strategic aims are set and operational plans made, and *indirectly* by being the arena in which decisions regarding size, culture, equipment and doctrine of the armed forces are made. In short the indirect impact influences the quality of the tools available to the political leadership for operations, while the direct impact determines the effectiveness with which these tools are employed. Without properly functioning civil–military relations, structurally as well as culturally, effectiveness in complex peace operations is, therefore, unlikely.

This framework is tested and refined in the book through the method of process tracing (George and Bennett 2004). Beyond the general discussion regarding causality, the empirical analyses seek to explain how specific patterns of civil–military relations affect operational conduct and effectiveness. To achieve that, the main section of the book involves the analyses of two cases: the United States and the United Kingdom. Each case involves the analyses of the patterns of civil–military relations, the strategic culture or the 'way of war', as well as the conduct and effectiveness of operations in Iraq from 2003. The case studies thereby involve two distinct patterns of civil–military relations. First, a divided approach is exemplified by the US case and involves limited interagency co-operation, a divided civil–military interface and military ownership of the functional imperative. Second, the integrated approach is exemplified by the British case, which involves relatively extensive interagency co-operation and civil–military integration within the Ministry of Defence, as well as civilian ownership of the functional imperative of the armed forces. The two cases are initially analysed separately, but in order to highlight the findings of the case studies, and to evaluate the assumptions of the theoretical framework, the book also includes a comparative analysis which compares and contrasts the findings of the case studies.

As mentioned, the analyses of the case studies show that the US is a clear example of the divided approach to civil–military relations, involving limited interagency co-operation, and a divided civil–military interface within the Department of Defense. Importantly, the functional imperative of the armed forces has always been defined by the military itself, which has meant limited political influence regarding the structure and culture of the military establishment. It has developed a rigid military culture and structure that is not well adjusted to face the challenges of the contemporary strategic context – complex peace operations. Reflecting the civil–military structures, the US system has always advocated purity of military and political advice to decision makers. The flaws of the US civil–military interface became obvious in Iraq as the operational plans failed to use the interagency apparatus and to co-ordinate the operational planning for all relevant actors – military and civilian. The US military culture, focused on conventional warfare, failed as it misinterpreted the operation at the strategic level in the planning process, and as the units in the field of operations were untrained, unprepared and unequipped for the more important post-conflict tasks.

The British case, although not as clear cut, is an example of the integrated approach to civil–military relations. It involves relatively extensive interagency co-operation and excellent civil–military integration within the Ministry of Defence. In the UK, the political leadership has always defined the functional imperative of the armed forces, and thereby, to a larger extent than in the US case, influenced the structure and culture of its armed forces. In contrast with the US case, the British system emphasizes integrated political and military advice and joint civil–military deliberation of issues before briefing the policy makers. British forces are, therefore, on the one hand flexible and adjustable to the political imperatives of the day, and, as a consequence, relatively well in synch with the demands of contemporary irregular warfare. On the other hand, the British armed forces are severely under-funded and undersized in relation to the tasks that the political leadership asks of them. In Iraq, Tony Blair circumscribed the traditional system of interagency committees which meant that the UK shared many of the strategic level planning mistakes with its coalition partner. In the field, British troops showed a familiar flexibility in adjusting to different situations and levels of threat. The inability to maintain enough troops in Iraq over time proved crucial in the failure to establish a safe environment in southern Iraq.

The study of American and British operational conduct in complex peace operations is intrinsically interesting as the two countries, for different reasons, are likely to participate in, and lead such operations in the future. The US has a particular role as the sole remaining military superpower and will in that role, as well as to protect its own interests and security, continue to be engaged in complex peace operations. The UK has a unique experience and capability of complex operations, including counter-insurgency. That experience, in combination with a large international presence, makes them likely to continue to engage in and lead operations of that kind, not least within the EU and/or NATO frameworks.

The design of the study, involving two cases and a comparative analysis, has created the possibility to contrast and compare different structures and methods of command and their effectiveness in contexts that have important similarities and differences. Again, the US and the UK are of great interest. Despite many relative similarities in culture and background, including extensive experience in both conventional large-scale warfare and counter-insurgency operations, the two countries operate very differently. They also have very different patterns of civil–military relations. Essentially, the cases were chosen based on their relevance to the theory of the book. They contain similarities and contrasts that make them helpful in understanding the causal relationship of the book (Denscombe 1998: 33).

The coalition's operations in Iraq have been chosen as the empirical testing ground of the book because it represents the latest and most interesting example of major powers conducting complex peace operations involving an asymmetric opponent. It also represents the complex far-reaching political aims often sought in contemporary operations, as well as the characteristics of a truly modern insurgency. Although a number of historical counter-insurgency campaigns are interesting in terms of reference for this book, they would not have provided the same contextual accuracy concerning contemporary irregular warfare. The case of Iraq also allows for a comparative analysis of US and British operational conduct within the same context, allowing for a number of different contextual variables to be isolated. It should, nevertheless, be emphasized from the beginning that, although US and British troops were, and are, operating within Iraq at the same time, the two armed forces actually operated within very different contexts. The Shia-dominated South where the British troops have operated is generally considered easier and less violent than the Sunni-dominated areas of the country where US troops are mainly operating. This problematic aspect of the empirical study is obviously further discussed in each of the case studies, as well as in the comparative Chapter 9.

Plan of the book

The book is constructed in four parts. The first part serves to set the scene and to construct a theoretical framework for analysis. Following this introductory chapter, Chapter 2 deals with the civil–military dimension of operational conduct by looking at the traditional theories of civil–military relations, as well as the concepts of mission command, trust and organizational culture. This review is concluded with the formulation of the theoretical framework to be utilized and refined within this scope of the book.

Part II of the book involves the case study of the United States. Chapter 3 looks at the history, culture and structure of civil–military relations in the US. This chapter, thereby, defines the independent variable of the patterns of civil–military relations in the US case. Chapter 4 examines the US way of war as well as its approach to complex peace operations. The aim of this chapter is to determine how the functional imperative is interpreted and if the US way of war is well adjusted to the contemporary strategic context. This involves the study of doctrinal content as well as reference to past operational experience. The final chapter in the US case study is an examination of its operations in Iraq. This analysis focuses on the planning process, the translation of political aims into military activity and the tactical behaviour of US troops. Have US troops conducted their operations in accordance with the US way of war? Have the operations been effective in relation to what is considered best practice in complex peace operations? Part III mirrors the US case study, but covers the British case in three chapters. Finally, Part IV of the book puts the data from the two cases together and provides a comparative analysis of the cases. The purpose is to evaluate the theoretical framework, and to draw conclusions regarding the impact of the different patterns of civil–military relations analysed in the book. This is achieved by comparing and contrasting the observations and conclusion of the study in relation to theory. A number of policy and theoretical implications are discussed in the concluding chapter.

Why complex peace operations?

Long gone is the hostile but stable and easily comprehensible Cold War environment. The conflicts of the new millennium seem ever more bewildering, complex and asymmetric. The last decade and a half has certainly seen the development of a plethora of studies on the changing nature of warfare. Much of the literature announces either the coming of 'New War', the proclamation of a generational shift in warfare, or declares the end of traditional large-scale warfare. Clearly, the fall of the Berlin Wall challenged the traditional strategic focus on large-scale interstate warfare. The challenge involved a shift of focus from great power conflict to civil wars and the management of small-scale conflicts. The greatest security challenges of today and the near future consist of failing states, rogue states, as well as regional insecurity with global repercussions, and the rise of global terrorism, which thrives in areas lacking political control.

The demise of large-scale conventional warfare is an important but disputed theme of the post-Cold War literature (Keegan 1993; van Creveld 1991; Smith 2005). 'War no longer exists' is the controversial opening statement of General Sir Rupert Smith's seminal work *The Utility of Force*. What Smith means by this is that traditional large-scale warfare has been replaced by irregular forms of confrontations, or what he calls war among the people. 'War, as cognitively known to most non-combatants, war as a battle in a field between men and machinery, war as a massive deciding event in a dispute in international affairs: such wars no longer exist' (Smith 2005: 1). Sir Lawrence Freedman, nevertheless, makes the sobering argument that while it is impossible to announce the end of major warfare, and the corresponding need to continue preparing for it, it remains clear that 'for the moment, the most perplexing problems of security policy surround irregular rather than regular war' (Freedman 2006: 7). The view that major warfare cannot be completely disregarded, but that different forms of irregular conflict are the more important in the near future, is a starting point of this study and the main reason why effectiveness in complex peace operations are at the forefront of the analysis.

Much of the debate regarding future warfare involves creating a suitable label for contemporary types of conflict. The critique of New War, or 4GW, is not so much about the content of the concepts, but more about the appropriateness of the label 'new' or the historical accuracy of the different generations of warfare. Frank Hoffman (2006) refreshingly argues that whatever form future warfare takes, it will not involve enemies 'choosing discrete options among conventional, irregular, catastrophic, or disruptive strategies'. Instead, a more likely scenario is the blurring of warfare categories. He calls this hybrid warfare, which includes any adversary capabilities used in custom-designed strategies and tactics to frustrate and impede Western efforts. Unnecessary categorization and labelling of conflicts may, therefore, be counterproductive in the understanding of them, and even more importantly, in the practical application of force in contemporary and future operations.

Nevertheless, to provide some clarity and consistency for the reader, this book uses the concept of *complex peace operation* to describe operations in the contemporary strategic context. The concept is used in a wide sense and thereby functions as an umbrella concept for most types of contemporary operations in which Western armed forces are most likely to find themselves involved in the near future. The concept includes the traditional concepts referring to different forms of operations other than war: complex irregular warfare, asymmetric warfare, stability and support operations, humanitarian interventions, small wars and low-intensity conflicts, as well as the many traditional concepts of peace operations: peacekeeping, peace enforcement and peace support operations. The concept of complex peace operations, as applied within this book, thereby captures the essential features of contemporary conflict without the historically imprecise connotations or generational shifts that are often announced within the New War literature. The concept, nevertheless, involves two important delimitations. The book avoids speaking of warfare in general as the term of complex peace operations serves to differentiate these types of operations from conventional large-scale warfare between nation states. The concept also serves to highlight the difference between complex peace operations and traditional forms of consent-based blue beret peacekeeping.

The use of complexity in the description of contemporary operations deserves some deliberation. What is complex and what is simple is relative and changes with time. This book does not apply the concept as it is used within science to describe the disorganized or organized complexity of a particular 'system' (Weaver 1948). Instead, a more general definition is used to characterize military operations with many actors, interests and activities. Further characteristics of complexity are the far-reaching, yet limited political aims of operations, as well as the importance of strategic narrative, global and local legitimacy – all taking place under the close scrutiny of real-time media coverage. IISS usefully refers to 'complex irregular warfare', highlighting complexity in terms of the physical, human and informational terrain. Operations are taking place in urban areas, among the civilian population, where it is difficult to distinguish friend from foe, and in which information flows and narratives are impossible to control (IISS 2008: 414).

In short, complex peace operations take place among the people and involve both sub-state and supra-state actors in a struggle for legitimacy and far-reaching political changes. For the most part, they involve low-intensity, counter-insurgency-type operations between the regular armed forces of the West and loosely formed networks of insurgents employing asymmetric tactics (Smith 2005; Hammes 2004; Kaldor 1999; van Creveld 1991). An important feature of contemporary conflict is asymmetry – of actors' will as well as means. In most smaller conflicts, one side, the great power, may have great means but often limited will because it is engaged in far away conflicts that do not threaten its homeland. This is contrasted with the other side, the local power or perhaps insurgency, in whose backyard the conflict occurs and which has limited means but is perceived to have a great will. Asymmetric warfare, therefore, means that the enemy adjusts itself to asymmetries by employing unconventional strategies like insurgencies or terrorist attacks (Freedman 2006). Contemporary conflicts and peace operations are also drawn out processes, often measured in decades rather than in months and years, involving a multitude of different actors, fighting for the hearts and minds of the local as well as the global population, whose perceptions of the conflict and the operation often determine the outcome (Smith 2005; Freedman 2006; Shaw 2005).

Moreover, all armed actors must reckon with comprehensive surveillance by global state institutions, law, markets, media and civil society (Shaw 2005). In the context of global surveillance, conflicts are fought under the critical gaze not only of the local population, and the people in intervening nations, but of the world as a whole. Such surveillance means that some tactics of the past are not politically acceptable in today's context where conveying the right message and winning hearts and minds of the local and the global populations are key features. Casualties must be minimized, laws adhered to and media managed. In particular, Western governments must pay constant attention to, and obviously also play by the rules of global surveillance, as these states generally make and enforce the rules (Shaw 2005). This is even more acute in the case of complex peace operations as they generally require higher levels of legitimacy in order to succeed.

Effectiveness in complex peace operations

The traits of contemporary and future complex peace operations, as briefly described above, create substantive new challenges for military organizations as well as the defence establishment as a whole, including the civil–military interface at the strategic level. Many of the strategies, tactics and organizations of conventional industrial warfare are obsolete. Applying traditional methods and organizations to new conflicts therefore risks leading to protracted conflicts and failure to achieve the political aims (Smith 2005: 306). This means a need for new thinking regarding what constitutes 'best practice' during operations. It also means a need for new takes on what military effectiveness is, how it can be studied, and how it can be improved.

What constitutes effectiveness?

What constitutes effectiveness in military organizations? This seems at first to be a simple matter. The semantic definition clearly implies that effectiveness should be related to the capability to achieve the desired outcomes of conflict – victory (Abrahamsson 2006). However, victory is not a characteristic of an organization, but rather a result of organizational activity. Therefore, outcome alone, or the more specific 'victory', is not a useful measure of effectiveness (Millet *et al.* 1986: 37). Outcomes in contemporary operations are also not about absolutes. The aims of contemporary military operations are changing from pursuing concrete military strategic objectives and 'victory' to establishing certain conditions from which political outcomes can be decided (Smith 2005: 269). In this context, battlefield victories, or other outcomes of military operations, are often only small parts of the comprehensive operations with far-reaching yet limited political aims. It is, therefore, more useful to speak in terms of success than of victory. A debate in the UK during the summer of 2007 has highlighted a more pragmatic approach to success among the military leadership. In June 2005 the British Chief of the General Staff, General Sir Richard Dannatt, spoke of the importance to achieve success in these theatres of Afghanistan and Iraq, interestingly adding: 'however you define success'. This pragmatic and flexible view of success stands in stark contrast to the traditional, absolutist view that requires victory.

Instead of analysing effectiveness in terms of outcomes, a more fruitful approach is to study the processes by which armed forces convert resources into fighting power: 'A fully effective military is one that derives maximum combat power from the resources physically and politically available' (Millet *et al.* 1986: 37). This means that effectiveness should also be related to the concept of *efficiency*. This concept is about the parsimony of resources, and is often the more important factor in the hierarchical bureaucracies of military organizations – 'doing more with less' (Snider and Watkins 2002: 9). While efficiency is often a precondition for effectiveness, it is certainly not sufficient. Effectiveness or goal attainment may also be achieved with little efficiency, as in the German airborne attack on Crete in 1941. While the Germans achieved the objective of defeating the British-led CREFORCE, and occupying Crete, the operation entailed severe losses and was considered a 'catastrophic victory' (Abrahamsson 2006: 15). Another problem with outcome as the measure of effectiveness is that contemporary operations often take place over a very long period of time. Waiting until the final verdict of history will thus deprive scholars of meaningful analysis until the very end of the campaign in question.

Effectiveness is, therefore, a combination of conduct and outcome. Outcome is evaluated through the course of history, but conduct can be measured on the spot by comparing it to what is considered best practice in operations. This book employs the concept of effectiveness as a measure of the quality of military conduct, and acknowledges that efficiency is an important part of this analysis, especially when the final outcome of operations is not applicable, as is the case in this book.

Traditional theories on military capability and effectiveness have overfocused on the physical military factor: numbers of troops and the quality of equipment, while paying less attention to the more intangible factors that influence state capacity to use its material resources effectively. The cases where the numerically and technologically weak win battles and campaigns, suggest that traditional explanations of military capability are misleading (Brooks 2003; Biddle 2004). In adhering to this broader view of military effectiveness, or 'fighting power', military theorists often describe military capability as a combination of physical factors (the means – meaning the size and materiel of the organization), conceptual factors (doctrine or the way the means are employed) and moral factors (the will of the soldiers) (Smith 2005). While most theorists agree upon the factors, they tend to emphasize them differently. As an example,

General Sir Rupert Smith gives greater importance to the moral and conceptual factors by creating the following formula:

$$Capability = Means \times Way^2 \times 3Will$$

The means available are multiplied by the way these means are used in relation to the opponent, again multiplied by the way, and finally multiplied by the morale or will times three. The way the means are used involves strategy, tactics and doctrine, and the will includes political will to employ force as much as the fighting morale of the forces (Smith 2005: 242).

Within this broader way of thinking about effectiveness, a large number of scholars have sought to explain and theorize military capability in relation to the often paradoxical outcomes in small wars, counter-insurgency operations and different forms of peace operations – the fact that physically and materially weak forces in Vietnam in the 1960s, Afghanistan in the 1980s and Somalia in the 1990s, Afghanistan and Iraq in the last decade, have been able to prevail and even achieve their objectives against substantially stronger opponents (see Merom 2003; Biddle 2004; Arreguin-Toft 2005; Angstrom and Duyvesteyn 2007).

While these studies and theories all contribute to a better understanding of the factors that determine military capability and effectiveness in complex peace operations, they fail to acknowledge the fact that engaging in these activities is seldom a solely military endeavour. Contemporary operations are inherently multifunctional and complex activities in which armed forces are but one tool in a toolbox also containing economic, social and political instruments of power. This means that a broader analytical perspective is necessary. Effectiveness in complex peace operations cannot be measured in military fighting power alone, but must also include traditionally civilian capabilities that also have an effect on the attainment of the political aims of operations. The sheer irrelevance of fighting power as a sole factor is perhaps best described by the infamous conversation between the American, Colonel Summers and Colonel Tu of the North Vietnamese Army: ' "You know, you never defeated us on the battlefield", said the American colonel. The North Vietnamese colonel pondered this remark a moment, "That may be so," he replied, "but it is also irrelevant" ' (Summers 1982: 1). The remarks also highlight the relevance of General Sir Richard Dannatt's (2007) pragmatic approach to 'some form of success' instead of the absolutist view of victory as the only measure of success.

Relating military effectiveness to that of the other instruments of power is one of the important contributions of this book as it uses civil–military relations as the point of departure in the study of operational conduct and effectiveness. However, as noted, effectiveness is complicated in that it involves both the outcome and conduct of operations. While outcome is difficult to measure in an ongoing conflict, conduct can be evaluated against what is considered best practice in certain contexts. In this book, such a list of best practices, or what we can call indicators of effectiveness, has been developed at the strategic as well as the tactical level, in order to provide a check list, against which the conduct and effectiveness of US and British operations in Iraq can be evaluated. Scholars, strategists and doctrine writers have somewhat different views regarding the content of such lists, but a reading of much of the contemporary strategic studies literature, as well as of military doctrines from different countries, actually reveals a surprising homogeneity in the field. The list below is, therefore, hardly controversial in any circles, although different actors are likely to emphasize the certain principles in different ways. The bulk of principles come from counter-insurgency doctrine, as that is often considered the actual nature of contemporary military operations (Mockaitis 2000). Importantly, the list is not exhaustive, but includes especially those indicators of effectiveness that are related to civil–military relations in some way. The strategic level factors included are:

1   the importance of clear and achievable political aims;
2   civil–military co-operation and co-ordination;
3   the importance of the strategic narrative.

The tactical level indicators somewhat overlap the strategic level and include:

1   civil–military co-operation in terms of unity of command and effort;
2   the hearts and minds approach – force protection and minimum use of force;
3   cultural understanding of the local context;
4   adaptability and learning.

A more comprehensive review of these principles is provided in the Appendix of this book. However, in summary they signify that at the strategic level a clear and achievable political aim informed by a joint civil–military, in-depth analysis of the conflict situation is necessary in order to provide clear direction for all involved actors. Clear aims create a common point of departure in the planning of operations and help to drive the different involved actors towards a common purpose. The planning and execution of operations thereby need close civil–military co-operation and co-ordination, if not integration, that provides comprehensive planning and co-ordination in the field of operations. Controlling the strategic narrative, or the perceptions of the events in the field, is of great importance to achieve legitimacy for the aims and conduct of operations. At the tactical level, the principle of civil–military co-operation and co-ordination is also of importance. While the aim should be unity of command, the realistic goal is often unity of effort through co-location of headquarters and close co-operation and communication. To win the hearts and minds of the local population – the centre of gravity in counter-insurgency operations – forces need good cultural understanding in order to apply minimum use of force that effectively links tactical activity with the strategic-level political aims. The hearts and minds approach should also be applied to force protection, which should be conducted softly by engaging with the local community, thereby winning consent and security. The diverse nature of complex peace operations also means that all soldiers at all levels will have to display unprecedented flexibility and adaptability to different situations and levels of threat.

A significant, final conclusion is that there are many indicators of effectiveness in complex peace operations that are related to civil–military relations – both at the strategic level and at the tactical level in the field of operations. The more specific civil–military aspects of effectiveness are, therefore, highlighted in the following chapter.

2 The civil–military dimension of effectiveness

A number of civil–military aspects of effectiveness are emphasized in the recent lessons learned coming out of complex PSOs such as Afghanistan and Iraq. Most often they stress the importance of increased co-operation and co-ordination of civilian and military instruments of power. As a result, a number of strategic concepts have been developed that serve to improve such co-ordination; comprehensive approach within the EU and NATO, integrated missions within the UN, effects-based approaches to operations, whole-of-government, 3D (diplomacy, development and defence), just to mention a few (Derblom *et al.* 2007). Civil–military aspects are thereby increasingly also becoming part of the strategic studies literature and military doctrine (Brooks 2008; Strachan 2006; US DoD 2006). There is, in other words, relative consensus regarding the importance of a number of civil–military aspects of effectiveness. However, the calls for increased civil–military co-ordination during operations are essentially based on assumptions rather than empirical data or sound theories that explain how such co-ordination can achieve increased effectiveness. Thus, the consensus is not matched by a corresponding body of work that increases the understanding of the relationship between civil–military relations and military effectiveness (Nielsen 2005). This is a serious gap in the existing literature that this book aims to start filling.

This chapter creates a theoretical framework that explains the impact of different patterns of civil–military relations on effectiveness in two important ways: *indirectly* by being the arena in which decisions regarding size, culture, equipment and doctrine of the armed forces are made, and *directly*, by providing the highest levels in the operational chain of command – the level where strategic aims are set and operational plans made. In short, the indirect impact helps determine the quality of the tools available to the political leadership, while the direct impact influences the effectiveness with which these tools are employed. After developing the theoretical framework, the chapter is concluded by a section that provides the method of analysis for the subsequent empirical chapters.

The indirect impact on military effectiveness

The term 'indirect' serves to highlight the fact that the nature of civil–military relations will have an impact on the size and quality of the armed forces, and thereby, indirectly influences the effectiveness of these forces when deployed. The impact on the size and quality of the armed forces has been a central problem discussed in civil–military relations theory as the normative aim of the field is the need to maximize the protective value that the armed forces can provide, and the need to minimize the domestic coercive powers that the same forces will inevitably possess, thus creating *effective armed forces under democratic civilian control* (Quinlan cited in Dandeker 2002). Despite the inherently dual aims of civil–military relations theory, the field has mainly focused on the issue of civilian control. The impact that civil–military relations has on military effectiveness is not nearly as well studied within the literature (Nielsen 2005). Despite this fact, civil–military relations theory is a useful point of departure for the development of a new theoretical framework.

The key to how the field connects different patterns of civil–military relations with effectiveness lies in the very starting point of civil–military relations theory – the assumption that the military institutions of any society are shaped by two forces: a functional imperative stemming from the threats to a society's security, and a societal imperative based on the ideologies, social forces and institutions that are dominant within the society (Huntington 1957: 2). How the functional and societal imperatives should be allowed to influence the structure and culture of the armed forces, and the impact this balance will have on the effectiveness of the military is, thereby, one of the main challenges of civil–military relations theory. One of the reasons for the centrality of this challenge is a traditional 'zero-sum' view of the civil–military problematique – thinking that it is only possible to maximize either military strength or civilian control (Dandeker 2002). As an example, the main conclusion of Samuel Huntington's work, *The Soldier and the State*, is that in order to increase the professionalism and effectiveness of the US military the American civil society had to adopt the more conservative and military values of West Point, which he describes as the military ideal at its best – 'a bit of Sparta in the midst of Babylon' (1957: 466). Political meddling in military affairs will decrease military professionalism and effectiveness, and the military should, in Huntington's view, therefore, only obey the functional and not the societal imperative for maximized effectiveness.

On the other side of the aisle are the theorists who tend to emphasize democratic civilian control more than military effectiveness – the societal imperative takes precedence. As argued by Dandeker (2002: 3), 'those of a liberal persuasion tend to expect the armed services to conform to civilian values and, in so doing, underestimate the unique character and demands of military life'. The challenge for political and military leaders is often expressed in terms of ensuring that a balance is struck between these competing imperatives. However, the conceptualization of the relations between functional and societal imperatives in zero-sum terms is misleading, as it assumes that military adjustments to civilian values necessarily undermine military effectiveness, and that the focus on military effectiveness must lead to decreased civilian control or non-adherence to the values of civil society (Dandeker 2002). It is clearly time to move beyond this zero-sum balancing of military effectiveness and civilian control, and also start looking for potential synergetic effects between the two imperatives.

A related debate concerns how the functional imperative of the armed forces should be interpreted. What is the main purpose and tasks of the armed forces, and how should the military be adjusted to perform those tasks effectively? Huntington (1957) sees the functional imperative as an external given, which can only be interpreted and adjusted to by military professionals, without interference from the political leadership. At the same time, Anthony Forster (2006: 46) makes the obvious but often overlooked argument that the purpose of military professionalism is the creation of a military 'fit for purpose' as defined by the political leadership. Professional, and thus effective, military organizations are, according to Forster, characterized by four factors, of which two constitute roles clearly defined by a government and widely accepted by the armed forces, as well as the development of military expertise necessary to fulfil these functions effectively and efficiently. Both the functional and the societal perspectives are, thereby, factors that help explain whether or not a culture is appropriate in relation to the actual tasks of the military. Forster clearly draws on constructivism within the field of international relations for his contribution. While the traditional view of civil–military relations sees the functional imperative as an objective constraint on decision makers, constructivists view them as 'being, in part, constituted by the values and aspirations of decision makers as they respond actively to their perceptions of both the external environment and the perceived "needs" of their own societies' (Dandeker 2002: 3). The functional imperative, thereby, takes on a subjective characteristic, that not only changes with variations in the strategic context, but also with the perceptions, values and aspirations of political and military leaders.

The position taken in this book is that the functional imperative can never be treated as an objective given. Instead, it alters with changes in the strategic context, political preferences, subjective perceptions of threat and societal needs. The armed forces must, therefore, constantly readjust its structure and culture in order to remain effective in relation to the tasks it is asked to perform. The functional imperative of the armed forces is a social construction and not a structural given.

Defining the functional imperative of the armed forces should instead be seen as a negotiation or an 'ongoing game of strategic interaction' within the civil–military interface (Feaver 2003). Importantly, this is a negotiation on which the nature of civil–military relations will, therefore, have a major impact. In fact, Peter Feaver's principal–agency theory of civil–military relations has provided much needed updates on the relationship between the political and military leaderships, and has, therefore, also provided the a number of concepts for the analyses of the empirical cases of this book. The problem that principal–agency theory seeks to answer is how a principal can ensure that the agent is implementing the orders in the manner that the principal intended, given that they have different incentives. In Feaver's language: is the agent working or shirking? The level of obedience is a direct function of the level of monitoring, which in turn depends on the perceived cost of such monitoring. The agent's incentives are determined by the probability that the shirking will be detected, and the likelihood of being punished for it (Feaver 2003: 37–38). The outcome of the ongoing game of strategic interaction between the political principal and the military agent is determined by a number of factors, including varying costs of civilian monitoring, the extent of the differences in policy preferences between civilians and the military, and the military perception of the probability of punishment in case of shirking (Feaver 2003: 103–104, 282).

Another useful perspective is provided by Risa Brooks, who has developed a link between civil–military relations and the quality of strategic assessment, defined as 'the process through which relations between a state's political goals/ strategies and military strategies/activities are evaluated and decided' (2008: 34). While the theory is mainly concerned with strategic assessment during international conflicts, this perspective is also useful when describing strategic assessment in peace, which can roughly be translated into the process of defining the functional imperative. The main question regarding the indirect impact on effectiveness is therefore: What type of civil–military relations will produce the most accurate analysis of the functional imperative and then adjust its troops and other security-related agencies accordingly?

The few theories of civil–military relations that take military effectiveness seriously differ greatly in terms of normative conclusions. This book highlights two distinct traditions: the divided approach – here represented by Samuel Huntington (1957), and; the integrated approach – as introduced by Morris Janowitz (1960), and later developed by the likes of Douglas Bland (1999) and Hew Strachan (2006). These two approaches will be tested throughout the empirical chapters and therefore require a more comprehensive discussion.

The divided and integrated approaches to civil–military relations

Since its publication in 1957, Samuel Huntington's seminal work, *The Soldier and the State*, has set the terms of debate about civil–military relations, and is commonly regarded as the 'normal' theory of the field, albeit a theory that has also been heavily criticized (Cohen 2002: 226). Huntington sees professional armed forces as a precondition for military effectiveness. The 'military professional' includes a professional ethic that can be described as an ideal set of universal values and capabilities that are 'pessimistic, collectivist, historically inclined, power oriented, nationalistic, militaristic, pacifist, and instrumentalist in its view of the military profession'. However, the most important feature of the military professional is that he or she is an objective and apolitical servant of the state, and, therefore, by definition subordinate to the political leadership (Huntington 1957: 79).

Huntington's conception of military professionalism assumes that it is possible to segregate an autonomous area of military science from political purpose. The autonomous military science, contrasted with the view of politics as art, is based on the functional imperative – to fight and win the nation's wars – as a structural given. The quality of the military can, therefore, according to Huntington, only be evaluated in terms of independent military standards, defined by the functional imperative, and should not be related to the political end for which it fights (1957: 56). As Huntington separates military means from political ends, the ideal purpose and identity of all armed forces become universal. The purpose of the military is national defence and its identity will, without interference from the political leadership or other societal imperatives, automatically be adjusted to fit this purpose through the development of military professionalism. Huntington thereby advocates the radical tradition of military professionalism, which emphasizes the isolation and autonomy of the military. It requires military obedience to civil authorities but, at the same time, allows complete military control over internal organizational matters (Larson 1974).

The armed forces' functional imperative in fighting wars and the resulting requirements this has placed upon the military have meant that, most often, a distinct military culture is formed. This professional culture is often perceived as threatening to civil society. Thus, an often-discussed problem is the extent to which the armed forces can be allowed to differ from the surrounding society (Dandeker and Gow 2000). Deliberate attempts by the political leadership to incorporate the values of civil society into the armed forces in order to control them are what Huntington called 'subjective control'. This form of political meddling in military affairs would, according to Huntington (1957), not only engage the armed forces in politics and, thereby, affect civilian control, but also decrease its fighting capabilities. Huntington argued that the military values feared by civil society are the very values that ensure civilian control and create military effectiveness. This is because the professional warrior values of conservative realism, self-sacrifice and being apolitical come from civilian non-interference in military affairs. If these values of military professionals are reduced, military effectiveness will also decrease.

Huntington's suggestion of how to achieve civilian control of the armed forces in democracies is, therefore, unsurprisingly, through civilian recognition and support of military professionalism and expertise, meaning no political interference in the military sphere (1957: 83). Huntington calls this 'objective civilian control', which, in practice, means a sharp division of labour between political ends and military means, as well as the idea that the military should be physically and ideologically separated from political institutions (Schiff 1995: 7). Peter Feaver summarizes Huntington's argument as 'autonomy leads to professionalization, which leads to political neutrality and voluntary subordination, which leads to secure civilian control' (2003: 18). A military organization well separated from the political leadership in a conservative civilian society will, therefore, according to Huntington, both be well adjusted for its purpose and under democratic civilian control. In paraphrasing Feaver, Huntington's causal chain regarding effectiveness would be: autonomy leads to professionalization, which leads to structural and cultural adjustment to the functional imperative, which automatically means military effectiveness.

While Huntington's work has become the normal, and most accepted, theory of civil–military relations, a parallel track has always existed in the sociological school of the field. The school, led by Morris Janowitz, instead advocates civil–military integration in order to achieve both effectiveness and civilian control. By adding a political dimension to the military profession, Janowitz suggested that the military professional must be 'sensitive to the political and social impact of the military establishment on international security affairs'. Civilian control cannot be achieved solely through the rule of law and a professional tradition not to intervene in politics, but must also come from 'self-imposed professional standards and meaningful integration with civilian values' (Janowitz 1960: 420). The practical solution to creating a professional military organization fit for purpose is thus the opposite to that of Huntington; the military should be integrated with the political leadership in order to develop increased political understanding and sensitivity. Importantly, the political leadership must control both the criteria and information for judging the effectiveness of the military establishment. 'The formulation of the standards of performance the military are expected to achieve are civilian responsibilities, although these standards cannot be evolved independent of professional military judgement' (Janowitz 1960: 420). In other words, the interpretation of the functional imperative and the consequent military adjustment should be controlled by the political leadership rather than by objective external factors, or by the military itself.

This school further argues that an integrated civil–military structure is a means of improving the process of strategic analysis and planning, thereby increasing effectiveness in operations (Strachan 2006; Brooks 2008). Brooks uses two causal variables in what she calls 'preference divergence' in the civil–military interface and in the power relations between the political and military leaderships (Brooks 2008: 23, 27). To achieve effective strategic assessment, both military and political leaders must, according to Brooks, 'participate fully in comprehensive dialogue at the apex of decision making to expose flawed reasoning, hidden and contradictory assumptions, and alternative views in the analytical process' of strategic assessment and planning. Ideally, and despite structural factors that are often working against it, military and political leaders should, therefore, be actively engaged with one another (Brooks 2008: 269–270).

Another significant argument is that integrated formal government and/or ministerial committee system should be used to support consensus-building procedures among the civil authorities, military leaders, and senior public servants (Bland 2001). Such an interagency system should ideally permit military and civilian leaders to develop co-ordinated advice for ministers. In the end, such co-ordinated advice produces policies that better command military support and loyalty, and thus simplify policy implementation (Bland 2001). This stands in stark contrast to the divided approach, which emphasizes the importance of pure military, as well as political advice.

In conclusion, the indirect impact means that the nature of civil–military relations is likely to have an impact on the size, structure, and equipment of the armed forces, which in turn affects the operational effectiveness of those forces.

The field of civil–military relations theory highlights the importance of the functional imperative as an explanatory variable in this process. As a consequence, the nature of the functional imperative will be a main feature of this study. How is it interpreted, and by whom is it decided? To what extent have the armed forces adjusted to that imperative and can be considered 'fit for purpose'?

A reading of the literature on civil–military relations theory highlights a striking range of normative conclusion relating to the essential question – what patterns of civil–military relations are likely to produce the most effective armed forces in the contemporary strategic context of complex peace operations. The section above has highlighted two distinct schools of thought in the divided and integrated approaches to civil–military relations.

The direct impact: the civil–military interface in the operational chain of command

While the traditional theories of civil–military relations create an understanding of the relationship between the armed forces, the political leadership and civil society at large, these approaches do not deal with the practical and operational aspects of civil–military relations when the military and other agencies are engaged in conflict – what this book refers to as the direct impact on effectiveness. What patterns of civil–military relations are effective when employed within the operational chain of command? What structure and organizational culture is necessary within the civil–military interface to apply the different military and civilian instruments of power with effectiveness?

A rare contribution from the field of civil–military relations is the argument that the nature of civil–military relationship in a particular state influences the quality of strategic assessment and planning during operations (Strachan 2006; Brooks 2008). As already noted, Brooks (2008: 270) highlights the importance of military and political leaders actively engaged with one another for effective strategic assessment. Hew Strachan, similarly, argues that instead of the traditional divide between civilian and military leaders, there should be civil–military integration, with the aim of harmonizing political aims and military capabilities and activities. 'There is no merit in the government trying to endorse a policy in Iraq or Afghanistan for which it does not have the military capability' (2006: 76). In a refreshing take on civil–military relations, Strachan also argues that we should completely rethink the fundamental questions in the field. The problem is not how the civilian leadership can control the military and avoid a coup d'état, but to create civil–military relations that would enable coherent strategy development (Strachan 2006: 79). This is a pragmatic and completely unsentimental view of civil–military relations that, in the language of the theoretical framework developed in this volume, focuses on effectiveness in terms of both the direct and indirect impact of civil–military relations. This section aims to pick up Strachan's trail and develop what this book calls the direct impact on effectiveness by marrying the fields of civil–military relations and military command and control theory.

The limited literature on how different structural arrangements in the civil–military interface affect operational effectiveness means that theoretical inspiration must be sought elsewhere. First, the following sections turn to military command and control theory to enhance the clarity of the direct impact of civil–military relations on effectiveness.

Mission command and trust

As the civil–military interface is an important link in the chain of command during operations, the field of command and control theory provides a number of useful perspectives on effectiveness. There are different methods of exercising command that are often placed on a continuous line between the extremes of direct (also detailed or centralized) command on the one side, and mission command on the other. In the contemporary context, involving politically sensitive wars of choice, scrutinized by global media coverage, means that political and military leaders have sought ways to control, or micro-manage, events from headquarters. However, such centralized, or direct, command is often ineffective as increased complexity generally requires dispersion rather than centralization of authority (Dandeker 2006). First, situations on the ground are very hard to assess if you are not there physically. Wrong or insensitive decisions may be the outcome. Second, micro-management often means that people with little understanding of soldiering will make the decisions, be it politicians with none or little experience, or high-ranking officers who have not experienced these situations for decades, or ever. Third, centralized command is time consuming. The reason is that when using centralized or detailed command, subordinates must refer to their headquarters when they encounter situations not covered by the commander's original orders (US Department of the Army 2003). In the short-term, this means a loss of operational speed and missed opportunities while waiting for new orders. In the long-term, it leads to a loss of quality and initiative of junior commanders and soldiers who are neither encouraged nor forced to make their own decisions and to learn from their own actions.

Therefore, most armed forces' doctrines on command and control emphasize the importance of mission command in complex environments – a philosophy of decentralized command based on trust and initiative. In essence, mission command involves giving orders about what to do and what the aims are, but not how those aims are to be achieved. Commanders can by explaining their objectives, and by communicating the rationale for military action throughout their commands, give junior commanders and their soldiers 'insight into what is expected of them, what constraints apply, and, most important, why the mission is being undertaken' (US Department of the Army 2003). Thus, commanders are allowed to hold a 'loose rein', allowing subordinates freedom of action, while at the same time demanding that they exercise initiative and adjust actions according to new input of information. This means that commanders make fewer decisions, and thus it allows them to focus on the most important ones (US Department of the Army 2003). Mission command was specifically developed to

deal with increased complexity in the operational environment. By decentraliz-
ing decision-making authority, the idea behind mission command is to increase
tempo and improve the ability to deal with fluid and disorderly situations (US
Department of the Navy 2006: 79). When commanders on all levels understand
their general roles within a larger perspective, as is ideally the case when
employing mission command, they are also more able to 'think laterally and
share objectives through unity of effort, decentralization, trust, understanding,
and timely decision making' (Lovelock 2002).

There is, however, always an element of increased risk involved in mission
command – the risk that the subordinates have not really understood the intent of
the commander, or the risk that the commander has made a bad decision or provided too few resources. Mission command theory, therefore, always involves a
trade-off between ineffective but safe command and effective but risky
command. Dealing with such risk requires mutual trust between superiors and
subordinates (Oliviero 1998). In sum, mission command requires high levels of
trust and understanding, initiative from subordinates and clarity of intent and
aims from commanders.

Interestingly, the practical application of civil–military relations can easily be
interpreted as a form of mission command, requiring a clear dividing line
between political decisions and military implementation. Operations are dele-
gated to the military and other agencies in a way that clearly resembles the ideals
of mission command, stating what to do, but not how to carry out the task.
However, as observed above, the successful implementation of mission
command requires the components of mutual trust and understanding, clear
intent from commanders, and initiative from subordinates. Without clear aims,
mutual trust and understanding, there is a risk that the political leadership
meddles in strictly military affairs and increasingly micro-manages what it considers to be politically sensitive situations. There is also a risk that the military
chain of command misinterprets the aims and intent of the political leadership,
and how these aims should be translated into military actions. Understanding
and showing what patterns of civil–military relations are likely to produce an
environment conducive to a strategic-level mission command type leadership is,
therefore, an important challenge for the argument of this book. The civil–military interface must be structured to create mutual trust and understanding across
the divide, to provide clarity of intent from the political leadership, and to
encourage a culture of initiative to act within that intent among the implementing agencies – not least the military.

The concept of trust is the key to successful mission command and deserves
further attention in order to distinguish different forms of trust and how they can
be achieved within the civil–military interface. The rich sociological literature
on the concept classifies different forms of trust relevant to the argument of this
book. First, *interpersonal trust* refers to trust between people. A useful distinction with reference to this analysis is provided by Khodyakov (2007) who differ-
entiates between thick and thin interpersonal trust. Thick interpersonal trust is
formed in relationships with strong ties and depends on the personalities of both

the trustee and the trustor. This form of trust involves personal familiarity with the counterpart, as well as strong emotional commitment to the relationship. It is essentially based on social similarities and shared moral codes – personal characteristics like gender, ethnicity and cultural background (Zucker 1986). This form of trust, thereby, depends on similarity and strong emotional relationships between people.

However, in governmental institutions, interactions and trust between people who do not often meet are of greater importance as this is the more normal form of interaction in these settings. This is referred to as thin trust, which is created through interactions of people who do not know each other well. This is a form process-based trust, built on experiences of reciprocity and relies on weaker ties. It is based on the assumption that another person would reciprocate and comply with our expectations of his or her behaviour, as well as with existing formal and ethical rules (Khodyakov 2007; Zucker 1986).

Social reality is nevertheless not only dependent on persons and their activities, but there are also institutions and abstract systems. Other ways to build trust than through personal relations are, therefore, necessary. This is where confidence or trust in systems or institutions becomes important. *System* or *institutional trust* refers to trust in the functioning of organizational, institutional and social systems. It flows from institutional arrangements that create and sustain trustworthy behaviour, such as broad societal norms, guarding institutional arrangements and organizational governance systems. These abstract principles can bring about varying degrees of embedded trust, of shared norms and expectations, and of reciprocity (Bijlsma-Frankema and Costa 2005). Trust in institutions depends on whether the institution is perceived as legitimate, has technical competence, and has the ability to perform its assigned duties efficiently (Khodyakov 2007).

How does knowledge about mission command theory and trust help in the analysis of civil–military relations for maximized effectiveness in operations? Mission command theory emphasizes that effective command and control in the political–military interface requires clear aims from the political leadership. It also requires an extensive understanding of how to use the military tool to achieve political aims, as well as a well-developed strategic conceptual framework. At the same time, mission command requires excellent political understanding within the military in order to translate political aims and directives into appropriate military activity. When the political leadership has no clear vision or strategic preference, and when there is a knowledge gap and/or a gap in analytical and conceptual tools, there is a risk that the military takes the position as an 'epistemic authority'. The military, thereby, controls the agenda of the civil–military interface and develops a political dependence on the military for information (Michael 2007a: 443–445). In order for the political leadership to wield effective substantive control, it must, therefore, develop sound knowledge and put forward high-quality challenging alternatives to those that the military presents (Michael 2007b: 541).

Mutual understanding and effective command and control in the civil–military interface also require trust. It is, therefore, imperative that the civil–military interface should be constructed to increase trust and mutual understanding across departmental and agency boundaries. Due to the different organizational cultures and interests of the civilian and military echelons, the inherent nature of the relationship is inevitably conflictual, but such conflict can be healthy and even stimulating as long as it is controlled. One important way to keep conflicts at a 'healthy' level is to increase mutual understanding and respect across the organizational boundaries.

The knowledge that interpersonal trust is based on social similarities and shared moral codes, and/or experiences of reciprocity, means that trust within the civil–military interface can be achieved by recruiting people with similar social background and moral code on both sides of the divide, or to promote a common civil–military culture of shared moral values within the interface. It also means that the civil–military organizations, such as the department of defence, or interagency planning teams, should strive to integrate staff from both sides of the civil–military divide, not only to widen the areas of expertise within the staff, but also to create interpersonal trust and mutual understanding through personal experiences of reciprocity.

Understanding that different institutional arrangements may evoke and sustain trustworthy behaviour means that the structures of the civil–military interface must be carefully constructed to promote co-operation and trust. If interpersonal trust is lacking within the organization, there can at least be a level of belief in the structure or culture of the organization to provide a basic level of trust. Competition between the different agencies of the civil–military interface may evoke distrustful behaviour within interagency structures. As an example, an operational planner may not know his/her counterpart from the other side of the civil–military divide, and the planner also feels that there are few shared values with the counterpart. Instead of instinctively distrusting the counterpart, the planner may instead fall back on institutional trust based on the fact that the different agencies have always co-operated well towards common goals, as well as the knowledge of a recruitment and promotion system within the other agencies that makes it highly unlikely that the counterpart is anything but competent and trustworthy. Finally, the planner may also fall back on previous personal experiences of working with people from other agencies with good results.

While much of the discussion on the civil–military interface aspects of effectiveness is about finding useful structural solutions, the cultural aspects are equally important. A number of the already discussed concepts that can have an impact on military effectiveness – mutual trust and understanding, as well as on co-operation and co-ordination – are more of a cultural nature than a structural one, and a basic level of understanding regarding the cultural and historical aspects of organizations is, therefore, essential.

History and culture as context

Showing that there is some level of causality between certain patterns of civil–military relations and military effectiveness is interesting in its own right.

However, if this can also be linked to a wider historical and cultural context, the findings become more significant by explaining where the different patterns of civil–military relations come from. Such understanding also provides a more solid foundation for policy recommendations that not only fit the ideal theoretical case, but are also firmly placed within the historical and cultural specifics of the political system concerned. A comprehensive review of the concept of culture and the debate regarding what culture is and how it influences behaviour is beyond the scope of this book. The contested nature of culture as a variable explaining behaviour nevertheless makes it essential to clarify some underlying conceptual and theoretical assumptions of the analysis (Johnston 1995; Gray 1999; Geertz 1973).

This book does not treat culture as a variable – something to which institutions, social events and behaviours can be causally attributed. Instead, this book treats culture as the context in which these events, institutions and behaviours can be intelligibly described (Geertz 1973). Clifford Geertz describes his method of research as 'thick description' of behaviour as a way of explaining not just the behaviour, but its context as well, thereby providing meaning to outsiders (1973). Thus, within this study, the analysis of history and culture as contexts provides meaning to the peculiarities of different civil–military structures, as well as to particular conduct during complex peace operations. As Dandeker (1999) argues, the historical context of the armed forces clearly has an effect on defence roles and mission, organizational structure, military culture, as well as the patterns of civil–military relations (Dandeker 1999). In sum, placing the nature of civil–military relations within a historical and cultural context is imperative.

Culture applied within the boundaries of a specific organization like the armed forces, a company, or a civilian government bureaucracy is referred to as organizational culture. Edgar Schein (1990: 110) defines organizational culture as 'what a group learns over a period of time as that group solves its problems of survival in an external environment and its problems of internal integration. Such learning is simultaneously a behavioural, cognitive, and emotional process.' He further describes culture as a pattern of invented or discovered basic assumptions by a given group as it learns to cope with its problems of external adaptation and internal integration. These assumptions are deemed to have worked well enough to be considered valid, and are, therefore, to be taught to new members as 'the correct way to perceive, think, or feel in relation to these problems' (Schein 1990: 110). It is worth emphasizing that culture, therefore, always seems to entail a normative aspect. Organizational culture is what is *considered* the right way of doing things within the organization. It is, however, not just a theoretical construction as the norms and values of the culture have to have worked well enough in the past to have an empirical aspect as well (Schein 1990).

The potential for flawed organizational cultures in relation to certain tasks is highly relevant with reference to the discussion regarding the functional imperative. Theories of organizational culture often focus on what type of functional imperative the particular organization is seeking to perform? It is clear that the organizational culture is an important factor in determining not only what the functional imperative is, but also in what manner the organization should address it. Thus, military organizations are likely to form norms and values that are adjusted to what is considered the functional imperative of the organization. What makes military culture unique is that its norms and values originate from the attempt to deal with the uncertainties and horrors of war (Burk 1999).

For reasons of bureaucratic self-defence, every bureaucracy has an organizational essence, a set of functions or activities that most clearly define it and justify its existence (Lord 1985). Left to themselves, bureaucracies, therefore, tend to undertake projects and pursue goals that reinforce this organizational essence. The problem is that such goals are often at odds with the larger goals that bureaucracies are expected to pursue on behalf of the government and the nation (Lord 1985: 17). Another interesting factor is that bureaucracies tend to value clarity of mission and autonomy even more than expansion. Expansion into areas that are only peripherally related to their organizational essence is, therefore, often viewed as potentially harmful, as it can increase demands for co-ordination of the bureaucracy's operations with other agencies and for oversight from above (Lord 1985: 19). Again, this is essential in relation to the debate regarding the armed forces' functional imperative, and helps us understand many armed forces' reluctance to accept 'new' roles such as peacekeeping and humanitarian assistance. Defining the 'organizational essence' or the organization's view of the functional imperative is, therefore, an important task of the case studies.

Military, political and societal cultures merge in the concept of strategic culture, which is here defined as the entire security establishment's values, assumptions and patterns of behaviour, regarding the use of force – a nation's 'way of war' (see Johnston 1995; Gray 1986; Lord 1985; Booth 1979; Katzenstein 1996). Lord identifies six factors which create a strategic culture: the geopolitical setting, military history, international relationships, political culture and ideology, the nature of civil–military relations and military technology (Lord cited in Longhurst 2000: 303). Strategic culture is significant in this book as it covers not only the military establishment, but, ideally at least, all the departments and agencies involved in security issues. Moreover, this book makes the argument that the functional imperative of armed forces is not fixed, but instead a function of the objective demands of the strategic context on the one hand, and on the other the outcome of strategic negotiation between political and military leaders, each with subjective perceptions of the strategic demands and the nation's needs. Again, the way the functional imperative is interpreted, and the extent to which the armed forces and other relevant agencies are adjusted to the strategic context, should, therefore, be significant parts of the empirical analyses of this book.

The result of the discussion above means this book treats culture as the context which conditions and constrains the behaviour of nations and organizations, rather than as one independent variable among others. Culture and history are used as 'thick description' in order to provide deeper contextual understanding of the causal mechanisms that lead to military effectiveness in complex peace operations. Culture as a context is better used to interpret the meaning of particular practice than to predict future behaviour. However, by understanding the nature of cultural conditions and constraints, predictions about the outcome of certain behaviour is likely to be more accurate. The concepts of military and strategic culture are in this book operationalized within the more generic term 'way of war' – a concept that includes past behaviour in the form of historical analysis, cultural expressions or artefacts in the form of texts and language, such as doctrines and statements, as well as 'classificatory systems' in the form of secondary sources about military and strategic culture in the particular cases. The analyses of the US and the British ways of war, thereby, involve US and British preferences in war – cultural and structural – interpreted as the outcome of past operational experience, certain patterns of civil–military relations, and different interpretations of the functional imperative, all within the constraining and enabling contexts of military and strategic culture. In the search for the US and British ways of war, descriptions of strategic and military culture are of importance, as they provide the context in which the practice or ways of war are formed.

In conclusion, beyond the indirect impact of the civil–military interface as an arena in which the most important decisions regarding the armed forces are made, the civil–military interface is also an important part of the operational chain of command, especially at the strategic level interface of civilian policy makers and military implementers. This is the level where strategic aims are created and translated into operational plans and activities, thereby affecting the planning and implementation of operations. The section above noted that the type of leadership exercised at this level of command is similar to what the military calls mission command – expressing what to do, but not how to do it. It was also argued that mission command requires mutual trust and understanding in order to function well – something that is often missing in the civil–military interface. Increasing trust within the civil–military interface and the interagency arena requires high-levels of both interpersonal and institutional trust – stemming from close working relationships and experiences of reciprocity. Finally, the theoretical section has emphasized the importance of historical and cultural understanding in relation to the link between different patterns of civil–military relations and military effectiveness.

Together, the theories of civil–military relations, in combination with command and control theory, provide a useful theoretical foundation for the development of a theoretical framework for analysis of how the nature of civil–military relations affects the conduct and effectiveness of operations. The following section not only puts together the discussions from the previous sections and formulates this framework in more detail. It also outlines the methodology for testing this framework empirically in the subsequent chapters of the book.

The civil–military dimension of effectiveness: a framework for analysis

As highlighted in the previous sections, the theoretical framework for analysis developed in this book involves dual causal links between different patterns of civil–military relations and the conduct of operations – one direct and one indirect.

The indirect impact

The structure and culture of a state's civil–military interface has an *indirect impact* on the conduct and effectiveness in complex peace operations. This is the type of influence on military effectiveness normally discussed within civil–military relations theory. It explains how the size, structure, training, culture, doctrine and equipment of the armed forces are affected by different patterns of civil–military relations. The key to understanding the indirect impact is the definition of the functional imperative. How and by whom is it interpreted, and to what extent are the armed forces adjusted to that imperative? In this book, the interpretation and consequential organizational adjustment are seen as the results of negotiations within the civil–military interface. The indirect impact of civil–military relations, thereby, asserts peacetime influence over the armed forces and determines whether they are 'fit for purpose' at the onset of operations. The civil–military interface must, therefore, be constructed in a way that can make an accurate interpretation of the functional imperative of the armed forces and other relevant agencies, and that is likely to produce organizations well adjusted to the demands of the contemporary strategic context of complex peace operations. This involves both the structure and the organizational culture of these implementing agencies.

The direct impact

The structure and culture of a state's civil–military interface also has *direct impact* on the conduct and effectiveness of operations by affecting the quality of command at the strategic and operational levels. Effectiveness in the contemporary strategic context requires the involvement and co-ordination of all instruments of national power in the planning and execution of operations. The nature of the civil–military interface determines the command and control structures of the strategic and operational levels of command, as well as the level of interagency co-operation and civil–military co-ordination of planning and execution of operations. In other words, the patterns of civil–military relations determine whether experts from all relevant departments and agencies are brought into the planning process, and whether a comprehensive approach to operations is applied. The command and control structures of the civil–military interface also determine the effectiveness of the execution of tactical operations through the facilitation of the necessary co-ordination and co-operation between the civilian and military components of operations.

Importantly, the practical application of civil–military relations within the operational chain of command is in this book interpreted as a form of mission command. However, command and control theory notes that effective mission command within the civil–military interface, as well as in the field of operations, requires clear political aims, initiative and high levels of mutual trust and understanding across civil–military boundaries within the entire chain of command. To co-ordinate the actors towards the common aim of the operations without micro-management, the political leadership must, therefore, trust the structures of the interagency system as well as the actors within it in order to give these structures the authority they need for effective planning and execution of comprehensive approaches to operations in the pursuit of the political aims.

The theoretical section has identified two typical patterns of civil–military relations – the divided and the integrated forms. While the main conclusions regarding the outcome of different patterns of civil–military relations are discussed in the final two chapters, a hypothesis is here derived from the theoretical framework and the previous discussions of the chapter. The complex nature of contemporary peace operations means that integrated civil–military approaches are necessary for effectiveness in achieving the often far-reaching political aims of democratization and economic development. Such integrated, or comprehensive, approaches to operations also require integrated institutions at the national strategic level, and at the international organizational level in cases of multinational operations within different organizational frameworks. There are two main reasons why integrated civil–military structures at the strategic level would provide better results in complex peace operations.

First, the indirect impact means that integrated structures provide more accurate and up to date interpretations and adjustment to the functional imperative of the armed forces. This means that the instruments of national power, not least the military, are better suited for the contemporary strategic context. Second, the direct impact of integrated structures is that they provide more inclusive command and control structures at the strategic level, which means that all relevant actors in complex operations are co-ordinated through integrated planning and execution of operations – providing a so-called 'comprehensive approach' to operations. Together, the direct and indirect impacts on the conduct and effectiveness of operations in complex peace operations are of great importance. The effectiveness of the command and control structures in the civil–military interface and the quality of strategic and operational level planning are of little value with a security organization that lacks the capability to effectively achieve the political aims of operations.

Design of the study

After constructing the theoretical framework for analysis, the next step of this book involves testing and refining this framework empirically, as well as to draw conclusions regarding the impact of the two approaches to civil–military relations on effectiveness, as highlighted in this chapter. This section, therefore, outlines the methodology for these tasks.

While causality itself concerns the effects or outcomes of different variables, causal mechanisms describe the processes of how these effects are exerted. In the words of King, Keohane and Verba: 'If we posit that an explanatory variable causes a dependent variable, a "causal mechanism's" approach would require us to identify a list of causal links between the two variables' (1994: 86). This book is interested in both causality and causal mechanisms. The causality aspect involves the effects of different patterns of civil–military relations, while the causal mechanisms deal with the important 'how question' and seek to explain the causal links between the explanatory and the dependent variables. In other words, through what processes do different patterns of civil–military relations affect operational conduct and effectiveness? To address these two concerns, the book employs a combination of two different methods – process tracing, and, what George and Bennett (2004) refer to as 'structured, focused comparison'.

Process tracing involves generating and examining data on the causal mechanisms, or processes, events, and other intervening variables that link putative causes to observed effects. George and Bennett argue that 'of the two kinds of evidence on the theoretical causal notions of causal effect and causal mechanisms, tests of co-variation attempt to address the former, and process tracing assesses the latter'. Within the general method of process tracing, this book employs process verification – a method which involves 'testing whether the observed processes among variables in a case match those predicted by previously designated theories'. This method involves uncovering and tracing the intervening variables along the causal chain between the explanatory and dependent variables (George and Bennett 2004).

To successfully test the theoretical framework, and to draw conclusions regarding the effects of different patterns of civil–military relations, the case studies need to provide several levels of evidence. First, the patterns of civil–military relations must be established in each case as the explanatory variables of both the direct and indirect causal chains, and as the starting points for process tracing. Second, the causal mechanisms in the intervening variables of the direct and indirect causal links between different patterns of civil–military relations and operational behaviour must be established. The causal mechanisms, the intervening variables, and the contexts of history and culture then provide further causal evidence and understanding in the final analysis of the dependent variable of operational conduct and effectiveness in complex peace operations.

As mentioned, the book involves two cases to achieve the above. These case studies are designed to test both the direct and the indirect influence on operational conduct and, therefore, involve multi-level analyses. The starting point of the case studies is to examine the independent variable of each case – the patterns of civil–military relations. However, as Christopher Dandeker (1999) has importantly argued, the historical context of the armed forces has an effect on defence roles and mission, organizational structure, military culture, as well as the patterns of civil–military relations. To place the pattern of civil–military relations within a historical context, a review of the historical background of the respective armed forces, therefore, precedes the analysis of civil–military relations in each case. Following the historical section, the patterns of civil–military relations are analysed in general terms, as well as by breaking down this variable into two parts: (a) interagency co-operation and co-ordination at the strategic level; (b) civil–military integration within the defence ministry. Finally, these analyses are discussed in relation to the two theoretical approaches to civil–military relations, as discussed in the section on civil–military relations theory – the divided and the integrated approaches.

Each case study contains an analysis of the indirect variables caused by the patterns of civil–military relations, and that in turn influences the armed forces' operational conduct. The intervening variables of this analysis involve the armed forces' structure, culture and doctrine. To perform that task, these sections discuss whether the structure, culture and doctrine of the armed forces in the US and the UK are suitable for complex peace operations. This is done with reference to the principles of best practice, as reviewed in the previous chapter. The historical and cultural analyses provide deeper contextual understanding of the nature of civil–military relations in the two cases, and thereby also enhance the significance and meaning of the empirical observations in the more institutional analyses. The main questions of these chapters are: How is the functional imperative of the armed forces interpreted and by whom? What are the structural and cultural consequences of this interpretation?

The answers to these questions not only reveal the extent to which the armed forces are fit for complex peace operations, they also create a number of expectations regarding the armed forces' conduct of operations in the field. Finally, to test these expectations, the two cases involve empirical studies of the two armed forces' respective operations in Iraq from 2003. This is the analysis of the dependent variable of operational conduct and effectiveness in complex peace operations. As previously discussed, the dependent variable of operational conduct or effectiveness does not involve neat dichotomies in victory or loss. Instead, it is measured in relation to a number of factors derived from the theoretical section on principles of best practice in complex peace operations. At the strategic level these factors involve the approaches to operations, the political and military aims, and the level of civil–military co-operation and co-ordination in the planning process. At the tactical level emphasis is placed on unity of command and effort, the use of hearts and minds approaches to operations, the level of cultural understanding and finally, adaptability. Outcomes of operations are nevertheless also briefly discussed in relation to the effectiveness of operational conduct.

The two case studies are followed by the comparative study, in which the cases are compared and contrasted. This chapter seeks to make inferences by further relating the empirical observations to the theoretical discussions of the first two chapters. The chapter, thereby, evaluates the hypothesis and the theoretical framework for analysis and discusses necessary refinements.

One of the main challenges when conducting case studies is the selection of cases. The cases analysed in the book are, as previously mentioned, the British and American civil–military relations, their approaches to complex peace operations, and finally their operations in Iraq from 2003. The cases chosen are justified for several reasons. First, in terms of relevance, the study of American and British peace operations is intrinsically interesting as the two countries, for different reasons, are likely to be leading these types of operations in the future. The US has a particular role as the sole remaining military superpower and will in that role, as well as protect its own interests and security, continue to engage itself in different complex expeditionary operations. The UK has a unique experience and capability of expeditionary operations, including counter-insurgency. That experience, in combination with a large international presence, makes the UK likely to continue to engage in and lead operations of that kind, not least within the EU and/or NATO frameworks. Methodologically, the comparison of the US and the UK is also relevant. Despite many relative similarities in culture and background, including extensive experience in both conventional large-scale warfare and counter-insurgency operations, the two countries have essentially different approaches to complex peace operations, despite a long history of co-operation in military, intelligence and other activities. Tracing the causes of that disparity is thus of great interest. The two cases are therefore chosen as contrasting instances of the same phenomenon (Denscombe 1998).

The choice of the operations in Iraq as the empirical testing ground for the book has been made because they represent the latest, and most interesting, example of major powers involved in complex peace operations against an asymmetric insurgent. A number of scholars stress the fact that contemporary insurgencies are quite different from yesterday's communist insurgencies – both in terms of aims and tactics (Mockaitis 2000). Although a number of historical counter-insurgency campaigns are of interest for this book, they would not have provided the same empirical strengths as a contemporary case of complex peace operations. Studying today's Iraq, which certainly involves a complex, networked, and, in some aspects, global insurgency, therefore limits the risk of producing lessons for past operations.

The empirical case of Iraq also allows for a comparative analysis of US and UK operational conduct within the same context, allowing for a number of different contextual variables to be isolated. It should, nevertheless, be emphasized from the beginning that although US and British troops were and are operating in Iraq at the same time, the two armed forces actually operated within very different contexts. This problematic aspect of the case selection is obviously further discussed in each of the cases as well as in the comparative analysis of the concluding chapters.

Another problematic aspect of US and British operations in Iraq as a case study is the fact that the operations are by no means concluded, and predicting an outcome is still, in the autumn of 2008, not easily done. The outcome of the operations is, therefore, impossible as a variable when evaluating operational conduct within the scope of this book. However, as noted in the previous chapter, in the discussion regarding military effectiveness, outcome is not the only variable of effectiveness, and the design of the case studies makes up for this problem by evaluating the independent variable of operational conduct and effectiveness in relation to what is considered best practice in complex peace operations. Outcome would also not have been useful as a variable of comparison as the outcome of British and American operations is inherently linked in Iraq.

Collection and use of data

This study employs qualitative research methods because of the limited number of cases and respondents as well as the type of data, which are, in some instances, based on subjective opinions and emotions and, therefore, less suitable for quantitative analysis (Marsh and Stoker 1995). The diverse nature of the research questions means that the data is pulled from many different sources. The first part of the book, involving the theoretical discussion and construction of a framework for analysis, has mainly involved the analysis of secondary sources. However, to establish a set of best practices in complex peace operations, primary sources in the form of doctrine and a few interviews have also been employed. The studies of different patterns of civil–military relations have involved a similar mix of sources, with more emphasis on interviews. The data necessary for these analyses includes the experience and opinions of military officers, politicians and civil servants, as well as observations of working methods and structures, for which interviewing was the best form of data collection. Again, the study of organizational culture and the approaches to irregular warfare has involved the same mix of sources, this time emphasizing historical writing and official doctrine publications.

Finally, gathering data from the operations in Iraq has produced a challenge. Initial hopes of research visits to Iraq were quickly abandoned due to security reasons. Instead, this book has relied on newspaper coverage, lessons learned documents, official reports, academic books and articles, and some interviews with returned military officers in Washington DC and London. The data collected in this manner is not ideal, but certainly sufficient for the purpose of this book.

Part II

Case study

The United States

3   The patterns of civil–military relations in the United States

This book advocates a broad view of civil–military relations, in which the study of history, in combination with cultural and structural factors, helps us to form a deeper understanding of how the civil–military relationship is rooted in societies' structures, and how they may affect the conduct of operational planning and execution. The analysis of US civil–military relations, therefore, starts with an analysis of US military history, before looking at the specific patterns of civil–military relations. The section on civil–military relations draws on the theoretical section of this book and seeks to relate the US patterns of civil–military relations to the previous discussion on divided versus integrated structures. The section focuses on interagency co-operation, civil–military relations within the Department of Defense, and the cost of civilian monitoring of the armed forces.

US military history

A comprehensive study of US military history is not feasible within the scope of this section, which, instead, highlights a number of events and currents in US military history that are likely to have had a major impact on the culture of the armed forces and its relationship with the political leadership. In practice, that means a closer look at the birth of the US armed forces, the era of professional development in the wake of the Civil War, as well as the Vietnam War and the lessons that came out of it. Finally, the section studies the latest developments within the changing security context of the post-Cold War world.

The early years

The American political and civil–military structures are as old as the nation itself, and the sentiments from the early years of the republic still form the relationship between the US and its military. Richard Kohn (1991) argues that few political principles were more widely known or more universally accepted in America during the 1780s than the danger of standing armies in peacetime. This fear was expressed by Samuel Adams with excellent precision:

A Standing Army, however necessary it may be at some times, is always dangerous to the Liberties of the People. Soldiers are apt to consider themselves as a Body distinct from the rest of the citizens. They have arms always in their hands. Their Rules and Discipline is severe.... Such a power should be watched with a jealous Eye.

(Cited in Millet 1979: 1)

The framers of the US Constitution feared that the military might try to take power, or that a government facing electoral defeat might use the military to hold onto power by force. Not only did the framers, therefore, seek to control the powers of the military, but also to limit political leaders' capability to exploit these powers. The solution was a system of checks and balances which institutionalized divisions among the civilian leadership and induced the executive and the legislature to monitoring one another as well as the military (Avant 1994: 21).

The basic elements of the new political system that were also used to control the military were the diffusion of power and shared responsibility. The American Constitution assigned the President the role of Commander-in-Chief of the armed forces. But it also reserved for Congress the power to declare war and the power to raise and equip armed forces. Appropriations for the army were limited to two years. Finally, the Constitution mandated state militias that were to provide an insurance against the power of the standing army (Johnson and Metz 1995: 3). From the very birth of the nation, the armed forces were thus distrusted and alienated from society, something that would have a large impact on the nature of its development into a professional corps.

The professionalization of the US military

After the relative peace of the early national period, mostly involving small wars along the Western frontier, the Civil War of 1861–1865 caught both sides unprepared, as they virtually had to build their armies from scratch. The Civil War is sometimes referred to as the first modern or total war, as it involved the entire societies, as well as introduced mass conscription, trench warfare, military railroads, as well as technological innovations, such as machine guns, submarines, and rifles. However, while the Civil War had a profound impact on the US, it was not until the war was over and the military went back to fight the indigenous people along the Western frontier that the US military went through what Samuel Huntington (1957) called the 'golden ages of professionalism'.

Despite, or perhaps because of, the broad participation of America's male youth in the Civil War, the hostility of American society towards the military institutions came back in peacetime and led to an isolation and rejection of the armed services after the war. This led the military to 'withdraw into its own hard shell' and develop a distinctively military character. No other period has, according to Huntington, been such a 'decisive influence in shaping the course of American military professionalism and the nature of the American military mind' (1957: 229). The size of the armed forces was kept small and as long as they did not ask for an increased budget, Congress left the armed forces relatively free to set its own training, promotion and evaluation standards. Moreover, the presidents, who at this time were free from any pressing external threats, left the armed forces to develop its professional standards free from civilian influence (Huntington 1957: 229).

One of the few post-Civil War political suggestions on the future of the US Army was the idea to change it into a police force. The army, not surprisingly, objected strongly to the use of the armed forces as a police force, since it was considered 'beneath the soldier's vocation' (Avant 1994: 26–27). Bernard Boëne has argued that, within the military profession, fighting other militaries and states is generally considered more charismatic than domestic policing. Defending the sovereignty of the nation state has given the military a unique role within the international arena as the most important security actor – a role worth preserving for the sake of status (2000: 7–9). In the US case the military was allowed to define its own functional imperative, and, as noted, the professional standards necessary to effectively address that imperative. Thus, the US military developed a doctrine of war based on the underlying principles of strategy. The inspiration for these developments came from an admiration and misreading of the Prussian military theorists of the nineteenth century, and relied heavily on the 'science of war'. Huntington writes: 'the German lessons were frequently misinterpreted and misapplied, but the desire to imitate German institutions was an important force in furthering American professionalism' (Huntington 1957: 235). Closely associated with the idea that war existed as an independent science was the notion that the practice of that science was the only purpose of military forces. The argument was, therefore, that the army and navy solely existed to fight wars, not for any other reason, and that the training and organization must be directed to the sole end of efficiency in combat (Huntington 1957: 256).

The American military profession differed from those of most other countries in that it was almost entirely the product of the officers themselves. In Europe, professionalism was normally the outcome of social–political currents at work in society at large. In the US, civilian contribution to the professional culture of the military was close to zero (Huntington 1957: 233). Thus, although most theorists in the field of civil–military relations claim that the culture and organization are a product of both functional and societal imperatives, in the US case the societal imperative was of little importance, and the functional imperative, which was left to be interpreted by the US military itself, was based on a misreading of European history and military theory.

The Cold War and the development of a standing army

The World Wars made sure that most military forces were adjusted for large-scale, conventional warfare. For the US military, this was nevertheless already the case and the World Wars simply confirmed and cemented its emphasis on large-scale offensive and decisive warfare. However, the military's role in policy-making had during the Second World War increased to the level where it essentially ran both the war and the country using the political leadership as political advisors. The military influence on decision-making did not prove easy to limit after the war (Huntington 1957: 315). Traditionally, the dislike for standing armed forces meant that the US military had been scaled back between wars. With the Soviet threat the US nevertheless for the first time since independence needed to maintain a large-scale peacetime military. This unbalanced the civil–military relationship by increasing the military's peacetime presence and influence in society and in security policy-making.

Strategically, the post-war era came to focus on a possible Third World War. To avoid the expansion of Communism, the US developed the grand strategy of containment, of which the first priority was the containment of Communism in Europe. The focus on Europe is important as it reinforced the US military's embedded bias towards large-scale warfare. The military's reward system, therefore, came to emphasize service in Europe and the continued focus on traditional principles of conventional war (Avant 1994: 34). The focus of the services in the early Cold War era was to demonstrate their necessity in a possible Third World War in order to secure congressional budgets, something that was demonstrated by the behaviour of the military services in the first containment war in Korea. In fact, none of the services saw Korea as the kind of war they existed for, and no lessons were learned in relation to limited warfare (Avant 1994: 35).

Korea, instead, provided the political and military leadership with almost opposing lessons learned. While the political leadership saw the benefits of the 'graduated response' and the possibility of limited political aims in wars to support the containment doctrine, the lesson learned by generals was that 'the only proper end of war was military victory', and they, therefore, found it hard to understand why this should ever be denied them (Huntington 1957: 389). As argued above, the political leadership that was in many ways relinquished to the military during the Second World War, and which allowed the military to define the aims of operations, was not easily regained in the post-war period. The Korean War, therefore, also provided a battleground over the control of strategic aims. General MacArthur, who was in charge of the operations in Korea, made his disgust with the limited aims clear as he, famously, argued that 'there is no substitute for victory' (Huntington 1957: 390). The civil–military conflict culminated in President Truman's firing of General MacArthur in 1951. This event, however, turned out to be somewhat of a pyrrhic victory as it proved politically costly, despite the fact that Truman in this matter had the support of the majority in Congress. The event made clear that the President's most important tool for controlling the military and generating change – control over personnel – was to be considered politically risky for the President. This risk was further exacerbated in the wake of the Second World War, as the heightened general interest in security policy also increased competition among the civilian branches of the government (Avant 1994: 35).

The military's historically successful resistance to innovation, caused by the high costs of presidential monitoring and incentives in forms of funding from

Congress that rewarded doctrinal focus on large-scale warfare in the European theatre, nevertheless had consequences. Avant argues that one such consequence was that the US never developed the type of military doctrine that is required for effective counter-insurgency operations (Avant 1994: 36). However, perhaps more importantly, it also lacked a military culture flexible enough to adapt to irregular operations. The cost of this deficiency became obvious as the US administration increasingly became involved in Vietnam.

The legacy of the Vietnam War

The Vietnam War is worth dwelling on, not only because it is arguably the most formative event for the US military in modern history, but also because it is a monumental example of a civil–military failure, and, therefore, highly interesting in relation to the later analyses of Iraq and Afghanistan. As part of the grand strategy of containment it is debatable whether the war was 'victorious' or not, as it was successful in limiting communist expansion in South-East Asia. However, in operational and tactical terms it is clear that the Vietnam War was a significant failure.

More than three million Americans were sent to Vietnam between the early 1960s until the main US withdrawal in 1973. About 58,000 were killed, and around 300,000 were wounded. A conservative estimate of civilian casualties in South Vietnam is the Senate Subcommittee on Refugees' estimates of 400,000 killed, 900,000 wounded, and 6.4 million turned into refugees. The total number of people who were killed during the American–Vietnam War has been estimated between one and three million people. Despite an enormous military and financial effort, the Americans never achieved the decisive victory they had always been seeking throughout their military history.

The mistakes and lessons of the Vietnam War have been thoroughly debated since, and the sheer diversity of lessons makes the issue very complicated. In a civil–military analysis of the Vietnam War it is obvious that the absence of clear objectives was very serious. On 19 May 1967, Secretary of Defense Robert McNamara drafted a memorandum redefining the goals worth fighting for in Vietnam. Since he argued that the goal of containing Chinese expansionism already had been attained, he no longer believed it vital that South Vietnam should remain independent or that it should remain non-Communist. The only American goal left was, therefore, to give 'the people of the South (Vietnam) the ability to determine their own future'. In 1984, McNamara broke his long silence about Indochina policy, and confirmed that he did not actually feel he had a compelling reason to go on fighting (Fromkin and Chace 1985).

However, equally weak as political strategy were military strategy and doctrine in Vietnam. The military strategy employed by General Westmoreland was one of a 'war of attrition', in which he sought to kill infiltrated and indigenous Vietnamese Communist soldiers more rapidly than they could be replaced. The infamous 'crossover point' was the point when the US would start winning as it killed more insurgents than were recruited. Counting bodies, therefore, became exceedingly important. During Westmoreland's four years in command of the US-led forces in Vietnam, and despite major setbacks and limited accomplishments, he remained faithful to his strategy and constantly asked for reinforcements to execute it. The lack of success was, according to Westmoreland, because of the effort's political limitations imposed on the military leadership.

Tactically, the search-and-destroy mission provided the basis for American military doctrine in Vietnam. This was an offensive attempt to bring as much firepower as possible to the engagements with the Communist forces (Avant 1994: 69). US Army doctrine was not in line with US grand strategy, which clearly required capabilities for limited and unconventional warfare. There was also an absence of institutional learning, as the army's offensive doctrine did not appreciate the constraints of counter-insurgency warfare (Cohen 1986: 296–297).

During the early years of the campaign, as the US military implemented its programme to train the South Vietnamese Army, its bias towards large conventional wars led the military to restructure the South Vietnamese Army from internal security, or counter-insurgency, to a defence against North Vietnamese invasion. The idea was that units trained to meet external aggression would also be able to handle the internal security (Avant 1994: 53–54). However, when President Kennedy took office, he sought to get the army interested in counter-insurgency. He asserted, in a message to Congress, that the nation needed a greater capability to handle guerrilla forces, and in 1961 he directed the army to examine its force structure in light of a possible commitment to South-East Asia (Avant 1994: 56–57). The army's response was minimal. General Lemnitzer, Chairman of the Joint Chiefs of Staff (1960–1962), argued that the administration overemphasized the importance of guerrilla warfare. Then Army Chief of Staff General Decker dismissed the idea of increased counter-insurgency competence by arguing that 'any good soldier can handle guerrillas' (Lemnitzer and Decker cited in Avant 1994: 57).

In a comprehensive analysis of US operations in Vietnam, John Nagl has argued that the main cause of failure was the inability to adapt to irregular warfare, caused by an inflexible military culture focused on conventional warfare (Nagl 2002). Avant (1994), similarly, argues that there are two reasons why the US Army failed to adapt in Vietnam. First, the incoherent civilian control of the armed forces in that the presidents were urging the army to adopt a counter-insurgency capability, while Congress, which controls the budgetary process, maintained a strong focus on Europe. The political leadership was, in other words, not in a strong enough position to enforce change. Second, the army was structured in a way that led to a doctrinal bias towards large-scale warfare, further institutionalized by rewarding those officers who focused on such warfare.

So what did the US military learn from Vietnam? Interestingly, in 1974 the Army War College commissioned a review of army strategy in Vietnam. The scope of the study nevertheless overwhelmed the War College and was turned over to the BDM Corporation, which published its findings in 1980. One of the major conclusions was that massive military power was not the best or the only weapon in low-intensity conflicts like Vietnam. In such cases, political aspects were more important than winning conventional military battles (Downie 1998). However, the findings of the BDM study disappointed the Army War College, which quickly published an alternative study, authored by Colonel Harry Summers. The main thrust of what was to become the US Army's approved version was that the 'lack of appreciation of military theory and military strategy ... led to the exhaustion of the army against a secondary guerrilla force' (Summers 1982: xiii). Summers contended that the problem in Vietnam was not that the army had failed to become unconventional, but that it was not conventional enough. The war was lost because the army was not allowed to use its firepower as widely and liberally as it would have liked (Nagl 2002: 207). The Army War College report, in other words, confirmed the conventional war bias of the US military.

It is clear that many important lessons that could have been learnt in relation to counter-insurgency and peace operations in general were lost in a military culture biased towards conventional warfare. The US military failed to learn from the mistakes in the Vietnam War, and made few significant conceptual changes to the Army's counter-insurgency doctrine in the post Vietnam War era, a doctrine that was also largely forgotten (Downie 1998: 109). Instead of facing up to the fact that army counter-insurgency doctrine had failed in Vietnam, the army decided that the US should no longer involve itself in operations of this type. The prevailing lesson of Vietnam was, therefore, printed in 1984, with the Weinberger Doctrine that allowed for the army to return to its organizational roots of conventional warfare for the purpose of decisive victory (Nagl 2002: 207). Thus, the radical approach to military professionalism prevailed despite the failures of the Vietnam War.

The Weinberger doctrine and the changing security context

The Weinberger Doctrine was created in the wake of the military disasters in Lebanon and Grenada, as the then US Secretary of Defense, Caspar Weinberger, proposed six major tests to be applied before deploying US combat forces abroad: Is a vital US interest at stake? Will we commit sufficient resources to win? Are the objectives clearly defined? Will we sustain the commitment? Is there reasonable expectation that the public and Congress will support the operation? Have we exhausted our other options? (Weinberger 1990).

The supposed soundness of the doctrine seemed to be confirmed in 1991 with what was then considered to be a tremendous success of military operations in the Gulf War. The criteria were in the wake of this success amended by the then Chairman of the Joint Chiefs of Staff Colin Powell, who made the addition that once Weinberger's conditions were met, the application of force should be overwhelming, swift and with a clear exit strategy (Powell 1992). The Gulf War, therefore, confirmed and strengthened the army's concept of purely conventional military battles with high-technology weaponry and overwhelming firepower. However, as John Nagl rightly argues, by refusing to acknowledge that most wars, unlike the Gulf, are and will be fought on battlefields populated by people who may support one side or the other (or one of many), the army continued to prepare itself to fight wars as it wants to fight them.

(2002: 207)

Because of the military success in the Gulf, the innovation that took place during the 1990s was completely in line with the military bias towards conventional warfare. The Gulf War was said to have started a revolution in military affairs, which with superior information and weapons technology would give the US a further advantage on the battlefield. However, in the meantime, the security context changed to place more emphasis on smaller, more complex conflicts as described in the first chapter of this book. Finally, with the terrorist attacks on the World Trade Center and the Pentagon in 2001, the luxury to choose suitable conflicts was lost. The strategy of containment had failed and even the most powerful nation in the world was incapable of protecting itself from unconventional attacks. Therefore, dealing with terrorist breeding grounds in failing states suddenly became a priority.

However, during the subsequent military campaigns in Afghanistan and Iraq, the US military has initially proved itself incapable of creating stability during the post-conflict phases of operations. 'By failing to learn the lessons of Vietnam, the US Army continues to prepare itself to fight the wrong war' (Nagl 2002: 208). It should nevertheless be noted that more recent developments point in a more positive direction. The Quadrennial Defense Review (QDR) of 2006 acknowledges the importance of irregular warfare (US DoD 2006). However, critics have noted that this acknowledgement of a new reality is in no way matched by programmes for transformation in order to face the new challenges. Instead, the QDR calls for more conventional capabilities (Lind 2006). A clearer break with past thinking is the new counter-insurgency doctrine, FM 3–24, also published in 2006. The doctrine involves an accurate and frank discussion regarding the difficulties for conventional forces to perform well in counter-insurgency operations, and produces a series of discussions and suggestions in an impressive attempt to catch up on lessons lost in the past. To a large extent, the doctrine involves a reappraisal of the counter-insurgency experiences from Vietnam, and has in Iraq been implemented to some extent. However, the degree to which the contents of the new documents will have an impact on the US military's training and culture in the long run remains to be seen.

After this historical introduction, let us examine the specifics of the US pattern of civil–military relations.

The US pattern of civil–military relations

When studying the civil–military interface it is of importance to acknowledge the fact that the national security apparatus is more than the organizational structures of civilian and military agencies; it is also the meeting of different organizational cultures. This section seeks to increase the understanding of the specifics of US civil–military relations by first discussing US civil–military relations in general, and, thereafter, studying the structural and cultural features of the interagency apparatus as well as the makeup of the US Department of Defense. The findings of the analysis of this section define the explanatory variable of the US case. A summary of features concludes the chapter, referring back to the theoretical discussion on the divided and the integrated forms of civil–military relations.

The birth of the modern US national security establishment came at the end of the Second World War, as the strategic context created a sudden requirement for standing armed forces. This led to a complete reorganization of the defence machinery with the National Security Act of 1947, which created what we now call the DoD, with the Departments of the Army, Navy and Air Force all under the authority of a Secretary of Defense with Cabinet rank. The legislation also provided a legal identity for the Joint Chiefs of Staff and created the Central Intelligence Agency, the National Security Council (NSC) and many other agencies (Stuart 2000: 5). The National Security Act of 1947 also created a clear division of responsibilities between the civilian and military leaderships. While the civilian leadership creates policy and objectives, the military commanders are supposed to use their professional judgement 'to execute the policy through the most effective and efficient means possible' (Libby 1993). This divide between political decision-making and military implementation, developed out of fear of military politicization and intervention in politics, has also in practical terms created a divide between the civilian and military sides of the Department of Defense, as well as in the interagency process.

The historical section revealed how the founding fathers' fear of centralized power led them to control the powers of the military, but also to limit political leaders' capability to exploit their powers. The basic elements of the new political system were the diffusion of power and shared responsibility. The diffusion, or the division, of power has taken the form of a federal system that guarantees a decentralization of power and a division of power between the central and non-central governments. It has also created the separation of powers between the executive, legislative and judicial branches of the government (Lijphart 1999: 186).

One of the main features of American democracy is the political system of checks and balances. The separation of powers and the system of checks and balances have led to a political culture that is marked by competitive, conflicting mindsets, rather than the consensual form of politics seen in other political systems. Not only do the branches of government check on each other, but also so do the different departments within the executive branch. The nature of the US political system, therefore, affects US civil–military relations in two distinct ways. First, the system of checks and balances has made the civilian leadership weak in relation to a comparatively unified military. The political system creates tensions and conflict between the different branches of government and, as a result, gives the military a chance to play them against each other on different policy issues. The US administration, thereby, has an incoherent and weak polit-ical side against the four coherent services of the armed forces (Avant 1994: 134–135). As noted in the historical section, the competition between Congress and the President has moreover resulted in the problem that the President's most important tool for controlling the military and generating change – control over personnel – is politically very risky. To use Feaver's terminology, the cost of political monitoring of the armed forces is high, and creates possibilities for mil-itary shirking without risks of punishment. This tendency was further exacer-bated with the introduction of the Goldwater-Nichols Defense Reorganization Act, which gave the Joint Chiefs a stronger and more unified voice in national policy-making.

Second, the system of checks and balances has created a political culture in which co-operation, consensus seeking and mutual trust are not very common-place. In a system of checks and balances, distrust and competition are con-sidered virtues in the protection of the democratic order. While this system is effective in certain respects, it is certainly not a tool for co-operation and co-ordination between different governmental agencies.

Although the US has never come close to a military coup, misunderstanding and distrust have underlain American civil–military relations from the very beginning, and have further deteriorated since the end of the Cold War (Weigley 2000: 246). Despite the relatively harmonious civil–military relations America enjoys compared with many other countries, the most dominant theme in the literature on US civil–military relations is, therefore, the presence of conflict (Feaver 2003: 12; Feaver and Kohn 2001). To illustrate the ebbs and flows of conflict in US civil–military relations, we can refer to the debate regarding the civil–military cultural gap and the extent to which civilian, societal values should be allowed to influence military culture. This debate was revived under the Clinton administration with the controversy over gays in the military and Presid-ent Clinton's lack of military experience. Conflict was again spurred by Defense Secretary Rumsfeld's technocratic ideas of military transformation against the wishes of the military leadership (Desch 2001: 317), as well as the tensions during the build-up to the war in Iraq, as described in Chapter 5.

The US interagency structures

US doctrine on interagency co-operation states that such co-operation forges a vital link between the military instrument of power and the economic, political and/or diplomatic and informational entities of the US Government as well as non-governmental agencies. It also states that 'obtaining coordinated and integ-rated effort in an interagency operation is critical to success' (US DoD 1996: v). This view is supported by the Center for Strategic and International Studies (CSIS) report on defence reform in the new strategic era. The CSIS report argued that the current operations in Afghanistan and Iraq show that success in major combat operations must be followed by success in post-conflict stability opera-tions. In many instances DoD success, therefore, hinges on how well it integrates with other government agencies and coalition partners (Murdock 2004: 22). The structure and culture of US interagency co-operation are, therefore, well worth studying further.

Despite the promising words of interagency doctrine documents, the US government often confronts problems that are beyond the capacity of any single department or agency to deal with, and it rarely develops comprehensive policies that span across the whole spectrum of government (Gorman and Krongard 2005: 52). Instead, the US government is structured to divide knowledge and expertise into component parts by disaggregating national security issues and then parcelling the parts to different departments and agencies. Krongard and Gorman refer to 'stove piped decision-making' – an approach that results in piecemeal US responses to most international issues. The independent solutions of the different departments and agencies vary greatly, and sometimes even conflict. Nevertheless, after going through the intra-departmental process, the separate solutions enter the interagency process and eventually end up at the highest levels of government. This means that only at the very highest echelons of government do integration, co-ordination and synchronization take place (Gorman and Krongard 2005: 53–54).

It should be noted that task forces and working groups designed to facilitate interagency co-operation and co-ordination have existed within the US government bureaucracy for years. However, they are usually ad hoc, narrow in scope, and limited in terms of decision-making or co-ordination authority. They are also viewed with suspicion by most government departments (Bogdanos 2005: 11). The lack of authority and meaningful mandates to create co-ordinated advice and policy means that meetings are not taken very seriously and primarily function as information sharing tools. Each agency informs the other of its stand on an issue, and then parts with little co-ordination or adjustment (interviews with Harris 2005; Parmly 2005; Stevenson 2005). Most organizational incentives of the US government work against an integrative interagency approach that is seen as providing unwelcome control over agency operations to other agencies or to a central planning staff (Lord 1998: 11).

The US interagency system also lacks a decisive authority – a central body in charge of strategic assessment and planning (Marcella 2000: 184). As already noted, the NSC, under the leadership of the national security advisor, is often highlighted as the bearer of this mantle. The NSC advises and assists the President in integrating all aspects of national security policy, and is thereby central to all interagency co-operation on matters regarding US security. Doctrine argues that 'together with supporting interagency working groups, high-level steering groups, executive committees and task forces, the National Security Council System provides the foundation for interagency coordination in the development and implementation of national security policy' (US DoD 1996: vi–vii). The NSC is, in other words, supposed to track and direct the development, execution and implementation of all national security policies for the President.

Although the NSC was created to integrate diplomatic, military, financial and other factors into a unified national security policy, it is, in practice, solely an advisory organ to the President, and, therefore, has little executive function (Crabb and Holt 1989: 9). It is not a planning of operations or co-ordination headquarters, and currently has neither the authority, nor the capacity to fulfil such a function. Despite the importance of integrating agency strategies and plans, as well as monitoring their execution, for the achievement of unity of effort and success in operations, there is actually very little capacity on the NSC staff dedicated to these functions (Murdock 2004: 61).

Limited interagency co-operation means few opportunities for staff from different departments and agencies to interact and develop interpersonal trust. As noted in the theoretical chapter, interpersonal trust comes either from similar backgrounds and values, or from personal experiences of reciprocity. Not only do the US institutional set-up and political culture promote competition and distrust, they also limit the possibilities to develop interpersonal trust as an alternative. While the interagency *structure* is limited in the US case, the *cultural factor* is perhaps even more important as a determinant of interagency co-operation. The stovepipe administrative culture also leads to increased parochialism and career development focused on intradepartmental proficiency rather than a more comprehensive expertise in dealing with national security threats. This leads to unnecessary interagency conflicts within the national security apparatus, which consequently focuses more on bureaucratic self-interest and resource allocation than on actual strategies to deal with threats (Gorman and Krongard 2005: 54).

A more practical problem in relation to interagency co-operation in complex peace operations is that, unlike the military, which has doctrines and standard approaches to operational planning, the US government in general and the Department of State in particular lack established procedures for developing integrated strategies and plans. Although the civilian agencies may theoretically have valuable inputs in operational plans, there are, except for the US Agency for International Development (US AID), no dedicated planning staffs, expertise or planning culture outside the DoD (Murdock 2004: 61). In essence, the State Department is not an operative or 'doing' organization.

A similar problem is the lack of rapidly deployable experts and capabilities in most civilian agencies. Again the US AID provides an exception by way of the Office of Foreign Disaster Assistance which rapidly deploys Disaster Assistance Response Teams (DART) (Murdock 2004: 62). In other words, even if all agencies were involved in the strategic and operational planning there would essentially only be the military to turn to for implementation of operations other than war. In the words of a CSIS report, 'the weaknesses of other U.S. federal government agencies have forced DoD to bear the main burden of nation-building' (Murdock 2004: 18). Robert Steele (2000) argues that the lack of civilian personnel for international operations is cultural, as the bulk of money in security policy is still invested in Cold War-type standing armies of relatively little use in these types of operations. The cultural bias towards conventional war and the conceptual war leads to skewed funding of different agencies involved in complex peace operations. The creation of the interagency Office of the Coordi-

nator for Reconstruction and Stabilization has not changed these skewed relations. Despite the obvious deficiencies in planning and field staff for the civilian
aspects of operations, the Office, as well as the Department of State in general,
have failed to secure the necessary funding in order to become serious partners
in complex peace operations.

The limited interagency structures as well as the limited civilian resources for
the planning and execution of international operations mean that, in the near
future, the bulk of operational planning and implementation will continue to be
the task of the Department of Defense. Therefore, the extent to which the policy
and military sections and units co-operate, and its staffs are receptive of input
from other government agencies is important. The next section, therefore, takes
a closer look at the US Department of Defense.

The Department of Defense

As earlier mentioned, the DoD, as we recognize it today, was created in the wake
of the Second World War. Since the late 1950s the Department of Defense has
remained remarkably similar, but the debacles in Grenada and Lebanon during
the early 1980s led to some major reforms in the Goldwater–Nichols Act, passed
in 1986. The first explicit objective of the Goldwater–Nichols Act was to
increase civilian authority. Therefore, the legislation strengthened the Secretary
of Defense's overall control over the Department of Defense. The second objective was to improve military advice, which by design gave the military a new
power base for military impact on civilians by centralizing the military leadership. This was done by making the Chairman of the Joint Chiefs of Staff the
head of an expanded and strengthened Joint Staff, and by making him the principal military advisor to the President, the National Security Council and the
Secretary of Defense. The Chairman of the JCS was also assigned to developing
joint doctrine (Murdock 2004, 15). Despite the Goldwater–Nichols legislation
and several other attempts to reform the national security since it came into place
in the late 1950s, 'what is most striking about the existing system is not how
much it has changed, but how little' (Stuart 2000: 2).

US civil–military relations consist of a clear divide between the political and
military leaderships. This divide forms the basic structure of the Pentagon as
well. Commentators speak of a military and a civilian side of the building, and a
demarcation line that goes between the Office of the Secretary of Defense
(OSD), and the Joint Chiefs of Staff (JCS) (interview with White 2004). As the
normal theory of divided civil–military relations is clearly the most prevalent
within the US administration, this is considered a strength that ensures that political advice stays political, and that military advice stays purely military. The idea
is also to limit the politicization of the armed forces by keeping the senior military leadership out of politics, as well as keeping politicians from meddling in
military affairs.

The structural divide between the military and the policy sides of the Pentagon, although unmistakeable, is nevertheless not as clear as one might expect.

The OSD employs roughly 30 per cent military officers, including military advisors to every civilian at Assistant Secretary level and above, and the Joint Staff employs roughly 10 per cent civilian civil servants (Grissom 2005). Former department officials moreover argue that there is daily formal and informal interaction between the two sides of the Pentagon (interview with Harris 2005). However, a closer look at the Joint Staff reveals that although there are many civilians working on the staff they are not evenly spread out in the office. While the J5 (Strategic Plans and Policies) understandably has a large number of civilians and frequent communication with OSD staff, there are also almost purely military sections in the J2 (intelligence) and J3 (operations) (White 2005). Where it really matters, in military terms, civilians are not a common feature. Even more importantly, it also makes a difference who the civilians on the staff are, and what type of function they perform. Many civilians within the Joint Staff are contractors and even former officers performing military staff functions. They are not there to provide a political perspective on military planning and operations, but to fulfil staff functions that military officers could just as well perform. There are not many professional civil servants on the Joint Staff (interview with Harris 2005).

As was the case in the analysis of US interagency co-operation, a closer look at the working culture between the different offices of the department reveals that, although the formal structures for co-operation are in place, the outcomes of interoffice meetings are often relatively limited and disappointing. Former DoD officials reveal that the meetings are often a show for the gallery. The joint staff representatives will argue that 'we give you best military advice'. The OSD staffers say 'thank you very much but we have a much larger plate of consideration to add into the equation' (White 2005; RAND roundtable 2005). There is, in other words, a very limited amount of give and take during these meetings, and, as previously noted, this format is also common in the interagency process. Although there is sometimes a structure for civil–military co-operation within the department, the culture of the department and the political system simply does not support it.

It is clear that the US DoD works in at least two different channels for policy and military affairs. An interesting question is, therefore, where does the necessary civil–military interaction take place? Johnson and Metz argue that the interface between the Secretary of Defense and the Joint Chiefs of Staff is the single most important one in American civil–military relations. The Secretary of Defense personally provides the interface between civilians and military. 'Whether he is seen as pro- or anti-military sets the tenor for all of civil–military relations' (Johnson and Metz 1995: 18). This view is, to an extent, confirmed by a former joint staff officer who claims that the most important relationship is between the Secretary of Defense and the combatant commanders (Harris 2005). Clearly the civil–military interface within the Pentagon is limited, which is, as previously argued, a recommendation of the divided approach to civil–military relations.

An explicit and successful goal of the Goldwater–Nichols Act was to attract the 'best and the brightest' to seek joint service in order to solve the problem of jointness between the different services in the armed forces. There has, nevertheless, been no parallel set of incentives or requirements to encourage professional development for civilians in the DoD or to broaden their experience base and skill set through training or interdepartmental and interagency rotations. According to the CSIS, this reflects a general lack of appreciation of the critical roles that civilian professionals play in the Department of Defense and the national security agencies more broadly. The CSIS report argued that there is currently too little civilian expertise in the US government generally and the Department of Defense specifically. This means that there is a serious imbalance between military and civilian expertise at the Pentagon. Civilian advice often cannot compete with that offered by their counterparts on the Joint Staff (Murdock 2004: 20).

This leads to another interesting aspect of the US case – the limited role of the professional civil servant. All of the senior management positions in the DoD at the Assistant Secretary level are occupied by political appointees, limiting the opportunities for advancement available to even the most capable and experienced career professionals. The CSIS contends that not only is this glass ceiling real – it is virtually impenetrable. It is also somewhat unique within the US government as both the State Department and the CIA, for example, have career professionals serving at the Under Secretary level. However, within the Pentagon, political appointees are also common at even lower levels, such as Deputy Assistant Secretaries, Deputy Under Secretaries, Office Directors and even action officers (Murdock 2004: 54).

Conclusions

American civil–military relations are, and always have been, marked by ebbs and flows of conflict. The US has, nevertheless, never been close to a military coup and the ideal of political primacy is strong within the military. However, in practice, the political control of the US armed forces is weak. A divided political leadership of checks and balances faces high costs of monitoring and controlling the relatively unified military leadership. Thus, the military can shirk political decisions without great risks of punishment. The development of military professionalism in isolation from the political leadership has, in combination with the high costs of civilian monitoring and control of the armed forces, meant that the US military's functional imperative has been interpreted and defined by the military itself.

The competitive political culture of checks and balances means that the US has poorly developed structures for interagency co-operation and co-ordination. Power is decentralized and national security issues, therefore, tend to be dealt with in departmental stovepipes. Where different forms of interagency structures exist, the culture of competition and distrust means that interagency working groups and committees lack the authority to conduct meaningful work.

Within the Department of Defense, the civilian and military sections are not well integrated. Instead, the department is purposefully divided to ensure the purification of military and political affairs. Pure military advice is highly valued and the Huntingtonian principle of objective civilian control, by ensuring that politicians stay out of military affairs and vice versa, remains strong. However, this divide between the policy and military sides of the building has led to another stovepipe structure in which civilian and military expertise is not co-ordinated until the very top levels of the department. The US administration contains a relatively politicized civil service, which, through regular replacements, limits the institutional memory of the different departments.

These findings are interesting with reference to the theoretical discussion on trust. The limited interagency structures as well as the divided civil–military structures within the Pentagon mean that there are few opportunities for civil servants and officers from different departments and agencies to meet face-to-face and, thereby, develop interpersonal trust that comes from previous positive experiences, mutual respect and at least some level of mutual understanding. The different backgrounds of military officers and civil servants also mean that no thick interpersonal relationships exist from common schooling or background. Moreover, there is little institutional trust as there are few positive experiences of working together. The interagency system is simply not trusted.

In conclusion, the US patterns of civil–military relations are divided. It is a structure in which political decision-making and military implementation are divided, and in which the cost of civilian monitoring of the armed forces is generally high. The theoretical framework of this book argues that the patterns of a state's civil–military relations will affect its conduct of operations in two ways: indirectly as the arena in which decisions regarding the size, structure, equipment and doctrine of the armed forces are made; and directly by being an important level in the chain of command during operations, in which strategic aims are created and translated into operational objectives and activities. The following chapters follow these causal chains in order to trace the causal mechanisms of the theoretical framework. First, the American way of war is analysed.

4 The American way of war

The US pattern of civil–military relations has an impact on the conduct and effectiveness of operations by affecting the organization, culture and doctrine of the armed forces. This chapter, therefore, examines these features, grouped into the concept of the 'American way of war'. Emphasis is placed on the cultural aspects of the US defence establishment. The relatively extensive inclusion of doctrine in this chapter denotes the importance that some scholars attach to this variable when explaining operational conduct. The central questions of this chapter concern the functional imperative of the US defence establishment: What is considered to be the main role of the armed forces, and the preferred way of fighting wars? To what extent have the armed forces adjusted to that imperative? Finally, in relation to the contemporary strategic context of complex peace operations, are the US armed forces prepared for the type of conflicts they are likely to find themselves involved in?

'We fight the wars but we don't do peacekeeping', is a comment from President George W. Bush that has bewildered scholars around the world. It is moreover commonly supported and expressed within the US military which has been notorious for its dislike of operations other than war. The author acknowledges that speaking in terms of 'the US military' implies great generalizations that fail to recognize the different service cultures of the US military. There is, in other words, a need to continue this research by breaking down the US armed forces into smaller units of observation. Regarding the tasks of nation building, Bush argued during the 2000 presidential campaign: 'I would be very careful about using our troops as nation builders. I believe the role of the military is to fight and win war and, therefore, prevent war from happening in the first place' (cited in Holt 2003). Moreover, the then National Security Advisor, Condoleezza Rice, declared that the US military, as the world's stabilizing force, was meant only for war-fighting: it is 'lethal', she said, 'it is not a civilian police force. It is not a political referee. And it is most certainly not designed to build a civilian society' (cited in Hirsh 2003). At first glance, the US approach to complex peace operations seems to be, 'we don't do it'. This is obviously perplexing since these forms of operations are precisely what the US armed forces have increasingly been doing since the end of the Second World War, and even more so since the fall of the Berlin Wall, an argument well made by Max Boot (2002).

As already mentioned, this remarkable position of the US government and defence establishment has changed somewhat after the terror attacks of 11 September 2001, and the wars in Afghanistan and Iraq. The changes are reflected in the 2006 *Quadrennial Defense Review* and the *National Security Directive*, as well as in the new counter-insurgency doctrine. Before looking closer at the US approaches to complex peace operations, it is important to understand the US military and strategic culture, and what the US military thinks it *should* be doing.

The functional imperative and US strategic culture

As discussed in the section on US military history, US military professionalism was developed in a state of isolation after the Civil War. The small size of the army, in combination with a lack of external threat, allowed the US military to professionalize without interference from either the President or Congress. As noted in the theoretical chapter, for reasons of bureaucratic self-defence, every bureaucracy has an organizational essence, a set of functions or activities that most clearly define it and justify its existence. Left to themselves, bureaucracies, therefore, tend to undertake projects and pursue goals that reinforce this organizational essence (Lord 1998: 17–18). The emphasis on principles of war, European continental warfare and a misreading of Prussian theorists defined the US military's functional imperative and the resulting professional ethos became biased towards large-scale conventional warfare. A trait that is still very much alive. In contrast, different forms of peace operations have low status and have despite extensive experience of such operations not been a large part of the US military ethos or training.

The US has always considered war an alternative to bargaining or politics, instead of as an ongoing bargaining process as described by Clausewitz's famous dictum about war as the continuation of politics by other means. In the US, politics ceases when war begins. This dualistic view of conflict means that the US either considers itself at war or at peace (Echevarria 2004: 43). There is, in other words, a grey area of operations other than war that the US military has never liked to tread, as well as a gap between military operations and political aims. As an example, Anthony Cordesman argues that the current US military transformation of technological innovation and network-based solutions fails to prepare for low-intensity combat and post-conflict reconstruction, and only creates possibilities to win 'half the war: winning the combat but not the peace' (Cordesman 2003a: 12). This argument is further developed by Antulio Echevarria, who maintains that the American concept of war rarely extends beyond the winning of battles and campaigns – activities at the operational level of war – and tends to avoid thinking about the complicated process of turning military victories into strategic success (Echevarria 2004: 1). US military professionals instead concentrate on winning battles and campaigns while policy makers focus on the diplomatic struggles that precede and influence the actual fighting. The US has, therefore, developed more of a way of battle than a way of war (Echevarria

2004: v). Carnes Lord (1998: 11) calls this an 'astrategic orientation of the US government', which is further reinforced by a political culture that lacks centralized direction and control. In essence, a dualistic view of war and peace has produced an equally divided bureaucracy in dealing with these issues. You are either a department of war or peace.

American strategic culture further views problems in isolation, according to Echevarria, as well as being oriented towards the present and immediate future. It thereby lacks both historical and long-term future horizons and sees peace as the normal state of things and war or conflict as unnatural or wrong. The US, therefore, tends to be poor at strategy, which is a field that requires holistic thinking and attention to the consequences of action over time. US security policy is as a consequence most often the outcome of considerations on specific issues as they arise, rather than 'an overall analysis of the current international situation and a comprehensive strategy for dealing with it' (Echevarria 2004: 11).

When at war, the preferred way of fighting is described by Russell Weigley (1973) as large wars of annihilation with a reliance on firepower, a quest for decisive battles, a desire to employ maximum effort and aggressiveness at all levels. The American way of war also involves an over-reliance on technology and firepower, as well as a strong preference for air power over troops on the ground. Another tendency is the reluctance to incur casualties (Nagl 2002; Cassidy 2004; Gray 1981). There is also a presumption that the United States must end military conflicts quickly and at minimum cost, as reflected in the Weinberger and Powell doctrines. This is not a presumption that has come out of 'the broad contours of American history', but of the specific context of the Vietnam War. The idea is that in order to maintain the support of the American public, military operations must be brief and efficient in terms of the human and economic price paid (Erdmann 2002: 48).

Miriam Becker (1994) claims that the US military often appears to fight for 'ideological' principles, such as democratic values, based on the belief that most countries want to be like the US and that the international community accepts its international leadership role. Nagl (2002), similarly, stresses the American faith in its liberal uniqueness and its moral mission. Rather than operating as a dispassionate professional, the US military personnel, therefore, act with a highly political and ideological motivation (Aylwin-Foster 2005: 6). Related to the idea of ideological righteousness is the assertion that the US has a continuing faith in progress: that somehow international politics could evolve towards a condition of greater security, and that US strategic culture is, therefore, oriented towards problem solving and does not accept readily the idea of continuing conflict. The idea that certain parties may not even want to agree on an issue, which is a main feature of contemporary conflict, is antithetical to the American assumption that issues must be resolved in order for commerce to prosper. American strategic thinking has therefore tended to be based on quick fix problem solving (Gray 1984).

Avant notes that American officers' training has emphasized military history in order to teach the principles of war and to create uniformity of both thought and procedure. This led to a rigid and inflexible understanding of the conduct of warfare. The idea was that through a uniform application of the principles of war, the army would make the individual qualities in leaders relatively unimportant, and would regardless of intellectual capabilities respond the right way to military uncertainties. The emphasis on the science of war also led to a strong bias against individual initiative. By rewarding and promoting officers who always adhered to regulations and the principles of war, the idea of 'safe leadership' took hold (Avant 1994: 26–28). This tradition is the root of what is often called the zero-defect culture of the US military. The zero-defect mentality is intolerant of mistakes by officers. The result is that military leaders become more concerned with 'making sure nothing goes wrong on their watch' than with achieving the aims of the operation (Steele 2004). The US approach to force protection in peacekeeping is an example discussed below.

Since the end of the Cold War the US military has undergone a defence transformation within the scope of the so-called revolution in military affairs, involving reliance on technology, firepower and air power. The hallmarks of defence transformation are speed, manoeuvre, flexibility, surprise, being heavily reliant on precision firepower, Special Forces and psychological operations. The goal is to increase the lethality of the US military forces by 'harnessing technological advances of the information age to gain a qualitative advantage over any potential foe' (Boot 2003). However, the force transformation is primarily focused on conventional warfare and the problem of defeating a regular enemy in battle. Its underlying concepts of information-centric theories such as network centric warfare, rapid decisive operations, and shock and awe, all focus on '"taking down" an opponent quickly, rather than finding ways to apply military force in the pursuit of broader political aims' (Echevarria 2004: 16). It can be noted that even the concept of Effects-Based Approaches to Operations, which by definition is constructed to better co-ordinate economic, diplomatic and military resources in order to achieve political aims, has also been high-jacked by the military and made into a new matrix for target value calculation for the air force, and for winning battles more efficiently (Mattis 2008; Egnell 2006).

Despite the fact that the US military has mainly been involved in irregular warfare since the end of the Second World War, US military and strategic culture is firmly fixed on what it sees as its core task – defeating conventional enemies that threaten the freedom of the American people. Given the constant perceived need to prepare for the Third World War during the specific context of the Cold War, this was more understandable before the fall of the Berlin Wall. However, the unshakable belief in the essence of the organization has precluded any organizational learning and adjustment to unconventional wars or operations other than war (Nagl 2002). It has also led to what John Nagl describes as 'a remarkable aversion to the use of unconventional tactics' (2002: 43–44). Studies of US counter-insurgency operations and doctrines show that US military leaders, since its infancy, have made little effort to capture lessons learned or to develop effective doctrine on counter-insurgency operations; the latter have instead been treated as mere diversions from the more important study of conventional warfare. The US military has during its history viewed counter-insurgency warfare as unglamorous, unwanted and diverting. It is a type of activity that detracts attention and focus from the military's primary role of fighting conventional wars (Birtle 2001).

Despite its many successes and evident professionalism and effectiveness in a number of military operations, the US military has been criticized for its conduct in recent peace operations, such as Bosnia, Somalia and Kosovo. Inflexibility, overemphasis on force protection and an indifference to mission success are commonly stated complaints. In the words of Thomas Mockaitis: 'Nothing underscores American discomfort with peace operations more than the emphasis on force protection at the expense even of mission success' (2004: 14). The US operations in Somalia during the 1990s were characterized by a propensity for maximum use of force and over-reliance on technology, resulting in a lack of tactical flexibility. It also highlighted the averseness to casualties with which the US military has conducted expeditionary operations in the post-Cold War era. Cassidy summarizes the US role in Somalia by arguing that 'maximalist and conventional attitudes about the use of force led the U.S. military to abandon the OOTW principle of restraint, and thus legitimacy' (2004: 155, 162–165).

The US military experiences in Bosnia-Herzegovina paint a similar picture of US behaviour in complex peace operations. First, US force protection policies generated tension both within the US military and between US and other militaries. At the tactical level during IFOR, force protection was the highest priority. Force protection was even part of the Operational Plan mission statement listed second on the 'Mission Essential Task List' only trailing the mission to sustain trained and ready forces. Interestingly, although many officers felt that the force protection policy was politically motivated rather than a result of actual threat assessment, and that any fatality would be considered a failure for which they would be held personally accountable, no officers felt that the force protection policies caused great damage to the mission. Instead, the force protection policy was seen as a wise approach given the nature of the mission (Garofano 2004: 245–246).

Second, US troops, although well prepared for their specific functions within their units, received minimal amounts and limited quality of cultural training. Platitudes, such as 'ethnic problems do not have solutions; thus, conflict must be managed', '[the local population] only respect strength of force', were common. Moreover, the depth of cultural and political training was very limited. Some units received less than one hour of cultural training before deployment in Bosnia (Garofano 2004: 243–244). Finally, limited civil–military co-ordination is presented as another problem in the Bosnian case. The US did not initially integrate plans with NATO or international partners and instead concentrated on military enforcement issues. The US, therefore, failed to plan for the more difficult political and civil tasks, and also failed to integrate military support with civil implementation (Garofano 2004: 254–255).

The US military has a long record of conducting various kinds of peace operations. As already noted, they nevertheless concentrate on warfighting and 'eschew the challenges of dealing with the battlefield after the battle'. When

American forces do undertake such missions, they try, as much as possible, to make them mirror traditional military warfighting (Carafano 2003: 2–3). This means that inherently unconventional campaigns, such as in Vietnam and Iraq, are still conceptualized in conventional terms, involving conventional tactics.

An explanation for the US reluctance to adjust its way of war to different types of operations and contexts is presented by the Triangle Institute for Security Studies that has conducted extensive surveys for a study on the cultural gap in civil–military relations. These surveys reveal a distinct US military dislike for operations other than war. In 1998–1999 only 1 per cent of US military leaders saw military interventions like the ones in Bosnia and Somalia as 'very important' roles for the military. This can be contrasted with 99 per cent support for the role 'to fight and win our country's wars' (Holsti 2001: 46). Thus, the US military seems to foster the cultural bias towards conventional warfare during military training. Moreover, Volker Franke's survey of West Point cadets demonstrates that they show less positive attitudes towards peace operations the longer they had been at West Point (Franke 1999: 111). Military training thus seems to increase the gap between the civilian and military institutions and creates a military mind that thinks less of peace operations in relation to traditional war.

The cultural aspects of the American way of war are adjusted to the functional imperative of conventional warfare in the defence of the nation. Structurally, the same pattern appears. Recent changes in the way US troops are organized indicate some alterations, but the US approach to war still remains industrial in scale and relies on mass and the use of decisive force (Mackinlay 2004). Cassidy argues that in contemporary US thinking 'the division is still the dominant organization that trains and fights as a team', and the division combined with armed teams is still the centrepiece of both the structure and doctrine of US Army warfighting. Suggestions to move away from the division to the smaller regimental-sized combined battle groups have faced strong resistance within the US Army (Cassidy 2004: 250). The equipment is largely adjusted for conventional warfare on the plains of Europe, or the deserts of Iraq. Heavy tanks and armoured vehicles and massive firepower in the forms of air power and artillery still remain the main investments in US military materiel.

In summary, the American way of war is focused on conventional warfare, which is also considered the functional imperative of the armed forces. The US military emphasizes massive firepower, high technology, a moral motive and quick fix solutions. In the specific context of complex peace operations, US troops often add a strong emphasis on force protection and a reluctance to incur casualties. The fact that the US military sees itself as an instrument of national survival has created an uncompromising focus on conventional warfighting that has left it ill prepared for post-conflict-type operations, and discouraged a quick adaptation to these types of operations (Aylwin-Foster 2005: 14).

US doctrine before Operation Iraqi Freedom

Before studying a selection of US doctrines concerning complex peace operations, a conceptual discussion regarding the impact of doctrine is necessary. What is doctrine and why does it matter? The modern definitions of doctrine vary slightly, but the US DoD dictionary defines it as 'fundamental principles by which the military forces or elements thereof guide their actions in support of national objectives. It is authoritative but requires judgment in application' (US DoD 2001). Doctrine is thus the officially sanctioned and written approach to military activity that describes the best way to go about things. Doctrines, moreover, provide educational documents and are thus meant to form the behaviour of armies in battle (Johnston 2000: 30).

Robert Cassidy maintains that doctrine is salient because 'it is central to how militaries execute their missions – it is how we operate'. In Cassidy's view, doctrine mirrors actual behaviour, and is, therefore, an important independent variable that affects the operational behaviour of the armed forces. Consequently, operational mistakes or successes can be explained by the quality of the doctrine (Cassidy 2004: 3–4). However, doctrine often lags behind events, and is, therefore, not always beneficial in conflicts. Doctrine, thereby, has a tendency to describe best practices in the last war, and may fail to attend to contextual changes and specifics between different conflicts (Bulloch 1996). Colin McInnes (2001) further argues that doctrine is 'wholeheartedly and unashamedly positivist'. It is presented as being founded in history and derives its authority from experience. Although reference is often made to the capacity of doctrine to evolve, doctrine has an enduring nature that emphasizes 'fundamental principles' of war much more than adaptation. This is problematic in relation to the fact that doctrine is inherently political, and often reflects service interests and political demands. The potential weaknesses of doctrine are notable in the case of Vietnam, where doctrine not only failed to prepare troops properly, but also prevented tactical adjustments. Sir Michael Howard, therefore, presents a rather bleak view of doctrine, derived from a historical perspective that correctly emphasizes the uniqueness of each conflict and its context:

> I am tempted to declare that whatever doctrine the Armed Forces are working on, they have got it wrong. I am also tempted to declare that it does not matter that they have got it wrong. What does matter is their capacity to get it right quickly when the moment arrives. It is the task of military science in an age of peace to prevent the doctrine being too badly wrong.
> (Cited in UK Army n.d.)

Another critique of doctrine is related to the important question of cause and effect: To what extent does doctrine actually influence behaviour in battle? A survey of the history of armies and their doctrines suggests that doctrine has a weak, or at best indirect, effect on the actual behaviour of armies in battle. Instead, how armies fight is more a function of their culture than of their doctrine

(Johnston 2000: 30). Doctrine reflects behaviour, which is in turn determined by the contents of doctrine. This reflexive view of doctrine makes it interesting in relation to culture.

Doctrinal publications are in this book treated as conceptual artefacts of a nation's strategic and military culture. Therefore, the language and content of doctrine help us understand a nation's way of war. Doctrine describes past behaviour of military organizations, and also serves to reproduce certain practices. If as influential as some commentators argue, doctrine should function as an important intervening variable that helps explain operational conduct and effectiveness. Even if doctrine does not have quite the causal effect as some commentators maintain it does, it is still an interesting artefact that helps us understand its function in relation to other explanatory variables, such as training and equipment, or in relation to the cultural context. Therefore, a highly relevant question for the following sections is: To what extent does doctrine reflect the US way of war?

Contents of US doctrine

The US has a fascination with doctrine, which means that in theory as well as in practice doctrine runs the training of especially the US Army (Cohen 1996: 193). The fact that doctrine is taken very seriously in the US becomes clear in the preface to the Doctrine for Joint Operations, which states that 'the guidance in this publication is authoritative; as such, this doctrine will be followed except when, in the judgment of the commander, exceptional circumstances dictate otherwise' (US DoD 2001: i). Most nations' doctrines include a similar statement, but the US case is certainly more authoritative, especially when considered in the light of the concepts of safe leadership and zero-defects culture. One of the arguments was that US military culture does not reward those who are innovative and flexible beyond the content of doctrine. Instead, for successful careers, officers are best advised to follow doctrine.

The *National Security Strategy of the United States of America* from 2000 declares that 'defending our Nation against its enemies is the first and fundamental commitment of the Federal Government'. However, the doctrine acknowledges that this task has changed dramatically. 'Enemies in the past needed great armies and great industrial capabilities to endanger America. Now, shadowy networks of individuals can bring great chaos and suffering to our shores for less than it costs to purchase a single tank'. The doctrine also acknowledges that the nation is now threatened less by conquering states than by terrorism and failing states. 'We are menaced less by fleets and armies than by catastrophic technologies in the hands of the embittered few' (US White House 2002: 1). An introductory observation is, in other words, that a new security context is clearly identified and acknowledged in strategic-level doctrine.

To effectively achieve the national goals, doctrine also identifies the need for the transformation of the national security institutions (US White House 2002: 1–2). *Joint Vision 2020*, a document that outlines a long-term vision of the US military, therefore develops a core concept in 'full spectrum dominance'. This means that the US armed forces should have the capability to defeat any opponent in a confrontation at any point on the conflict scale.

> The threats and enemies we must confront have changed, and so must our forces. A military structured to deter massive Cold War-era armies must be transformed to focus more on how an adversary might fight rather than where and when a war might occur.
>
> (US White House 2002: 29)

The way to achieve this goal is a steady infusion of new technology as well as the modernization and replacement of equipment (US DoD 2000: 3). Innovation is supposed to be based on 'experimentation with new approaches to warfare, strengthening joint operations, exploiting U.S. intelligence advantages, and taking full advantage of science and technology' (US White House 2002: 30). The second observation is that, while a new and more complex context is acknowledged, the proposed changes are mostly reinforcements of the traditional US way of war, with a heavy reliance on technology and firepower. The traditional functional imperative of the US armed forces is clearly confirmed in the *National Military Strategy*:

> Our Armed Forces' foremost task is to fight and win our Nation's wars. Consequently, America's Armed Forces are organized, trained, equipped, maintained, and deployed primarily to ensure that our Nation is able to defeat aggression against our country and to protect our national interests.
>
> (US DoD 1997)

Operational-level doctrine describes wartime campaigns as the synchronization and integration of any necessary air, land, sea, space and special operations in harmony with diplomatic, economic and informational efforts to attain national and multinational objectives (US DoD 2001: xi). Combatant commanders and subordinate joint force commanders (JFCs) are therefore, according to the doctrine, likely to operate together with other government agencies representing the other instruments of national power, as well as with foreign forces, NGOs and international organizations. The doctrine further argues that the interagency nature of operations means that commanders and planners have to consider all instruments of national power when creating strategies for achieving policy objectives (US DoD 2001: viii).

Significantly, the operational-level doctrine on joint operations emphasizes the division of military operations into two distinct categories – war and military operations other than war (MOOTW). MOOTW are described as encompassing a wide range of activities where the military instrument of national power is used for purposes other than the large-scale combat operations usually associated with war (US DoD 2001: vii). The document notes that the military is often not the primary player in MOOTW, and that these operations are more sensitive to political considerations. Therefore, more restrictive rules of engagement often apply. The doctrine further acknowledges the importance of all military personnel understanding the political objective and the potential impact of inappropriate actions. Moreover, commanders must be aware of changes in the operational situation, as well as changes in political objectives that may warrant a change in military operations (US DoD 1995: vii).

Interestingly, the joint doctrine on MOOTW includes the traditionally un-American operational principles of restraint, perseverance and legitimacy. Another significant feature is the emphasis on campaign plans that include a transition from wartime operations to MOOTW to ensure the achievement of the political objectives (US DoD 1997: viii). The joint doctrine even identifies a number of special planning considerations for MOOTW, which include interagency coordination, post-conflict operations, command and control, intelligence and information collection, constraints and restraints, training and education (US DoD 2001: xiv).

One month before the invasion of Iraq the US Army published a field manual on 'stability and support operations'. The manual sees the concept of MOOTW replaced by 'Stability Operations' and 'Support Operations'. Stability operations are supposed to promote and protect US national interests by influencing the threat, the political and information dimensions of the operational environment through a combination of peacetime developmental, co-operative activities and coercive actions in response to a crisis. Included in the concept of stability operations are different forms of peace operations, support to insurgencies, combating terrorism, counter-drug operations, arms control, etc. Support operations include domestic support and humanitarian operations (US DoD 2003).

The doctrine on stability operations comments on suitable tactics by arguing that the centre of gravity in counter-insurgency operations is public support, and that in order to defeat an insurgent force, US forces must therefore be able to separate insurgents from the population. The problem, as expressed in doctrine, is that at the same time, US forces must act in a manner that enables them to maintain popular domestic support. In the more recent counter-insurgency doctrine this is presented as a paradox in that excessive or indiscriminate use of force is likely to alienate the local populace, thereby increasing support for insurgent forces, while insufficient use of force is likely to result in increased risks to US and multinational forces and perceived weaknesses that can jeopardize the mission. To achieve the appropriate balance in the use of force, the doctrine seeks a thorough understanding of the nature and causes of the insurgency, the end state, and the military's role in a counter-insurgency operation (US Department of the Army 2004).

The doctrine on stability operations further stresses the importance of adjusting the conduct of military operations for counter-insurgency to avoid alienating the population with excessive violence. 'Collateral damage destroys government legitimacy' (US DoD 2003: 3–6). In the process of planning counter-insurgency operations, 'it is imperative that leaders and soldiers understand that military force is not an end in itself, but is just one of the instruments of national power employed by the political leadership to achieve its broader objectives'. It also stresses that military action and the use of force are limited by 'a variety of political and practical considerations, some of which may not seem sensible at the tactical level'. All personnel involved in the operations must therefore understand the nature of such limitations and the rationale behind them in order to make sound decisions regarding the application of or restraint in the use of force (US DoD 2003: 2–14).

Operational-level doctrine leads to two important observations: first, the division between war and operations other than war, which also reflects the US conceptualization of war in dualistic terms. This would also mean that if different doctrines were implemented in different contexts, US troops would also operate in fundamentally different ways. This has not been the case. Second, doctrines on operations other than war, and stabilization operations are, in several aspects, well up to date with the principles of best practice in complex peace operations.

Tactical-level doctrine

Tactical-level doctrine essentially leaves the concept of operations other than war or stability and support operations behind. Tactics are, according to the US Army doctrine, the employment of units in combat. 'It includes the ordered arrangement and maneuver of units in relation to each other, the terrain and the enemy to translate potential combat power into victorious battles and engagements' (US Department of the Army 2001: ch. 1, 1). However, this narrow definition of tactics should be understood in relation to the higher-level doctrines on operations. In other words, to employ the tactics as described in doctrine, one must, according to the doctrine, 'understand how the activities described in FM 3–07, *Stability Operations and Support Operations*, carry over and affect offensive and defensive operations and vice versa' (US Department of the Army 2001: ch. 1, 1). The theory is that with an understanding of the type of conflict and context the unit is operating in, the tactical concepts of offensive, defensive and security operations can be appropriately adjusted for each context and situation. What this means for the individual soldier is unclear.

In the US Army field manual *Tactics*, conventional warfare is clearly emphasized. As an example, it argues that success in tactical problem-solving results from the 'aggressive, intelligent, and decisive use of combat power in an environment of uncertainty, disorder, violence, and danger'. Moreover, tactical-level commanders 'win decisively through the rapid application of available combat power' (US Department of the Army 2001: 1–13). Another example is the emphasis on offensive action, which is considered key to achieving decisive results. 'Tactical commanders are instructed to conduct offensive operations to achieve their assigned missions and objectives – destroying enemy forces or seizing terrain – that cumulatively produce the theater-level effects required by the operational commander' (US Department of the Army 2001: 1–13). How such tactical operations relate to strategic-level political aims is not discussed – especially not in the context of complex peace operations. Except for civilians in the area of operations possibly restricting the use of force, there are no other pointers within the entire doctrine on how to adjust tactics with reference to the type of operation one is part of, or the different aims of operations. In sum, there seems to be a mismatch between the operational-level doctrine on stability and support operations on the one hand, and tactical-level doctrine on the other.

Four significant observations have been made in the analysis of US doctrine. First, strategic- and operational-level doctrine before the operations in Iraq clearly recognized a new strategic context. Second, major reforms of the national security apparatus were considered necessary in order to adjust to the new context. However, the suggested reforms are essentially based on the traditional American way of war, and involve technological improvements to increase the lethality and precision of weapons systems to deliver massive firepower. The functional imperative of conventional warfare in defence of the nation still dominates US doctrine, despite the recognition of contextual changes. A third observation is that the operational-level doctrine on operations other than war, such as stability operations, is well up to date with the principles of best practice in complex peace operations. However, the principles of complex peace operations are nowhere to be found within tactical-level doctrine, which strongly emphasizes the American way of war by promoting massive use of force and offensive operations. The observations are contradictory in relation to the above discussion on the American way of war.

Finally, an important feature of US doctrine is that the dual view of war and peace is reflected in doctrine as a divide between doctrines on warfare and doctrines on operations other than war. The doctrines on warfare treat war in its traditional form where political influence is limited, and where the principles of overwhelming force, firepower, technology, and manoeuvre are emphasized. Doctrines on operations other than war underscore a rather different set of principles and define other important imperatives for success, such as interagency co-operation and political understanding at all levels. However, let us put culture and doctrine together in some concluding thoughts regarding the American way of war and the US approach to complex peace operations.

The US approach to complex peace operations

The American way of war begins with a conceptual division between war and peace, which means that there is really no conceptual space for 'grey area' operations between war and peace – such as most complex peace operations. The isolation of the armed forces during the professionalization meant that the officer corps was allowed to define the functional imperative of the armed forces. The cost of civilian monitoring of the armed forces means that despite variations in civil–military conflicts and contextual changes, the military ownership of the functional imperative prevails. The resulting military culture's preferred way of war is large-scale conventional wars fought quickly at minimum cost. It also involves the maximum use of force, and the application of high technology to maximize firepower. US troops are, therefore, organized around the division as the defining organization, and the warrior ethos as the foundation of military culture is emphasized. Another significant feature of the US way of war is the astrategic culture, stemming from the dualistic view of war and peace that has essentially detached military operations from political purpose.

The uncompromising focus on conventional warfighting has left the US military ill prepared for complex peace operations and post-conflict type settings. Yet the realities of the contemporary strategic context put US troops in precisely the types of operations they do not prepare for – sometimes with abysmal results, as displayed in Somalia. Within such contexts the US military still seeks to apply the traditional American way of war. However, the limited and complex political aims of such operations mean that a low tolerance for casualties is added to the list as an 'American way of peacekeeping'.

Beyond the doctrines on traditional warfare, the US doctrinal library also contains a number of operational-level doctrines that are well up to date with the principles of complex peace operations. In other words, US doctrine is not simply a mirror of US military culture and the US way of war. As noted above, the diversity of doctrine is also not mirrored by US troops in the field. Thus, US doctrine is clearly more than simply 'how we operate'. Rather it should be seen as the outcome of what Peter Feaver (2003) describes as a game of strategic interaction in the civil–military interface. The diversity of doctrine reveals a debate regarding the functional imperative of the armed forces, with increasing emphasis placed on non-traditional tasks, such as stability operations. However, US doctrine has not had a large impact on the military culture, or the US way of war, which means that culture is currently the stronger variable when determining US conduct in operations. In the specific context of complex peace operations, there is, in other words, a gap between the contents of doctrine and actual behaviour on the ground – where the cultural emphasis on traditional war generally prevails.

Another significant aspect of US political and military culture is the dualistic view of war and peace and the corresponding divide between warfare and operations other than war in US doctrine. Since the US military is uncomfortable conducting operations other than war, an operation of strategic importance is likely to be interpreted as war. This means that regardless of the reality on the ground, which, in most cases, involves operations between the extremes of war and peace, the US military is likely to invoke conventional doctrine within the cultural comfort zone. As the following chapter will show, the campaign in Iraq is an obvious case in point.

In terms of theory, the patterns of civil–military relations have, in the US case, led to a conventional definition of the functional imperative and the creation of a corresponding structure and culture of the US armed forces. The resulting American way of war is not well adjusted to the contemporary strategic context. In the words of Andrew Garfield (2006: 29): 'The U.S. military appears to have the wrong organizational culture to fight the war in which it is currently engaged, [Iraq], which is the most likely type of warfare it will face over the next twenty years'. The US armed forces are not 'fit for purpose'. The effect of the divided patterns of civil–military relations and the high costs of civilian monitoring of the armed forces have failed to achieve the necessary adjustments of the armed forces, something that is likely to have consequences in the conduct and effectiveness of operations in complex peace operations. To test this notion, the following chapter analyses US operations in Iraq from 2003.

5 Civil–military aspects of US operations in Iraq

The analysis of US operations in Iraq serves as an empirical test of the hypothesis of this book, and, thereby, adds some insight to the growing literature on the Iraq War by adding the civil–military perspective to the analysis. The chapter examines the total outcome of the US patterns of civil–military relations by tracing the causal chain to the dependent variable of operational conduct and effectiveness in complex peace operations. Both the direct and indirect effects of civil–military relations are, thereby, taken into account. However, this chapter does not provide a comprehensive analysis of US operations in Iraq. Instead, this analysis focuses on a number of thematic discussions that are relevant to the hypothesis of the book. The themes have been provided by the theoretical review of best practice in complex peace operations. They involve: (a) the US approach to operations in Iraq; (b) civil–military co-operation and co-ordination; and (c) tactical behaviour. The first thematic discussion seeks to answer how the operation was interpreted and conceptualized by the military and civilian leadership in the US, as well as how this was translated into political aims and operational plans. The discussion on civil–military co-operation and co-ordination involves two sub-categories in the civil–military aspects of the planning process and of the command and control structures. Finally, the section on tactical behaviour analyses the conduct of tactical operations with reference to the hearts and minds approach, minimum use of force, cultural understanding and adaptability.

As noted in the theory chapter, the conduct and effectiveness of operations are in this book less concerned with the outcome of operations than conduct in relation to the principles of best practice in complex peace operations. By comparing US conduct to the principles of best practice, a number of inferences regarding US effectiveness can be made. However, to set the stage for the thematic discussions, the chapter is introduced by a brief overview of the invasion phase.

The invasion of Iraq

The military campaign to liberate Iraq was a four-phase operation, including the entire spectrum of conflict, from combat to peace support to humanitarian and security assistance. Phases I and II involved setting the conditions for neutralizing the Iraqi defence forces, by deploying forces, securing regional and international support, as well as by 'shaping the battlespace'. Phase III involved the decisive offensive operations, which marked the beginning of the conventional combat operations. Phase IV involved post-conflict operations, such as the transition from combat to stability and support operations, humanitarian assistance and reconstruction (Center for Army Lessons Learned 2004). The strategic goal of the campaign in Iraq included establishing a stable, secure, prosperous, peaceful and democratic Iraqi nation that is a fully functioning member of the community of nations (Bush 2003). Therefore, strategic success would require success in each phase, inextricably linking all actions into a campaign that is truly an extension of politics by other means.

The invasion phase of the campaign in Iraq not only displayed a known technological superiority of the American military, but also an operational and tactical flexibility that took the world by surprise. Instead of the expected 'shock and awe' involving heavy bombardment and a massive frontal attack, the US troops displayed a shock in its surprise tactics, and awe in its speed and effectiveness. The advance on Baghdad displayed a logistics operation that is unprecedented in military history and the fall of Baghdad was forced with speed and accuracy. Although some preliminary operations were conducted on 19 March 2003, including a decapitation attempt on Saddam Hussein, the main coalition attacks began early on 20 March. Already on 9 April the regime in Baghdad effectively ceased to function, the Iraqi defence, including the Republican Guard, was beaten and scattered around the city sometimes creating pockets of resistance throughout the city and many parts of the country. However, by 13 April the organized resistance by major Iraqi units faded and the invasion phase of the war was won.

On 1 May 2003, President Bush declared the end of major combat operations. This was a piece of theatre that highlighted the US emphasis on the major combat phase as opposed to the following Phase IV. However, at this stage no senior Iraqi government official had surrendered, and several pockets of resistance still existed – most notably in Fallujah. Most importantly, an embryo of a serious insurgency had started revealing itself. Like in Afghanistan the war, therefore, had no 'clean ending' (Cordesman 2003b: 144–145). It would quickly show that declaring an end to the war was wishful thinking. In many parts of the country the insurgency was growing and the number of attacks against coalition troops steadily grew. The insurgency has subsequently evolved into a complex mixture of Shia militias, former Baath party members and former army members supporting Saddam Hussein's regime, Iraqi Sunni Islamists, and foreign Islamist volunteers, often linked to al Qaeda (Baram 2005). A British battalion commander even argued that the very day President Bush declared the end of major combat operations, was the day the real war started (interview with Lowe 2004). Let us, thereby, start the thematic discussion of US operations in Iraq.

The US approach to operations in Iraq: strategic assessment

In his seminal work, *The Utility of Force*, General Sir Rupert Smith underscores the importance of analysing and understanding the nature of conflict, and of having a clear political purpose, from which military strategic objectives can be derived (Smith 2005: 291, 373). This section studies these aspects of the US campaign in Iraq. After a quick look at the political objectives of the campaign, the analysis and interpretation of the campaign are discussed in relation to the previous chapter on US military culture.

A clear list of aims and objectives was provided as early as August 2002 when the National Security Council drafted a Presidential Directive entitled 'Iraq: Goals, Objectives and Strategy'. The secret Directive that the NSC also agreed on stated:

> U.S. goal: Free Iraq in order to eliminate Iraqi weapons of mass destruction, [...] to prevent Iraq from breaking out of containment and becoming a more dangerous threat to the region and beyond. End Iraqi threats to its neighbours, to stop the Iraqi government's tyrannizing of its own population, to cut Iraqi links to and sponsorship of terrorism, to maintain Iraq's unity and territorial integrity. And liberate the Iraqi people from tyranny, and assist them in creating a society based on moderation, pluralism and democracy.
>
> (Cited in Woodward 2004: 154–155)

Among the objectives stated in the document were a few imperatives regarding the conduct of operations, such as minimizing the risk of a WMD attack, to reduce the danger of regional instability and disruption to the international oil market. Elements of the strategy included employing all instruments of national power to work with the Iraqi opposition in order to demonstrate that the US was liberating and not invading Iraq, and to establish a broad-based democratic government, respecting the basic rights of all Iraqis and adhering to the rule of law (Woodward 2004: 155). The goals were confirmed by President George Bush on the eve of battle: 'My fellow citizens, at this hour, American and coalition forces are in the early stages of military operations to disarm Iraq, to free its people and to defend the world from grave danger' (Bush 2003).

The translation of US policy into a military campaign in Iraq was carefully planned. Planning for what would become 'Operation Iraqi Freedom' started on 27 November 2001, as Secretary of Defense Donald Rumsfeld and General Tommy Franks, the commander of United States Central Command (CENTCOM), started examining the assumptions and requirements of the old war plan, at the request of President Bush (Franks 2004; Woodward 2004). The outcome of this process was presented by Secretary of Defense Donald Rumsfeld in a number of specific objectives of the military operations of the campaign. The coalition's military operations were said to be focused on achieving eight specific objectives:

1   To end the regime of Saddam Hussein by striking with force on a scope and scale that makes clear to Iraqis that he and his regime are finished.
2   Next, to identify, isolate and eventually eliminate Iraq's weapons of mass destruction, their delivery systems, production capabilities and distribution networks.
3   To search for, capture, drive out terrorists who have found safe harbour in Iraq.
4   To collect such intelligence as we can find related to terrorist networks in Iraq and beyond.
5   To collect such intelligence as we can find related to the global network of illicit weapons of mass destruction activity.
6   To end sanctions and to immediately deliver humanitarian relief, food and medicine to the displaced and to the many needy Iraqi citizens.
7   To secure Iraq's oil fields and resources, which belong to the Iraqi people, and which they will need to develop their country after decades of neglect by the Iraqi regime.
8   To help the Iraqi people create the conditions for a rapid transition to a representative self-government that is not a threat to its neighbours and is committed to ensuring the territorial integrity of that country (Rumsfeld 2003).

The main problem was that the political aims included far more than what could be translated into *military* objectives and activities. While the general contours of the war plan were finished and mostly agreed upon in August 2002, civilian planning had barely begun (Bensahel 2006: 455). Furthermore, the post-conflict planning process was limited by a number of false assumptions. Among them were the beliefs that the military campaign would have a decisive end that produced a stable security environment, that coalition troops would be greeted as liberators by the bulk of the population, that the government of Iraq would continue to function after the ministers and their closest advisors were removed from power, and that the infrastructure of Iraq would remain largely intact. The only serious post-conflict planning that took place, therefore, dealt with an anticipated humanitarian crisis (Bensahel 2006: 455–458; Bensahel *et al.* 2008: 234–235). Thus, the civilian objectives were, at the beginning of the campaign, vague at best and non-existent at worst.

A congressional hearing was held on 11 February 2003 because of concerns regarding the planning process of Phase IV operations – concerns that were not eased afterwards. A number of vague objectives were presented without any specifics on how to achieve them, although Douglas Feith, Under Secretary of Defense for Policy, argued that administration officials were thinking through the lessons of Afghanistan and other recent history. 'We have learned that post-conflict reconstruction requires a balance of efforts in the military sphere and the civil sphere' (Feith 2003).

A number of other institutions also expressed concern early in 2003. The January 2003 CSIS report argued that recent experience in Haiti, the Balkans, East Timor and Afghanistan has demonstrated that 'winning the peace is often

harder than fighting the war', and that it would be important to step up preparations for addressing post-conflict needs as the United States and its allies intensi-
fied military preparations for a war with Iraq. The report's verdict on the
post-war planning was severe:

> So far, however, signs of military build-up and humanitarian contingency
> planning have not been matched by visible, concrete actions by the United
> States, the United Nations, or others to position civilian and military
> resources to handle the myriad reconstruction challenges that will be faced
> in post-conflict Iraq. This situation gravely threatens the interests of the
> United States, Iraqis, the region, and the international community as a
> whole.
>
> (Barton and Crocker 2003: 7)

It was obvious that the US administration was running late on these issues: 'To
win the peace and secure their interests, the United States and the international
community must commit the resources, military might, personnel, and time that
successful post-conflict reconstruction will require in Iraq – and they must start
doing so *now*' (Barton and Crocker 2003: 7). Concerns were also expressed by
the closest coalition partner. The British complained internally about the planning of the nation building process in a memo written in advance of a Downing
Street meeting on Iraq held on 23 July 2002 (Pincus 2005).

An important aspect of the failure to provide comprehensive plans for the
campaign lies in the military and political leadership's failure to analyse and
interpret the conflict. Unwillingness to accept the cautionary advice of allies was
part of the same syndrome that led the highest levels of the Bush administration
to dismiss the concerns of generals, the caveats of intelligence analysts and the
counsel of the State Department. Ricks quotes an American four-star general
who described the syndrome in these terms: 'There was a conscious cutting off
of advice and concerns, so that the guy who ultimately had to make the decision,
the president, didn't get the advice.' All post-Saddam concerns were blown off
or disregarded. 'They were making simplistic assumptions and refused to put
them to the test' (Ricks 2006a: 99). This can also be attributed to a structural
problem of the interagency process, which failed to force alternative input and
buffer zones against the false assumptions of the mighty few. Bensahel is correct
in noting that 'the fundamental problem was not the content of these particular
assumptions, but the fact that a *single* set of assumptions drove US government
planning efforts, and no contingency plans were developed in case that one scenario did not occur' (Bensahel 2006: 458).

The work of General Tommy Franks, Chief of US Central Command and the
head of US military planning for Operation Iraqi Freedom, has been placed
under particular scrutiny. Ricks argues that Franks had little understanding of
strategy – seeing the bigger picture. Instead, Franks expressed himself in tactical
terms and based his planning on technological and mechanical advantages and
speed as a substitute for feet on the ground (Ricks 2006a: 127–128). Clearly,

Franks thought that planning for phase IV operations was not his job. The purpose of the campaign, according to Franks' plan was to force the collapse of the Saddam Hussein regime and deny him the use of WMD. The endstate of operations was identified as 'regime change'. Accordingly, Franks' plan only won the Battle for Baghdad and failed to address the political aims of the campaign and the aftermath of major combat operations. Major General Jonathan Bailey went as far as arguing that the short and decisive campaign plan was counterproductive with the more ambitious political aims of stabilization and democratization in mind (Cited in Ricks 2006a: 119).

The false assumptions about post-Saddam Iraq and the consequential emphasis on the invasion phase created a number of blind spots in Phase IV operations. Defense Secretary Rumsfeld was at first dismissive of the looting that followed the US arrival in Baghdad and then for months refused to recognize that an insurgency was taking place and growing. Ricks cites a meeting between Rumsfeld and a reporter who in the summer of 2003 asked Rumsfeld if he was facing a guerrilla war: 'I guess the reason I don't use the phrase "guerrilla war" is because there isn't one', Rumsfeld responded (Ricks 2006b). It took a long time, and many failed opportunities to seize the initiative in Iraq before the political and military leadership acknowledged the fact that it was involved in a complex counter-insurgency operation, involving an inherently irregular and asymmetric enemy. Another consequence is noted in the US 3rd Infantry Division's after-action report:

> Because of the refusal to acknowledge occupier status, commanders did not initially take measures available to occupying powers, such as imposing curfews, directing civilians to work and controlling the local governments and populace. The failure to act after we displaced the regime created a power vacuum, which others immediately tried to fill.
>
> (Cited in Lumpkin and Linzer 2003)

Moreover, whatever the contents of the Phase IV plan, it was not transferred effectively down through the chain of command, before the invasion, or even before the transition. The 3rd Infantry Division's after-action report reads: 'Higher headquarters did not provide the Third Infantry Division (Mechanized) with a plan for Phase IV. As a result, Third Infantry Division transitioned into Phase IV in the absence of guidance' (O'Hanlon 2004). An American officer argued that

> a plan for phase four was never passed from CFLCC [Combined Forces Land Component Commander] to V Corps and on the 3ID [3rd Infantry Division]. There was no guidance on which targets we needed to protect once we got into Baghdad. We weren't told to protect museums or banks and we didn't expect the scale of the looting [we saw].
>
> (Major Hylton cited in Graff 2004: 62)

A campaign with such complex political aims for a large and oppressed country containing several ethnic minorities should, in hindsight, or even in good foresight, given what was known before the invasion and what we have learned from previous complex operations, have led to a humble approach and comprehensive plans for a complex stabilization and reconstruction phase – a long-term occupation. Instead, it was interpreted and approached as a conventional war that would essentially end with the fall of Saddam Hussein. The invasion phase was, therefore, well planned and executed, while, at the same time, post-conflict issues, such as security and reconstruction, were treated as less important. The divided civil–military interface of the US system certainly contributed to this failure. Moreover, the strategic culture and the American way of war further contributed to the failure to grasp that this was a different kind of conflict. John Nagl has argued that due to the military culture of the US military, it does not adapt well to changed situations unless they are 'within the parameters of the kind of war it has defined as its primary mission' – conventional warfare (Nagl 2002: 218). The same can be said about US strategic culture and the conceptual definition of conflicts. The result was also that the US military invoked conventional doctrine rather than doctrine on operations other than war, which, in hindsight, would have been more useful.

Civil–military co-ordination and co-operation: a comprehensive approach?

The comprehensive and effects-based approaches to operations involve planning that not only covers the entire continuum of conflict, but also includes and co-ordinates all relevant actors towards a mutual political aim in the planning and execution of operations. This section, therefore, examines the civil–military aspects of US operations in Iraq by studying US post-conflict planning as well as the command and control structures. Were all relevant actors included? Were civilian and military contributions to the operation well integrated or co-ordinated?

Post-conflict planning

Planning for a post-Saddam Iraq commenced within the Department of State in April 2002, and the launch of the 'Future of Iraq' project. The project developed a large number of working groups with the purpose to begin practical planning for Iraq after the fall of Saddam Hussein's regime. Each of the working groups brought together about 10–20 Iraqi experts to discuss the Iraqis' thoughts and plans for what could be done to improve the lives of the Iraqi people (Grossman 2003). The project produced an extensive report, which was nevertheless later completely neglected by the Pentagon, as they took over the planning process. However, Ambassador Paul Bremer, head of the Coalition Provisional Authority (CPA), argues that the purpose of the Future of Iraq project was to engage Iraqi-Americans thinking about their country's future, and that it was never intended as a post-conflict plan (Bremer and McConnell 2005: 25). Notwithstanding its initial purpose, the 15-volume document included some important information about the terrible state of the Iraqi infrastructure and the high risk of post-conflict looting and disorder.

During the summer of 2002 the Pentagon started planning the post-conflict phase within the newly established Office of Special Plans, created out of the expanded Iraq desk of the Near East South Asia directorate (NESA) of the Office of the Secretary of Defense (Kwiatkovski 2004). However, the limited planning within the Pentagon was not formalized until 20 January 2003, when President Bush ordered the creation of the Office for Reconstruction and Humanitarian Assistance (ORHA), appointed retired General Jay Garner as its director, and released $15 million to fund its efforts (Lugar and Biden 2003: 10). Although Secretary Rumsfeld argued that this was the first time, to his knowledge, that the US had created an office for post-war administration before a conflict had even started, this was a very late start for serious planning of post-conflict reconstruction and security (Wolfowitz 2003). Another planning process for the civilian aspects of operations took place within the National Security Council, which established an interagency Executive Steering Group (ESG) for that purpose. The ESG included representatives from the State Department, Defense Department, the CIA and the Office of the Vice President, and could, thereby, have provided the ideal set-up for interagency planning (Bensahel 2006: 455). However, as already noted, this planning was seriously hampered by false assumptions about post-war Iraq and the competitive interagency culture.

Although post-conflict planning involved several problematic aspects, arguably the most serious problem in the planning process was the lack of civil–military co-operation and co-ordination. The failure of the interagency system in the specific case of Iraq is discussed by a special task force report on the improvement of US post-conflict capabilities, sponsored by the Council on Foreign Relations. The report argues that the lack of a body or an arm within the US government formally responsible for post-conflict stabilization and reconstruction operations is a major reason for poor post-conflict planning. 'Policy and implementation are divided among several agencies, with poor interagency coordination, misalignment of resources and authorities, and inadequate accountability and duplicative efforts' (Nash 2005: 7). Cordesman (2003b) has a similar explanation but points more specifically at the National Security Council, which failed to perform its task of interagency co-ordination. Instead of forcing effective interagency co-operation where formal and informal structures had failed, it acted in a largely advisory role and, therefore, had little influence. An interesting observation that confirms the analysis of US civil–military relations is that interagency structures for post-conflict planning were, in fact, in place within the NSC, but that the competitive and distrustful cultural climate of the US political system hindered these structures from being effective. The NSC failed not only to consider other planning alternatives than those based on the false assumption outlined above, but also to provide strategic guidance on US policy for the post-war period. Several requests from Central Command and the Office of Reconstruction and Humanitarian Assistance (ORHA) went unanswered and the planning of Phase IV operations was, therefore, conducted without the co-ordination and guidance that a coherent policy and consistent objectives could have provided. Not until late March 2003, with the war under way, was such strategic guidance issued (Bensahel *et al.* 2008: 238).

There were deep divisions between the State Department and the Department of Defense over how to plan for conflict stabilization and nation building. The rift began at the top with personal problems between Secretary of State Powell and Defense Secretary Rumsfeld, and extended down to the 'working levels' of the departments. President Bush's National Security Directive 24 on 20 January 2003 put the Office of the Secretary of Defense in charge of the nation-building efforts, and effectively led to the efforts of the State Department and other agencies being 'dropped, ignored, or given low priority' (Cordesman 2003b: 498). The background material and human expertise from the Future of Iraq project were all dismissed, and when appointing the ORHA staff for General Garner the Pentagon removed a number of highly qualified experts from the State Department's list (Ricks 2006a: 109). Having a lead department or agency in charge of planning and operations is something that is generally done to create unity of command and effort. However, the Pentagon lacked the expertise to plan and lead a post-conflict operation in Iraq, and the competitive culture of the system led to the opposite effect. The campaign in Iraq was stovepiped and command was dispersed.

There was also a rift between the civilian and military sides within the Pentagon, with the military leadership feeling steamrollered by Rumsfeld's Office of the Secretary of Defense in the planning process. One concern was the number of soldiers needed for post-conflict stabilization. General Shinseki broke ranks when he confessed in a congressional hearing that an occupation of Iraq would require several hundred thousand troops – a figure he came to, by comparing Iraq to historical occupations of Japan and Germany. The general was publicly reprimanded for these estimates by the Deputy Secretary Paul Wolfowitz. However, General Shinseki was not the only one on the military side of the Pentagon to be unhappy. Inside the military, officers kept publicly quiet. But, according to Ricks, privately their unhappiness ran deep (2006a: 96–98).

Michael O'Hanlon argues that going to war without a complete Phase IV plan was the biggest mistake of the whole campaign. 'Invading another country with the intention of destroying its existing government yet without a serious strategy for providing security, thereafter, defies logic and falls short of proper professional military standards of competence' (O'Hanlon 2004). The US military was, therefore, not prepared or trained for dealing with looting or the difficult task of distinguishing hostile and non-violent civilians and irregular forces and enemies. As Cordesman states, 'troops were trained to fight asymmetric warfare up to the point of dealing with the consequences of victory'. This resonated well with the US military tradition to avoid deep involvement in the complex political issues of nation building and to avoid prolonged military commitment to missions other than direct warfighting (2003: 499). Steven Metz asserts that 'an insurgency is born when a governing power fails to address social or regional polarization, sectarianism, endemic corruption, crime, various forms of radicalism, or rising expectations'. The early mistakes of the stabilization and reconstruction phase, in combination with the fact that an outside power has a smaller margin of error than an inept or repressive national regime would have in dealing with popular discontent, in Metz's view, meant that the insurgency gained popular support and developed a recruiting base among the Iraqi youth (2003: 26–28). The failure of the interagency system and of civil–military co-operation and co-ordination may, therefore, have had greater strategic consequences than any tactical adjustment in the field of operations could have had.

The politically imposed limit, i.e. Secretary Rumsfeld's intervention in the planning process, regarding the number of troops sent to Iraq, meant that, as the regime of Saddam Hussein fell, there were simply not enough soldiers on the ground to provide security and stability during Phase IV of the campaign. Another consequence was that the borders with Syria and Iran were never secured, thereby failing to block important supply routes for the insurgency groups (Ricks 2006a). An important observation is that the false assumptions of the political and military leadership were allowed to influence the entire planning process, which, as noted, had dire consequences. There were, in other words, no safety nets for flawed assumptions present in the US system. A well-established interagency structure, in which experts from all relevant departments would have participated, as well as a better established civil–military co-operation and integration within the DoD could have provided such safety nets. Without that web of co-ordination and co-operation, a few misinformed people had too much influence, and alternative interpretations were kept out of the planning process.

The fault of failing to create appropriate plans for the campaign in Iraq is shared by the political and military leaders. The flawed assumptions about Iraq must be attributed to the political leadership that effectively cut out dissenting voices from the planning process. However, US Central Command under General Franks created a half-baked plan based on these assumptions. Planning for only part of the campaign and basing that planning on best-case assumptions is a gross military mistake. The fact that so few officers in the military leadership did not raise their voices against the planning of Operation Iraqi Freedom is significant.

US command and control of the post-conflict phase

As already noted, the DoD and Office of the Secretary of Defense (OSD) were put in charge of the planning and execution of post-conflict operations in Iraq. Unfortunately the divisions between the State Department and the Pentagon meant that rather than achieving unity of command, this decision cut all non-military agencies out of the planning process. In other words, from the beginning of the campaign, and at the top levels, the US command and control structure failed to achieve co-operation and co-ordination between the different actors involved. A decision that was hoped to achieve unity of command instead created fragmentation and lack of co-ordination. The command and control structures at all levels later came to reflect this initial set-up.

Under Secretary of Defense for Policy Douglas Feith said in the congressional hearings before the war that the coalition officials responsible for the post-conflict administration of Iraq – whether military or civilian, from the various agencies of the governments – would report to the President through General Tommy Franks and the Secretary of Defense (Feith 2003). However, after the initial invasion phase, the chain of command was far from clear. The relationship between the civilian and military sides of the occupation, the Coalition Provisional Authority (CPA) and the military headquarters, was inherently stormy. The Combined Joint Task Force Commander, the US military commander in Iraq, General Sanchez, reported to General Abizaid, commander of US Central Command, who reported to Defense Secretary Rumsfeld. On the civilian side, Ambassador Paul Bremer, head of the CPA, reported directly to Secretary Rumsfeld. Further complicating matters is the fact that Ambassador Bremer often gave the impression that he believed he reported directly to the President. One general was clearly puzzled by the command and control structures: 'If you held a gun to my head and told me "Tell me what the chain of command is for your people in Baghdad!" – well, I'd just be babbling' (Anon. cited in Ricks 2006: 179).

At the tactical level the chain of command was not geared towards co-ordinated civil–military operations. Civil affairs units were divided among the combat units, and their actions were not synchronized nation-wide. Not only did civil–military operations as a consequence have little effect, but also structurally, these arrangements subordinated civil–military operations to ground combat operations, and the task of targeting insurgents took precedence over working with the people (Varhola 2004). During the first year of the occupation there appeared to be no effort at co-ordinating the reconstruction and reform processes necessary to eliminate the root causes of unrest. Instead, the 90-day rotations of Coalition Provisional Authority advisors and personnel, in combination with limited security, restricted their work to the 'Green Zone'. The CPA, therefore, gained little respect among the Iraqi population and the military units in the country (Graff 2004: 68–69).

Not only was there confusion about the chain of command, there was also friction between the military and civilian sides of the operation. Different views about how to stabilize, reconstruct and democratize the country led to frequent conflicts between the military and civilian leaders in the field (Ricks 2006; Bremer and McConnell 2005; Diamond 2005). Confusion and friction, combined with ORHA's refusal to co-locate headquarters with the military from the start of operations, also limited civil–military co-operation and co-ordination. In other words, the failure to achieve unity of command was reinforced by the even more serious failure to achieve unity of effort (Diamond 2005: 299). General Garner's refusal to co-locate ORHA with the military command meant that ORHA and later the CPA remained out of touch with the conditions in the field, adding to the lack of expertise or experience with peacemaking and nation building. Key issues like jobs and economic security were as a consequence addressed much later than should have been the case in a campaign for the hearts and minds of the Iraqi population (Cordesman 2003b: 499–500).

Another important aspect of command and control, discussed in the theory chapter of this book, is the importance of mission command and decentralized command structures that rely on the initiative of subordinates at the scene of action. However, according to British Brigadier Nigel Aylwin-Foster (2005), while the US military champions mission command in theory and doctrine, in Iraq it did not practice it. He notes that commanders and staff at all levels rarely, if ever, questioned authority, and were reluctant to deviate from the precise instructions which were often preferred by commanders rather than mission-type orders. A common trend of US command was that of micro-management, with many hours devoted to daily briefings and updates. The result was highly centralized decision-making, which tended to discourage initiative and adaptability at a lower level of command.

In sum, the level of civil–military co-operation and co-ordination was seriously inadequate from the initial strategic and operational planning processes to the planning and conduct of tactical operations in the field. The interagency structures completely failed the planning process in Washington, which, in combination with a lack of constructive dialogue between the civilian and military sides of the Pentagon, failed to provide comprehensive analyses and plans for the occupation of Iraq.

Post-conflict operations in Iraq

With the fall of Saddam Hussein's regime, a power vacuum of anarchic disorder, involving widespread looting and the first signs of a growing insurgency, took its place. Thus, as the combat phase ended, it quickly became clear that the US military forces were not manned, equipped, trained nor mentally prepared to occupy urban areas, or to secure the country. Moreover, the impressive jointness displayed between the military forces during the war certainly did not translate into jointness between the military and the civilian components in the work to secure and rebuild the country (Cordesman 2003b: 145). Before looking at the conduct of military operations at the tactical level, the civilian activities are quickly analysed.

The civilian administration in charge of the stabilization and reconstruction phase was initially ORHA, with retired General Jay Garner as its director. However, ORHA had not been created until two months before the invasion and was not ready to perform its duties as Baghdad fell. Garner and ORHA did not arrive in Baghdad until 21 April 2003, almost two weeks after the Iraqi regime fell. Once ORHA arrived on the scene it made the cardinal mistake of moving into Saddam Hussein's Republican Palace, a place of symbolic value for all the wrong reasons, and, in practical terms, nothing more than a shelter. The palace was without telephones or working showers, and situated far from the military headquarters where knowledge of the situation on the ground existed. The situation led to what commentators called 'a complete mess' (Philps 2003). Not only was the palace symbolically and practically a grave mistake, but by refusing to collocate with General Franks and the military command centre in Baghdad, ORHA missed most of the military intelligence and they themselves lacked escorts to get out of the palace to get an idea of what happened in the city (Cordesman 2003b: 501). ORHA, therefore, had little idea of the situation in Baghdad, and few resources to do anything about the situation had they known (Hirsh 2003).

On 7 May 2003, the President attempted to reverse the deteriorating situation by appointing former Ambassador Paul Bremer to replace General Garner. Unlike Garner, Bremer and the CPA reported directly to Secretary Rumsfeld and also enjoyed the support of Secretary Powell (Perito 2004: 317). However, the CPA's first decisions were very controversial, and have in hindsight been described as contributing greatly to the failure to stabilize Iraq. Among Bremer's first acts was to ban those who had held one of the top four ranks in the Baath Party from holding government jobs. This reversed ORHA's policy that banned only the most senior Baathists and effectively removed about 30,000 senior bureaucrats, the entire leadership from government ministries, including the police. Although this decision answered previous criticism from some Iraqi groups, it also created great bitterness, mistrust and confusion, thereby, slowing down the reconstruction of government services (Perito 2004: 316). The CPA also decided to disband the entire Iraqi Army and ordered the few soldiers who had returned to the barracks to go home without any promise of pay, or of a future in the new Iraq. This decision increased the number of disillusioned, 'angry young men' on the streets. The decision was also culturally insensitive as honour is a major value in Iraqi society, and the decision to disband the army dishonoured the entire military profession by making them unemployed and, thereby, losing their status in society. Ricks argues that these decisions helped spur the insurgency by providing almost unlimited sources for recruitment in the shape of disenfranchised former Baath party members as well as unemployed and armed former soldiers (Ricks 2006: 190–191).

A June 2003 report on the conditions in Baghdad argued that the capital was in 'distress, chaos, and ferment'. Two months after the termination of major combat operations, the CPA had failed to provide security and to restore essential services, such as water and electricity. According to the report, it was conventional wisdom that the Americans had blundered by failing to protect vital institutions and impose public order from the outset. They had, in other words, abdicated the occupying power's moral and legal obligation to protect the local population (ICG Report cited in Perito 2004: 316). The occupying forces thereby seriously undermined the political aims of the operation, as well as giving early impetus to the insurgency (Nash 1995: 4).

Tactical behaviour of the US military

Notwithstanding initial interpretations of the campaign in Iraq, the reality on the ground quickly proved to involve a complex irregular war and counter-insurgency-type operations for the coalition. This section, therefore, studies US military tactics, discussed in relation to the principles of best practice in complex peace operations, as reviewed in the first chapter of this book. The main argument is that heavy-handed tactics and limited cultural understanding, made explicit by local media coverage, worsened relations with the local Iraqi community and, thereby, destroyed the legitimacy of the occupation. This boosted the insurgency that won easy propaganda victories by provoking disproportionate responses from the US military.

Failure to apply the hearts and minds approach to operations

The hearts and minds approach requires restraint in the use of force, accurately applied force protection policies and good understanding of the local culture and context. Little of this is seen in Iraq. An important example of US military tactics took place in Fallujah during Operation Vigilant Resolve in April 2004. The Americans were initially welcomed in Fallujah – a town that had never really been a Baath party stronghold, but that was known for its religious and social conservatism, and its nationalist fervour. However, early clashes, that often involved insensitive or heavy-handed US tactics, quickly alienated Fallujah's inhabitants (Hills 2005: 192). The security situation deteriorated gradually in Fallujah during 2003 as the city developed into a stronghold of anti-coalition elements. At the end of 2003 two US helicopters were shot down, killing 25 Americans, and in March 2004 four American security guards were killed by a mob as they drove through the city. Both the local commanders on the ground at the time, and subsequent analysts, have argued that these killings were classic examples of insurgency doctrine, conducted as a 'come-on' designed to evoke a disproportionate response (General Mattis cited in Ricks 2006: 6). If that was the intention it worked perfectly.

Despite concerns expressed by the local marine commanders, orders to launch a full-scale attack on Fallujah came from the Pentagon. The US command simply could not allow the city to develop into a no-go zone for the American troops and a precedent needed to be set. On 5 April 2004, the city was cordoned off and heavy fighting began almost immediately (Hills 2005: 192). Fighting was intense, involving both artillery and close air support. Thus, there was large-scale damage to civilian lives and property in the city. As one marine inside Fallujah put it: 'We will win the hearts and minds of Fallujah by ridding the city of insurgents. We're doing that by patrolling the streets and killing the enemy' (Bunting 2004).

The siege and battles for Fallujah were concluded by a final heavy US assault on the city. Amid reports of hundreds of civilian deaths the fighting ended in a 'truce'. The agreement turned over security to the 'Fallujah Brigade', a force led by former officers of Iraq's demobilized army. However, this entity quickly collapsed, and control of the city passed into the hands of insurgents. The operations in Fallujah, therefore, not only failed to achieve the objective of increased security. The Americans also lost control of the city, reinforcing it as an insurgent stronghold, and certainly did not win any hearts and minds in the process.

Instead, the US-appointed Iraqi governor of Fallujah's city council resigned, claiming that 'American behaviour is increasing the size of the resistance ... [making] everyone seek revenge'. A US senior officer argued that as a result, as many as 25 per cent of the new Iraqi security forces 'quit, changed sides, or otherwise failed to perform their duties' (both cited in Hills 2005: 193). Aylwin-Foster goes as far as to argue that in the case of Fallujah, the sense of moral righteousness combined with a strong emotionality 'served to distort collective military judgement'. Those US commanders and staff who 'generally took the broader view of the campaign were so deeply affronted on this occasion that they became set on the total destruction of the enemy. Under emotional duress even the most broad-minded and pragmatic reverted to type: kinetic' (Aylwin-Foster 2005: 6).

Cordesman suggests that US military commanders do not seem to have fully understood the importance of peacemaking and nation-building missions in Iraq. They often did not provide the proper support for civilian activity, or did so with extensive delays and little real commitment. Even where military resources were clearly available, too little emphasis was placed on immediately securing key urban areas and government buildings. The initial security efforts in Baghdad were, moreover, generally reactive rather than part of a cohesive or coherent effort to provide security for the entire area. This meant constant security gaps that allowed looting, firefights and ambushes to occur before an effort was made to act. The emphasis on force protection, especially within the US Army, further meant that the political impact on the Iraqi population was ignored, and the security enforcement mission often proved more provocative than helpful to already frustrated Iraqis (Cordesman 2003b: 502). Varhola notes that despite the talk of hearts and minds approaches, a brigade commander argued that his forces were in Iraq to 'kill the enemy, not win their hearts or minds'. It should, therefore, come as no surprise that Iraqi acceptance of the coalition has not been widespread (Varhola 2004).

Speaking on the transition from combat operations to post-conflict operations a company commander reveals the limited change in attitude and posture: 'When we do operations, like when we do patrols ... they are organized from combat patrols, they move like combat patrols, and they have objectives like combat patrols. So, we really didn't change anything, we just can't shoot everybody' (William Jacobs cited in Graff 2004: 66–67). Another interesting observation is a contradiction within the Army Lessons Learned Report from December 2003. The report maintains that the greatest intelligence assets were soldiers on foot patrol, who were able to quickly establish 'ground truth'. However, the same report claims that the number of patrols is limited by the number of *vehicles* available in a task force (Center for Army Lessons Learned 2004: 35–36). Force protection clearly took priority over effectiveness in tactical behaviour.

US preoccupation with force protection meant that they quickly moved into large camps outside the cities, thereby alienating themselves from the local population (Aylwin-Foster 2005: 6). The civilian administration of the CPA resided in the so-called Green Zone in the centre of Baghdad, which was completely isolated and disconnected from the harsh realities outside the zone. People seldom left the zone and had little understanding of the situation in the country (Ricks 2006: 206–208). The military alienation from the local population was exacerbated by the conduct of patrols, which were most often done in armed vehicles, with the usual offensive posture of pointing guns at those who happened to pass by. The US military further instinctively turned to technology to solve problems. The instinct was 'to seek means, including technology, to minimize frequent close contact with the local population, in order to enhance force protection, but this served further to alienate the troops from the population' (Aylwin-Foster 2005: 6).

A Center for Army Lessons Learned Report notes that American soldiers wore full body armour and carried loaded weapons everywhere, muzzles pointed at the Iraqis, which is an insult in their culture (cited in Graff 2004). In Graff's words: 'Every layer of armour is another layer of isolation from the population with which the security force needs to interact' (2004: 59–60). The lack of cultural understanding is discussed further below. There are certainly situations in which a posture of complete combat readiness should be maintained, but when it is maintained indefinitely, regardless of current events and surroundings, it indicates not only a lack of situational understanding, but also a lack of trust, as well as signalling a lack of general security.... 'If security forces do not feel secure, should the population have reason to fear?' (Graff 2004: 60).

It should be underscored that even before the major tactical shifts during the surge of 2007, there were a number of important exceptions in terms of tactical behaviour and leadership. As an example, Major General Peter Chiarelli, commander of the 1st Cavalry Division in Baghdad between March 2004 and March 2005, immediately noted an almost perfect correlation between the areas with high insurgent activity and the areas lacking electricity, water, functional sewer systems and that had high unemployment rates. When faced with the insurgency statistics and a first-hand look at the miserable living conditions in Sadr City, where the electricity and sewage did not work, where running water was unavailable and where unemployment in April 2004 was 61 per cent, he revisited his campaign plan and started concentrating on a combination of lethal and non-lethal effects (Chiarelli cited in Hoffpauir 2005). Thus, water, rubbish collection and unemployment became key components of the 1st Cavalry Division's counter-insurgency strategy. Although combat operations were frequent throughout the division's deployment in Iraq, Chiarelli argued that 'we also tried to concentrate on the other operations that were just as important, sometimes, more important'. Besides the reconstruction tasks, Chiarelli also pointed out the importance of training the Iraqi Army and police, as well as 'helping the people learn about the democratic process ... to teach people what it was like to live in a democratic society.... When we went in and started reconstruction projects, things got better', he said (Hoffpauir 2005).

A few years into the campaign the US military started displaying a distinct improvement in tactical behaviour. The previous chapter noted that a new counter-insurgency doctrine was published in 2006. This doctrine, as well as a number of changes in pre-deployment training, started reflecting the needs of complex peace operations to a much larger extent. This initially had limited effects on the ground in Iraq as the security situation deteriorated into outright civil war during 2006. The adaptations were, moreover, displayed by a few exceptional officers rather than as a sign of a major cultural shift. An example is the 3rd Armoured Cavalry Regiment's attack on Tal Afar led by Colonel Herbert R. McMaster in the spring of 2005. Instead of staging a major raid into the city for suspects and then moving back to operating bases, McMaster said he took a sharply different tack, spending months making preparatory moves before attacking the entrenched insurgents in Tal Afar. That indirect approach demonstrated tactical patience. The attack followed most of the classic counter-insurgency principles, including the clear and hold approaches used by the British in Malaya (Ricks 2006c).

In 2007, the US began the so-called surge in Baghdad, or *Operation Fardh al-Qanoon* (imposing the law). The operation to root out the insurgents from large parts of Baghdad was conducted with reinforcements of almost 45,000 troops and has displayed a complete reversal of the US approach to operations in Iraq. Essentially, the tactics applied by Colonel McMaster in Tal Afar are being implemented on a larger scale in the context of Baghdad. US forces are being moved from the large and heavily fortified military bases on the edge of the city to be stationed among the population in so-called Joint Security Stations and Combat Outposts. They share these bases with members of the Iraqi Army and police force. The co-operation with Iraqi forces puts a 'local face' on the operation, providing both language skills and an attempt to reduce friction between the population and the new security stations. Selected areas are first cleared of insurgents and militias. They are then 'gated', or cordoned off with roadblocks and security checks. Residents are issued with security passes, and movement in and out of the area is monitored. Finally, once order has been imposed, reconstruction money is channelled in using funds from the Commander's Emergency Response Programme (CERP) (see Robinson 2008; Odierno 2008; Ucko 2008). Earlier heavy-handed tactics are, thereby, sought to be replaced by activity more in line with the hearts and minds approach and classical counter-insurgency tactics of clear, hold and rebuild (IISS 2007).

The question is, if we are witnessing a cultural shift within the US armed forces, or merely the logical reaction to operational and tactical challenges in the specific contexts of Iraq and Afghanistan, is a topic for the following chapter. The outcomes of the surge and the tactical adjustments are discussed in the concluding section of this chapter.

Lack of political and cultural understanding

The US joint doctrine on military operations other than war (MOOTW) comes to the conclusion that 'all military personnel should understand the political objective and the potential impact of inappropriate actions' (US JCS 1995). In complex peace operations, involving politically charged situations and global media following every step, the smallest event may have strategic consequences. The US military's institutional mechanism for advising on cultural considerations, and for establishing guidelines for interaction with the civil population, rested with US civil affairs forces. However, due to what Varhola describes as 'the overwhelming requirements of the invasion', civil affairs forces were deployed with no training in the Middle Eastern culture or introduction to Arabic. In other words, the task of advising ground commanders on how to deal with the local community fell on the shoulders of people with no such training in the Middle East (Varhola 2004).

Thus, on numerous occasions, US troops displayed that this part of doctrine has not been a priority during pre-deployment training. One example took place on 10 April 2003 in Baghdad when Corporal Edward Chin of the US Marines covered the face of the Saddam Hussein statue with an American flag to celebrate the fall of the regime (*ABCNews* 2004). The event was broadcast by global media and completely contradicted President Bush's insistence on describing the invasion as 'a liberation, not an occupation'. Second, the US forces did not even understand that the very reason they were in Iraq was to create a political transition. A remarkable display of bad leadership and lack of understanding was displayed by Captain Dave Gray of the US 4th Infantry Division, who complained about the post-war transition job.

> I don't like it, but I'll do it. There is no NATO, so we're doing the NATO thing now. But it's kinda f-ked: to take a bunch of infantry who're trained to kill, not mediate who ran over somebody's dog.
>
> (Cited in Hirsh 2003)

Varhola has noted that it is not uncommon to hear American soldiers explain that the only thing the Iraqis understand is 'force'. At the same time 'these soldiers do not speak Arabic and have had little or no interaction with Iraqis'. While force as a means of communication is certainly understood in Iraq, as in most places, these tactics may also undermine the political aims of the operations, and do not help when it comes to the struggle for hearts and minds (Varhola 2004). While the highly publicized criminal behaviour and inhumane treatment of prisoners by US forces are an extreme example of US military conduct that serves to alienate the local as well as global population, many of the daily and less publicized activities are perhaps more alarming. The reason is that these are activities condoned by the chain of command, and have direct effects on the lives of ordinary Iraqis. A number of examples are:

> 'test firing' weapons from moving vehicles in urban areas, shooting at Iraqi vehicles on major highways, destroying walls that have anti-American graffiti painted on them, collectively detaining all males in a given area or village for up to several weeks or months, and detaining preadolescent family members of suspects in an effort to force suspects to turn themselves in.
>
> (Varhola 2004)

The most abhorrent example of failing to connect the political purpose of operations with tactical behaviour on the ground was the systematic abuse of prisoners contained in the Abu Ghraib prison. The abuse, and the slow response to the reports from the prison displayed a complete lack of understanding of the political role that the US armed forces are playing in Iraq. The cases of prisoner abuse in Iraq as well as the treatment of prisoners at Guantanamo Bay mean an immeasurable loss of credibility for the United States as a force for good, and as a promoter of democracy and respect for human rights. It should also be noted that the cases of abuse have a domestic dimension in both the US and British cases. The cases of abuse and other immoral acts may decrease the respect which the domestic population has for the military and what it does – thereby breaking the Military Covenant between the nation, the military and each individual soldier.

There is also a number of disturbing cases of illegal behaviour of US troops in Iraq. During 2006 a story of mass killings in the village of Haditha came to public attention. On the morning of 19 November 2005, a roadside bomb struck a Humvee carrying Marines from 3rd Battalion, 1st Marines, on a road near Haditha. The bomb killed a Lance Corporal in the unit (Duffy 2006). The marines responded by going on a rampage in the town. The rampage killed 24 civilians, among them women and children. The killings were 'methodical in nature' and occurred over a period of three to five hours (Poole 2006). The incident also involved the attempt of a major cover-up at several levels of command before the story broke. It is also notable that it was not an issue of bad training as the unit was well prepared for their duty in Iraq. Several members of the unit were on their second tour; one was on his third. They were, moreover, veterans of the house-to-house fighting in Fallujah during previous tours, and should have been well-prepared for the conditions in Iraq (Duffy 2006). Following the high-profile Haditha allegations, pressure from the Iraqi government on military commanders to curtail excessive force by soldiers, and an initiative to cut down on civilian casualties by Lieutenant General Peter Chiarelli, commander of the multinational forces in Iraq during 2006, caused an intensification of investigations into US troop behaviour in Iraq. This has led to a number of disturbing incidents being revealed. Among the cases are rapes of minors, killings of unarmed civilians, including a crippled man. In most of the cases there are also cover-ups involved (Finer 2006).

However, the basic training and values of the US soldiers in general do not seem to have been questioned. After the Haditha incident became public, Lieutenant General Chiarelli ordered a 'core warrior-values training' – a four-hour refresher course and an information packet reminding soldiers of the values with which they were trained (Knickmeyer and Hernandez 2006). In other words, rather than rethinking the values of the military, they were further reinforced. The criminal activities in themselves, the failure to react quickly and harshly in condemnation of the activities, and especially the institutional cover-up attempts, point towards a systemic failure to understand the importance of the strategic corporal and the strategic consequences of such behaviour. The strategic narrative was, therefore, before the surge of 2007, beyond the control of the coalition, creating further dissent by the day.

US counter-insurgency learning and the surge of 2007–2008

Once the US administration faced the fact that it was dealing with a protracted and growing insurgency rather than the remnants of Hussein's regime, it started seeking ways to overcome the initial failures. Subsequent institutional innovation has occurred on three levels. Many of these efforts centred on relearning the forgotten lessons of counter-insurgency. David Ucko (2008) describes US learning in Iraq in conceptual, institutional and operational terms. Conceptually, the US military has been forced to develop counter-insurgency doctrines and strategic documents that are more up to date with the demands in the field of operations. Institutionally, counter-insurgency warfare has become an integral, albeit limited, part of military training, education and planning. Finally, the operational learning has meant that the US military has radically changed its mode of conduct in Iraq, to some extent implementing the conceptual development of the counter-insurgency doctrine. The best example is the surge, started in February 2007 with Operation Fardh al-Qanoon, which can be described as the first time since the Vietnam War that the US military has conducted a 'community-oriented, population-centred counterinsurgency campaign' (Ucko 2008: 293).

From February 2007, the number of US troops steadily rose from 130,000 to a peak of 175,000 in November the same year (IISS 2008: 205). The surge in troop numbers was accompanied by a complete change of tactics in a number of ways as briefly described above with reference to Operation Fardh al-Qanoon. Against the odds, and certainly proving many sceptics wrong, the US military surge has contributed to a significant reduction in violence, and, in military terms, it is obvious that it has worked.

However, as Stephen Biddle (2008) accurately argues, violence in Iraq did not decrease simply because of US troops killing insurgents or forcing them out of Iraq, nor was it because of improvements to the Iraqi Security Forces (ISF). While al Qaeda suffered heavy casualties in Iraq during 2007, and while the ISF steadily increased numbers and improved its capabilities, the numbers hardly explain the large reduction in violence after the surge. There are a number of contributing factors and an important one was the so-called 'Anbar awakening'. The awakening was an unanticipated and unplanned opportunity for stabilization in Iraq that arose through bilateral contractual agreements with a group of Sunni tribal sheiks. In exchange for the recognition as legitimate security providers with a salary of $300 per member per month, local armed groups would wear uniforms, take care of security in their home districts, provide accurate information on all members, and fight al Qaeda rather than US troops. The successes of these agreements have been startling and in 2008 95,000 Iraqis under more than 200 of these contracts are controlling and providing security in much of Western and Central Iraq. If the decision to disband the Iraqi Army created hundreds of thousands of armed potential enemies, these contracts are precisely the opposite. Sectarian fighters become allies and providers of security (Biddle 2008). Although neither planned nor anticipated, the Anbar awakening was not just pure luck or coincidence. A conceptual revolution within the military leadership in Iraq gave the US forces the ability to carry out new policies and take advantage of new dynamics in Iraqi politics. Without the intellectual openness, these contracts would not have come about.

Outcome of US conduct of operations in Iraq

While the military campaign in Iraq has been described as a success by quickly outmanoeuvring the Iraqi forces and toppling the regime of Saddam Hussein, the post-conflict period has, until some positive signs began to appear during the second half of 2007, been largely unsuccessful. A dramatic military victory has, therefore, been overshadowed by chaos and bloodshed on the streets of Baghdad, difficulty and delay in establishing security or providing essential services, and a deadly insurgency. Human, military and economic costs are high and continue to rise. Michael O'Hanlon (2004) writes that 'one of the most brilliant invasion successes in modern military history was followed almost immediately by one of the most incompetently planned occupations'.

The final verdict regarding the outcome of US operations in Iraq remains for history to decide, but a number of conclusions can be made at this stage. In the summer of 2008 Iraq was calmer than it had been since April 2004, overall violence in Iraq was down by 80 per cent since the surge began, and ethno-sectarian violence is down by at least 90 per cent (Robinson 2008: 345; Biddle *et al.* 2008; Odierno 2008: 3). However, five years after the coalition's invasion of Iraq, the country remains deeply violent and divided. In April 2008, Refugees International reported that there are still 2.7 million internally displaced Iraqis and that in a 'Hezbollah-like' fashion 'militias of all denominations are improving their local base of support by providing social services in the neighborhoods and towns they control' (Younez and Rosen 2008: 1).

Moreover, the purpose of the surge, as expressed by General Petraeus, head of the Multinational Force in Iraq from January 2007 to September 2008, was to create a condition from which to establish a long-term political settlement. By suspending the civil war and thereby creating a window of opportunity, the idea was that Iraqi leaders would use this opportunity by moving towards a process of national reconciliation. Despite the surprising military achievements of the surge, the political process has not moved forward. The political leadership of Iraq is still dominated by highly divisive and sectarian agendas. This means high levels of inefficiency and corruption, as well as a weak and divided parliament that is unable to pass crucial legislation (IISS 2008: 206, 215). The achievements of the surge should not be understated, but the absence of the fundamental political changes and processes towards reconciliation it was supposed to facilitate, means that the long-term effects of the surge remains highly unstable, fragile and quickly reversible (ICG 2008; IISS 2008).

A further problematic aspect of the new US approach is the fact that it supports a set of local actors and traditional power structures that operate beyond the state's realm. While the long-term consequences of this approach are difficult to predict, there is an obvious risk that long-term stability and state capacity to control its territory in Weberian terms is weakened by the actors that have recently been strengthened by the US support. The International Crisis Group (2008) notes that the *sahwat*, the local awakening councils of the Anbar province, have already generated new divisions within the local society, which may create new potential sources of violence in the already multilayered conflict. Some Iraqi tribes have benefited heavily from US assistance, while others receive much less. The resulting redistribution of power risks engendering instability and rivalry, which in turn could trigger violence, something that the remaining insurgency groups would make use of (ICG 2008). Moreover, without integrating the local structures into the national political process, they do not constitute progress towards consolidation of the central government or institutions. Although highly successful in quickly bringing stability to much of Western Iraq, the local councils are, therefore, also a liability that could just as quickly bring the country back into civil war (Hanna 2008; ICG 2008).

In grand strategic terms, has the invasion of Iraq made America and the rest of the world a safer place? Dana Allin has argued that the Iraq War 'has been a counter-strategic diversion that has weakened America, strengthened global jihadist terrorism and has arguably failed, so far at least, to bring humanitarian betterment to the Iraqi people' (2007: 128). Similarly, Francis Fukuyama contends that a result of the Iraq War is that the US has squandered the overwhelming public mandate it had received after 11 September, and instead, alienated most of its allies, 'many of whom have since engaged in "soft balancing" against American influence, and stirred up anti-Americanism in the Middle East' (Fukuyama 2005). Interestingly, while seven of eight military objectives were said to have been achieved in May 2003, the failure to achieve the last objective of reconstruction and democratization has, therefore, led to the failure of the campaign in relation to the political aims of the operation.

The US troops in Iraq have largely conducted their operations in accordance with the American way of war and their doctrine on conventional warfare throughout the campaign, including the post-conflict phase until the dramatic shift in 2007. The campaign was interpreted as an essentially conventional war, which is also what the US military planned and trained for. The invasion was an overwhelming display of superiority in terms of technology and organization on the conventional battlefield. However, when Saddam Hussein's regime fell, it quickly became clear that the US leadership had failed to create a serious strategy for the post-conflict phase. Interagency co-operation failed in the planning process and did not produce a comprehensive approach. Civil–military co-operation within the Pentagon also failed to produce plans that effectively connected operational and tactical activity to the strategic aims. The limited interaction over departmental boundaries, with the subsequent limitation in expertise in the planning process, allowed a small number of people to plan operations on a number of flawed assumptions about Iraq.

In the field, the civilian and military components failed to create unity of command, which made co-operation difficult. Confusion about the chain of command, in combination with different views on how to get the task done across the civil–military divide, meant that the activities of the different instruments of power were not co-ordinated, thereby violating the principle of unity of effort.

The tactical behaviour of US troops in Iraq, especially the first three years of the campaign, revealed that they have neither been trained, nor mentally prepared for post-conflict-type operations, or complex peace operations. Instead, the US military resorted to conventional tactics based on firepower and technology, with the addition of an overemphasis on aggressive force protection policies, which separated and alienated the US troops from the local population. US forces also lacked cultural sensitivity and understanding of how the political aims of the operation must be reflected in their behaviour on the ground. This is noted in the heavy-handed day-to-day work of US troops. The tactical principles of complex peace operations, as discussed in the introductory chapter, were, therefore, also violated. Instead of hearts and minds operations, involving minimum use of force, force protection through closer connections with the local communities and an understanding of the political primacy and consequences of operations, the intended strategic narrative has been lost in heavy-handed tactics and a failure to understand local culture as well as the nature of the enemy and the strategic aims. The incidents of abuse at Abu Ghraib, in combination with the criminal investigations of serious crimes committed by US troops in Iraq, thereby, raise questions regarding the warrior values which are the foundation of US military training.

The previous chapter suggested that the functional imperative of US forces – defined too narrowly by the military leadership – has left the US armed forces inadequately prepared for complex peace operations – structurally and culturally. This has been confirmed by the analysis of US operations in Iraq, although the remarkable learning curve in terms of tactical adjustments during the last three years requires a discussion whether a major shift of organizational imperatives has taken place, and in that case – why? However, before engaging in that discussion, the analysis of British civil–military relations and operations in Iraq is due.

Part III

Case study

The United Kingdom

6 The patterns of civil–military relations in the United Kingdom

The theoretical chapter advocated a broad view of civil–military relations in which the study of history, in combination with cultural and structural factors, forms a deeper understanding of how the civil–military relationship is rooted in societies' structures and how they may affect the conduct of operational planning and execution. This chapter, therefore, starts with an analysis of some important aspects of British military history. The historical section is followed by the analysis of British civil–military relations. This section uses the discussion from the theoretical chapter and focuses on the interagency structures and the patterns of civil–military relations within the Ministry of Defence. The central question is whether the civil–military structures are integrated or divided with reference to the normative theories outlined in Chapter 2. Another central issue is the level of civilian control of the armed forces.

Historical background of the British military

This section is designed to illustrate a number of themes in British military history that are likely to have had a major impact on the culture of the armed forces and its relationship with the British political leadership. It, thereby, functions as 'thick description' in order to provide increased meaning to, and understanding of, the civil–military structures and modes of operational conduct that are subsequently described. The themes studied are the development of professionalism in the British armed forces, Victorian values and lessons from colonial policing and the counter-insurgency operations of the Cold War era, and finally, the operations in Northern Ireland and the post-Cold War era.

The early years

In 1688, King James II was expelled and William III installed during the so-called Glorious Revolution. Before the revolution, England had experienced a dual system consisting of the New Model Army under the authority of Parliament, and the Army of James II, of course, controlled by the Crown (Strachan 1997: 44). The new system, created in the wake of the revolution, was based on having just one army managed in a system of dual control. This meant that control of the armed forces was shared by the Crown and Parliament – a form of checks and balances that provided the military with the opportunity to play its masters against each other. However, at the same time, Parliament successfully kept the British Army disorganized in order to ensure control. To play one civilian branch off against the other the military needed some form of integrity, which it lacked. The army was, thereby, prevented from being able to take advantage of the divided civilian rule in the eighteenth century. However, the disorganization, with a lack of structured education and the system of purchased commissions, also hindered the professionalization and effectiveness of the British armed forces (Avant 1994: 36).

Empire and professionalism

With the defeat of Napoleon on the European continent, the British Army's focus turned to the colonies. Since 1815 the British have only fought three wars on the European continent: the Crimean War and the two World Wars. More often, British military campaigns have taken place on the fringes of the Empire, and, as Hew Strachan describes it: 'Extra-European warfare has been the army's dominant experience' (1997: 74). The Empire has, therefore, been the most consistent and most continuous influence in shaping the British military, as well as the most important variable in the process of military professionalization. In essence, the British development of military professionalism took place in an era when the functional imperative consisted of colonial policing and administration, and with a very large influence of what Huntington (1957) calls the 'societal imperatives'.

In the 1870s, three major reforms of the military establishment took place that would open the way for a more professional army, by removing any royal authority over the military outside of parliamentary action, by creating a new system of service and reserves, and by abolishing the purchase of commissions (Avant 1994: 38). At the same time, the political institutions had by this time been changed to centralize authority over policy to the Cabinet, which made political monitoring and control of the military less costly. The Cabinet's ability to intervene in military policy without major political costs affected the development of military professionalism in Britain. The Cabinet exercised control over the military personnel by replacing officers who did not produce the desired results. In this way the military leadership and the officer corps in general became closely attuned to the preferences of the political leadership (Avant 1994: 40). Moreover, since the British Army became professionalized under conditions of low cost civilian intervention, the military purists were not able to set the agenda as to what counted as the military's functional imperative or proper warfare. The training and promotion of the British military came to reflect civilian concerns of solving immediate threats and problems in the Empire. The functional need to face all kinds of immediate threats within the Empire as well as the political or careerist need to pay close attention to the civilian leadership in order to be promoted developed a military culture that emphasized adaptability, and political understanding.

The types of operations the British Army conducted during this period caused a further politicization as well as political awareness of the military. The soldier in the colonies was more than a soldier. He was also part of the administration of the colony and therefore a civiliser and settler. The soldier's role was not simply to win wars and conquer territory, it was also to administer and police the land he had conquered (Strachan, 1997: 75). Military responsibilities and civil administration were closely linked, and the most obvious manifestation of this fact was in the common combination of the jobs of commander-in-chief and governor (Strachan 1997: 76). This was, moreover, a pattern that continued into the twentieth century and even its second half with the appointment of General Sir Gerald Templer as High Commissioner *and* director of operations in Malaya, as an example (Nagl 2002: 104).

The British military went through the process of professionalization in an era when the functional as well as the societal imperatives created close links with the political leadership and what Huntington would call politicization of the armed forces. The political interventions led the armed forces to become closely attuned to the wishes of the political leadership. Moreover, the imperial policing and administration conducted in the colonies also politicized the armed forces by giving it tasks that are normally executed by civilian administrations. Although the normal theory of civil–military relations would argue that this is a prime example of subjective civilian control that should lead to the decrease in military effectiveness, the British armed forces were successful in their tasks of colonial policing within the Empire. We shall also later come back to the importance of the politicized professional mindset in the development of effective counter-insurgency doctrine.

Victorian values and counter-insurgency operations

The British way of war, as described in the following chapter, can be traced well into the nineteenth century and the combination of pragmatic lessons from colonial policing and counter-insurgency operations, as well as the societal influence of Victorian values (Thornton 2004a: 85). The Victorian values of British society are based on Christian protestant sentiment and the values of individual liberty and responsibility that are inherent in both Protestantism and the basis of British liberalism. Built into the British view of the law was the belief that individuals must take responsibility for their own lives and suffer the consequences of their actions. The purpose of the law was not to coerce citizens into the right actions, but to free them from the state and leave them to mind their own business as well as to attend their duties. The most important of these duties was the chivalric 'to do what you ought ... [in relation] to the duty of care which each person owes the innocent stranger' (Scruton 2000: 57, 121).

It was certainly expected of the British gentlemen officers and soldiers to act within these sentiments. The concept of minimum force was also supported by another derivation of Victorian values in the idea of the British gentleman. The nineteenth century saw a revival of the idea of medieval chivalry and the ideals of bravery, loyalty, courtesy, modesty and honour. The gentleman was the front figure of this movement and, of course, the imperial officer was part of it. The reason why the concepts of chivalry and humanitarianism were so successfully ingrained in British society was thanks to the British public school system and the popular literature of the time (Thornton 2004a: 89). The public schools in Britain were established with the sole purpose of creating a future upper class and governing elite of the British Empire. They would produce men of character who would 'provide the benefits of Christian civilization to the heathen peoples of the Empire, without cruelty and excess'. Through the public school system, and please note that 'public school' actually refers to private elite schools in the British case, the Christian or Victorian values were moreover embedded in society long after Queen Victoria. The same values have been taught by the public schools to this day as 'British' values and thus still inform the British officer corps (Barnett 1972: 27–28).

The Victorian values that were taught to the young elites were, moreover, strengthened by the popular culture of the Victorian period. The juvenile literature was often centred on military figures who, filled with patriotism and courage, and fuelled by a strong sense of duty and honour, imposed the British ideals throughout the Empire. This juvenile literature also had the effect of spreading the Victorian values beyond the upper class as it had the capability of reaching a far wider audience than the public school system (Thornton 2004a: 90). The British male youth, even if he did not attend a public school, was thus socialized into knowing the standards of behaviour for a British gentleman and officer. These values have, to a large extent, survived until today within the British armed forces. One reason for this can be ascribed to the conservative nature of the public school system and the military recruiting and education system. While the traditional Victorian values have been maintained within the public school system, the British armed forces, to a disproportionately large extent in relation to the rest of society, still recruits from these institutions (Thornton 2004a: 94).

Plenty of research has been conducted concerning the link between public school education and commissions in high status regiments and career success in the British armed forces (Otley 1973; Garnier 1975; Macdonald 1988; Macdonald 2004). Relatively recent data supports the notion that there is still a strong link between commissioned officers and 'top' public schools.

> The proportion of public school cadets reached a high point of 91% in 1910, remained around 80% until World War II, and fell to two-thirds in the nineteen-fifties and sixties. It has declined by 15 percentage points since then and now seems to have fallen below 50%.
>
> (Macdonald 2004: 111)

The statistics become even more striking when looking at the 'elite regiments', the Guards Regiments (Grenadier, Coldstream, Scots, Irish and Welsh), as well as the Royal Green Jackets. The recruitment to these regiments in the period between 1999 and 2000, involved 57 entrants of which 51 came from public

schools (Macdonald 2004: 112). Equally, when studying the continued importance of public school education in the military career the same pattern continues, as most positions of senior officers have been, and continue to be, filled
by ex-public schoolboys. 'In 2000 89% of senior generals and field marshals had
been to public school, as compared with 63% of cadets in 1967, which is the
period when these men would have been at the RMA [Royal Military Academy
Sandhurst]'. This is despite the fact that public school recruits do not stand out
in terms of merit during military training (Macdonald 2004: 119).

The Boer War, the World Wars, the Cold War and the return to old principles

The Boer War, or the South African War of 1899–1902, was a watershed event
for the British armed forces, and showed that all was not well. After the Crimean
War between 1853 and 1856, the British Army had enjoyed 40 years of fighting
ill-equipped and ill-organized forces in the colonies. This legacy made for an
over-confidence that was quickly shattered by the opening battles in South
Africa. The British generals had a difficult time adjusting to the different tactics
of the Boer Army. The Boers constituted a fast and highly mobile guerrilla force,
employing hit-and-run tactics that caused severe losses to the British forces, and
that frustrated the British officers' view of a 'fair fight'. The South African War
turned out to be a pyrrhic victory, not only because it cost the British society
many lives and £217 million (compared to the £68 million for the Crimean War
and £1 million for the Zulu War), but also because it broke the imperial spirit of
British society (Morris 1976). Not only was public support quickly lost as the
war dragged on and even caused some spectacular defeats. There was also public
outrage due to the brutal tactics used to try and subdue the Boers' guerrillas in
the latter part of the war. An example was Lord Kitchener's scorched earth
tactics. This took the form of the destruction of farms in order to prevent the
guerrillas from obtaining food and supplies, and to demoralize them by leaving
their women and children homeless and starving in the open. When these tactics
proved unsuccessful, the Boer women and children were instead herded into
concentration camps where as many as 30,000, or about 25 per cent, of the
inmates died due to appalling conditions (Porter 2000: 635). Thus began the
long, slow decline of support for the imperial idea in Britain.

Despite the treatment of the Boer War as a dark moment in British history, it
can be argued that it was also a case of relatively quick and successful adaptation to guerrilla tactics after initial losses. 'For all its barbarism, however, the
policy worked ... Kitchener instituted a plan that was not quick or easy, or even
popular; but it was effective and, ultimately, successful' (Avant 1994: 113–114).
The changes instituted by the British were not the result of orders from civilian
leaders in London, but were initiated by the army itself. Interestingly, within six
months of the start of the war, all high-ranking commanders had adjusted their
tactics in their own personal way. As noted, this adaptability can partially be
explained by the nature of civil–military relations which allowed for strong

civilian control over army personnel. The civilian leaders at the time had favoured flexible and adaptable military leaders in the years before the Boer War. Civilian control over personnel had affected the bias of British military professionalism to be more concerned with adaptation and flexibility than with standard manners of strategic and tactical thinking (Avant 1994: 115).

When the First World War broke out, the British were, despite the hard-won lessons of the Boer War, used to small and relatively cheap wars and, therefore, had little appreciation of the nature of warfare against industrialized powers. However, in the wake of the Boer War a royal commission was set up to investigate the military problems in South Africa and to suggest reforms. Radical technological changes were made to naval vessels and rapid-firing guns, and the institutional integrity of the defence establishment was strengthened and included an institutionalized system of military advice to civilian leaders. Another result was increased civilian appointments of the offensive minded 'continentalist' officers of the British Army, who had until then been out of fashion within the British defence establishment. These officers were more interested in continental defence than in colonial warfare and favoured the scientific and Prussian view of war, shared by their continental and American counterparts (Avant 1994: 46, 115–116). The war caused enormous casualties on the European continent, and one of the most salient British lessons of the First World War was that the cost of victory had been too high. Thus, the First World War created strong reactions and developed an essentially anti-military environment in Britain during the interwar period (Cassidy 2004: 49).

Against this background, Basil Henry Liddell Hart developed what seemed like an attractive alternative to the mass killings of the First World War in the 'traditional British way in warfare', involving the indirect approach. The British approach to complex peace operations is further discussed in the next chapter, but, in essence, the indirect approach was a return to old principles of imperial policing, and Hart sought to return wars to the periphery and 'on the cheap'. As a consequence, after the war the army was again dismantled and as the interwar governments treated another continental war as an unlikely contingency, the army returned to its duties in the colonies (Nagl 2002: 40).

The anti-military climate of the interwar period, in combination with Liddell Hart's indirect approach, led the British Government to a number of defence reviews that in essence stated that Britain would not commit an army on the continent under any circumstances (Cassidy 2004: 49). This political environment of 'the imperial defence mission', together with the historical organizational focus on colonial policing, is thought to have impeded the important development of armoured warfare in Britain before the Second World War (Winton 1988). Although many officers saw the need for armoured mechanization, the way the army should be equipped depended on what the purpose of the army was supposed to be – the functional imperative. The colonial commitments in India especially, therefore complicated the process of mechanization; militated against the creation of an Expeditionary Force in peacetime. It also prevented a radical redistribution of imperial garrisons in response to changing strategic conditions in Europe. Ultimately, the creation of armoured divisions was considered too costly when infantry resources were needed for the continued policing of the Empire (Bond 1980).

At the onset of the Second World War, the UK was, therefore, ill prepared to face the reformed German forces, including armoured formations and blitzkrieg strategy. The war obviously led to another vast expansion of the British military establishment. The lessons of the Second World War were nevertheless mixed because of the wide variety of experiences in different theatres, but it is clear that the emphasis on conventional war changed the training and mindset of the British Army. However, the two world wars precipitated three new strategic realities for the British: the loss of great power status; divestment of the Empire; and a larger role for the British Army in Europe. Britain, therefore, faced the challenge to balance reduced economic resources with both the security requirements in Europe, and maintaining the remaining colonies. The post-war period was therefore transitional, whereby the army lost its overseas role and gained one in Europe. It fought small wars but became more focused on defence of continental Europe (Cassidy 2004: 41, 52).

The experience of sending a larger conscription-based army into the high-intensity warfare of the Second World War, nevertheless, paved the way for a more permanent inclusion of a second military subculture of warfighting in the British armed forces (Mäder 2004: 82). The Army's new role in defending Northern Germany, and the large forces stationed in continental Europe, created, as a result, the British Army consisting of two distinct organizational cultures: first, a camp that emphasized traditional expeditionary warfare of counter-insurgency and small wars in the former colonies, and, second, a camp focusing on large-scale, armoured warfare in the European theatre of war, within the NATO framework. The second strand became embodied in the so-called British Army of the Rhine, which was responsible for the defence of Northern Germany. This created a somewhat uneasy co-existence of two distinctly different modes of operations, which also created two conceptually different groups of officers and soldiers. A rivalry between the two cultures was also obvious in the post-war conceptual debate over how to divide the decreasing financial resources among the different services, as well as among different parts of the Army (Mäder 2004: 83).

In the post-war period the British found it difficult to readjust to the traditional way of war in the old colonies. In 1955 the training and doctrine of the British army were still essentially that of a nation in arms, 'dedicated to the principle of unlimited war fought by massive forces and only reluctantly discarding the organization and tactics of El Alamein and the Normandy beaches' (Jones 1966: 315–316). However, by the early 1960s the British armed forces were once again absorbing the traditional values and tactics of its colonial history. To an even greater extent than before the Second World War the British emphasized civilian leadership in the execution of counter-insurgency operations. A comprehensive package of economic, political, social and military measures was wanted (Thornton 2000: 44). To emphasize the transition from the continental operations of the Second World War with the relearning of counter-insurgency principles, this following section takes a closer look at the British operations in Malaya. It is also an interesting example of quick learning and adaptation after initial failures.

Malaya

The post-Second World War British Army looked much more like a conventional army than during the pinnacle of the colonial period, and the problems faced by the British in Malaya were, therefore, somewhat similar to those faced by the US in Vietnam. Malaya was a British colony that was first lost during the Second World War during the Japanese invasion of South-East Asia. However, long before that, the Malayan Communist Party (MCP) was created out of a very active anti-colonial movement, especially among the Chinese community, during the 1930s. During the Second World War, the MCP organized a guerrilla army that fought the Japanese with the support of the British who provided them with weapons. After the Japanese capitulation in 1945, the MCP resisted the return of the British-supported government of Malaya. After negotiations had failed the MCP turned to insurgency. The counter-insurgency campaign in Malaya started on 19 June 1948 when the British High Commissioner declared a state of emergency (Farrar-Hockley 2003: 330).

Initially, the British were struggling due to a weak command and control structure. However, in 1950, due to the rising number of terrorist incidents, the British Government was convinced of the need for drastic changes. Lieutenant General Sir Harold Briggs was placed in a new position as director of operations, directly under the High Commissioner, and in charge of planning, co-ordinating and directing the operations of the police and the military. Moreover, the government was reformed into a structure of executive committees which connected the central government to the states and districts for more effective co-ordination of the counter-insurgency campaign. At the state and district levels the state and district war executive committees (SWECs and DWECs) were implementing policy with local knowledge and sensitivity. This was the start of a solution to overcome the operation's ineffective civil–military relationship (Hamby 2002: 55; Avant 2004). Another innovation by Briggs was the 'New Village' system, which was a scheme to resettle the Chinese population that was thought to provide the insurgents with supplies. By moving them and improving their standard of living, three aims were achieved: the insurgents were starved out, the support for the government was strengthened, and the flow of information from the local population increased (Short 1975; Nagl 2002: 75). It should be noted that the British tactics of forced population movement is today considered a war crime close to ethnic cleansing. It would, therefore, be a completely unacceptable tactic in the age of global surveillance warfare.

However, even with the committee system and the New Villages in effect, Briggs found difficulties in directing and co-ordinating the efforts of the police and the military. Briggs felt that this was because of too limited powers invested in the director of operations and, therefore, suggested increasing the powers of his successor. Finally, the assassination of the High Commissioner, Sir Henry Gurney, led the British Government to respond to Briggs' request. The solution was the merger of the posts of High Commissioner and director of operations with General Sir Gerald Templer in charge (Nagl 2002: 104). The exceptional powers invested in Templer created a highly effective command and control structure and a close co-ordination of the operation's civil and military aspects. The Briggs plan could be effectively implemented.

The smoothly running command and control structure also led to good civil–military co-operation at the tactical level. Most units formed their headquarters in a joint operations room usually run by the police. Moreover, there was no separate military intelligence chain created, and the police special branch was instead used. Although the policing measures were sometimes very harsh they were often done with restraint and under the established rules. Those who violated the regulations of the troops were severely punished (Avant 1994: 58). The legitimacy and coercive power of the campaign was moreover strengthened through a well-executed information campaign that was waged from centralized headquarters, and implemented by the SWEC–DWEC system. Also the security problem, for both the local population and the counter-insurgency troops, was established by making the local population responsible for their own security.

With the Briggs plan, as implemented by Templer, the government continually increased its legitimacy while the insurgents were further isolated from the population (Avant 1994). Initial difficulties at the operational and tactical levels were dealt with in a highly flexible manner. It was the flexibility and innovation of the civil–military relations and the command and control structures that created a campaign of flexibility, sound civil–military relations and the minimum use of force.

Northern Ireland and the post-Cold War era

With the exception of a few diversions of more traditional warfare in the Falklands campaign and the Gulf War, the British military experience has continued to be filled by different forms of complex peace operations of the counter-insurgency type.

In Northern Ireland, the British military was reluctantly called in to give military aid to the civil power in August 1969. With experience limited to counter-insurgency operations in the colonies, the British Army used what was considered rather heavy-handed tactics at the start of the operations in Northern Ireland. Such tactics reached their nadir on the infamous 'Bloody Sunday' early in 1972, when soldiers from the Parachute Regiment killed 13 men and wounded 13 others. However, the British Army subsequently improved its tactics and training so that by 1975 it was relatively successfully managing the conflict with more sophisticated tactics and intelligence operations. As a result, the British military gained unique experience in urban patrolling, covert surveillance and bomb disposal (Dewar 1990: 15; Strawson 2003).

Colin McInnes has underlined a number of key features of the British Army's experience in Northern Ireland:

> The civil authorities remained in control; minimum force was generally used; new tactics were constantly developed and tactical control devolved; close relations were established with the police; and finally the Army recognized that it could not resolve the conflict on its own, but that a broader-based political strategy was required.
>
> (1996: 182)

Against this rather positive view of British operations in Northern Ireland, one must still also emphasize that it took over 30 years and more than 3,500 casualties before the British could establish an acceptable level of stability. It was an internal conflict within the UK, and elsewhere Protestants and Catholics lived in complete harmony. Regardless of the important lessons learned from the Ulster experience, one can hardly claim that it was effectively or efficiently handled.

Nevertheless, the operations in Northern Ireland perpetuated the British Army's experiences and attitudes about low-intensity conflict (Cassidy 2005). Despite the traditional operations in the Falklands and the Gulf War, the operations in Northern Ireland have greatly influenced the British Army's training, movement, deployment, logistics and morale. It has shaped British soldiers' lives (Strachan 2003). Not only have the British had the chance to perfect their urban patrolling, civil–military co-operation, and counter-terrorist techniques, they have been forced to do so under the close scrutiny of the British legal system as well as the media. Northern Ireland has, therefore, often been referred to as the perfect training ground for units bound for the complex peace operations of the 1990s and after.

Since the end of the Cold War the British armed forces have increasingly been used 'as a force for good' in Prime Minister Blair's terms, meaning state-building tasks, peace support and humanitarian operations. While the rhetoric surrounding these operations speaks of reconstruction and peacekeeping, the forces on the ground often experience fierce fighting and Anthony Forster notes that retired senior officers have increasingly criticized the political leadership for failing to give proper moral and financial support to the military in such contexts (Forster 2006b: 1046). A further strain in the civil–military relationship has recently been made public by the fierce criticism of government policy by the head of the Army, General Sir Richard Dannatt, as well as his predecessor, General Sir Mike Jackson. The criticism is not limited to operational matters, but also covers the management of British forces in peacetime, in terms of personnel management, housing, salaries and procurement of equipment (Sands 2006). Forster also observes that in recent years the political leadership has been more inclined to micro-manage the armed forces. As noted, in contemporary operations, tactical operations may have unforeseen strategic consequences, thereby giving the political leadership an incentive to intervene at lower levels – an imperative that is supported by technological advance that makes such micro-management of day-to-day operations possible (Forster 2006b: 1046).

The perceived strain in the civil–military relationship is, to a large extent, based on a discussion regarding the Military Covenant in the UK. The Military Covenant is part of formal British doctrine, which states that, as soldiers are called upon to make great personal sacrifices in the service of the nation, and forgo some of the rights enjoyed by those outside the armed forces, 'the British soldiers must always be able to expect fair treatment, to be valued and respected as individuals, and that they (and their families) will be sustained and rewarded by commensurate terms and conditions of service'. The unique nature of military operations also means that the armed forces must be allowed to differ from all other institutions, and must be provided for accordingly by the nation. As formulated in British doctrine: 'This mutual obligation forms the Military Covenant between the nation, the Army and each individual soldier; an unbreakable common bond of identity, loyalty and responsibility which has sustained the Army and its soldiers throughout its history' (UK Army 2000).

The budgetary limits on personnel, housing and equipment can be seen as a violation of these obligations on the part of the British Government. Apart from housing, equipment and pay issues, the military is feeling a considerable overstretch of the armed forces, which are required to do too many tasks with too few troops. This has serious consequences. Forster cites a study carried out by the Ministry of Defence in the last quarter of 2005, in which almost 25 per cent of members of the armed forces wanted to leave at the earliest opportunity. The Army also has trouble recruiting (Forster 2006b: 1047). Moreover, there is a widespread sense among the lower military ranks that their interests are not well defended by the senior military leadership or by the civilian officials within the MoD (Smith 2007). As a consequence, calls are also being made for a unionization of the British military (Alexandrou 2004; Bartle 2006).

At the same time, criminal behaviour, such as a number of cases of abuse in Iraq, can be seen as a violation of the moral obligations placed on all soldiers who bear arms in the service of the nation. In the end, popular support for the military and what it does may be decreased. The mutual obligations of the covenant are broken on all sides as the nation, or the people, fail to show support for the troops fighting abroad (Forster 2006b: 1046–1047). The Military Covenant between the British nation, her military and each individual soldier is certainly under some strain. On that note, let us take a closer look at the pattern of civil–military relations in the UK.

Civil–military relations in the UK

As in the US, the presence of a large standing army has in Britain been considered a threat to civil liberties. The British Army's role in aid of civil authorities has contributed to this fear (Cassidy 2004: 73–74). After failing to control the highly organized army after the English Civil War, Parliament's strategy for civilian control was to 'staff it with leaders representative of Parliament, that is, gentlemen of the land' (Avant 1994: 36). During the eighteenth century and part of the nineteenth century, officers were gentlemen first and officers when duty called, and the army was essentially dismantled after each war. Like most armies in Europe, social class was the most important qualification for both entry and advancement for army officers, and the level of military education was considered largely irrelevant. Therefore, effective action of the British military was at this time highly dependent on the personal qualities of individual officers. As officers' capabilities and strategic preferences varied greatly, so did the performance of the British armed forces. Parliament's strategies for civilian control of the armed forces created an unprofessional military with highly variable leadership and effectiveness (Avant 1994: 36–37).

During the imperial period, civilian officials and military officers alike were allowed to rule the colonies and conduct counter-insurgency operations with relatively little interference or direction from London. There was a high-level of trust that both civilians and officers would run the colonies in a way that would not discredit the government (Thornton 2004b: 12). During this period the British armed forces also inherited an understanding of the importance of close civil–military co-operation. Officers understood that because most insurgencies were caused by legitimate grievances that could only be dealt with by the civil authorities, political primacy was necessary. As an example, General Sir Charles Gwynn wrote in 1934 that while the army can deal with the symptoms of insurgencies, it is up to the civilians to deal with the causes (Gwynn 1934). Officers and civilian administrators, moreover, worked closely together, which meant that they developed mutual trust and understanding.

Apart from a historical tradition of close civil–military co-operation, an enabler of smooth civil–military relations is the fact that the civilian and military leaderships have historically been recruited from the same social group. The two groups received the same schooling and were taught the same values (Thornton 2003: 54–55; Avant 1994: 13). As noted in the previous section, although British officers as well as civil servants are today recruited from a slightly broader social background, the socialization into a common belief system among political and military leaders is a tradition that has largely been maintained until today (Thornton 2003). The common background of officers and civil servants means that the problem of a civil–military cultural gap is more limited than in the US case. The following sections analyse the structure and culture of the interagency system as well as the civil–military relations within the MoD.

The British interagency structures

In the British system, ultimate responsibility for policy lies in the Cabinet. As it is always necessary to bring together the different perspectives of the various government departments, this is centralized in the Cabinet Office, which is a government department that serves the government as a whole and not just the Prime Minister (Hopkinson 2000b: 24). Crises are controlled and directed at the Cabinet level which directs all instruments of national power. Crises may, more specifically, be handled at the Cabinet level by a ministerial Committee on Defence and Overseas Policy, or by a special, ad hoc Cabinet committee set up specifically to co-ordinate the work of all the different departments and agencies involved (UK JDCC 2004a: 2–8). In principle, the Committee on Defence and Overseas Policy deals with defence policy. However, in practice, the more important defence policy issues are dealt with in trilateral correspondence between the Foreign Secretary, the Defence Secretary and the Prime Minister. How business is handled at this level is nevertheless much the responsibility of the Prime Minister (Hopkinson 2000b: 24).

Underneath the Cabinet is a structure of ministerial and official committees and sub-committees that help achieve coherence across Government and to ensure that issues of interest to several departments are properly discussed, and that the views of all relevant ministers are considered. One of the key purposes of the Cabinet Committees is to support the principle of collective responsibility, meaning that Cabinet members make decisions collectively, and are, therefore, responsible for the consequences of these decisions collectively. This principle, in combination with the committee structure, ensures that, even though a question may never reach the Cabinet itself, Cabinet Committee issues will be considered by representatives from across the government and are thereby essentially given the same authority as Cabinet decisions (Cabinet Office 2005).

The traditions of collective responsibility and interagency committee deliberation mean that Cabinet or Cabinet Committee decisions are, at best, more than the sum of their parts. The idea is that by bringing the different knowledge and perspectives of the different departments, as well as the varying judgement and experience of ministers and civil servants, ministers are able to arrive at a better outcome than would be possible for any one department head, or the Prime Minister for that matter. However, there are also problems with the committee system. One risk is that decisions become weak but acceptable compromises after being diluted within the interagency committee structure. The most pressing problem of the committee system is, nevertheless, that it does not seem to be quick or integrated enough for contemporary military operations. Interagency deliberation in committees requires time. In the current British system, there is, in other words, a trade off between a subsequent delay in decision-making and the benefits of better decision-making. In practice, big decisions are, therefore, taken collectively, while many small decisions are taken within a single department, the Defence Ministry typically, often after consulting with other departments with a direct interest (Cabinet Office n.d.).

The interagency deliberation process in the UK is also limited by departmental stovepipes and turf wars – something that was recently made evident during the operations in Afghanistan and Iraq. Therefore, defence ministry officials argue that new and more effective structures are needed for successful implementation of contemporary military operations. The argument is that firm structures would speed up the deliberation process, thus removing the process of setting up new ad hoc structures for each major contingency (presentation by Samuels and Russell 2006). The deficiency of the British interagency system has, therefore, sparked the development of the Comprehensive Approach. This approach seeks to achieve more effective integration of the different government agencies – structurally, as well as by making sure that professional education and career development match this imperative (UK MoD 2006).

During the Labour Government of Prime Minister Tony Blair there was an intense debate regarding what is described as his presidential style of leadership (Allen 2001; Foley 2000; Hennessy 2000; Norton 2003; Heffernan 2005). A widely held conviction is that Tony Blair accumulated a level of personal influence that is at variance with the normal configuration of the office. In the words of Michael Foley: 'Blair has developed a reputation not only for acquiring a preeminence in conventional prime ministerial power but also for drawing upon alternative resources of leadership in respect to organizational management, media cultivation, populist outreach, party cohesion and representational innovation' (Foley 2004: 295). Blair had centralized the party as well as the working culture of the government. The influence of the Cabinet as a whole declined and the Prime Minister instead relied on bilateral meetings with his ministers and his own, substantially increased, staff in Downing Street (Jones and Kavanagh 2003: 181–183). The presidential style of leadership was also confirmed by Lord Butler's *Review of Intelligence on Weapons of Mass Destruction*, popularly known as the Butler Report, which investigated the use of the use of intelligence in the run-up to the War in Iraq. The report stated that 'we are concerned that the informality and circumscribed character of the Government's procedures which we saw in the context of policy-making towards Iraq risks reducing the scope for informed collective political judgement' (2004: 160). The increased centralization of the British Government is further discussed in Chapter 8 with reference to British operations in Iraq.

Apart from including an intricate interagency committee structure below the Cabinet, the British political system is highly centralized in the Cabinet and the Prime Minister's office. Interestingly, while the British system of government is formally centralized, it is also known for its decentralization of responsibility. Thus, apart from the collective responsibility within the Cabinet, there is also a tradition of individual ministerial responsibility for all the actions within the ministry. In other words, there seems to be a form of mission command exercised within the British political system, giving ministers the authority and responsibility to act. This is combined with the committee system's tradition of interagency co-operation and collective responsibility, meaning that despite the authority to act alone, the actors with direct interest will at a minimum be consulted, if not involved in issues through an inter-departmental committee.

The British system allows the government departments to work together to create national policies and not simply for departmental advantage. The inter-departmental friction which hampers the work in Washington is more limited in the British system (Hopkinson 2004a: 25). However, while the British interagency co-operation is well developed in relative terms, it does include the same turf wars that all government bureaucracies experience. The relatively close interagency co-operation of the committee system is confirmed by defence ministry officials who assert that, in terms of defence policy, the co-operation and communication between the Foreign and Commonwealth Office and the Ministry of Defence are very close. This co-operative relationship does not extend to all departments and agencies, and the relations between the military and development agencies have in interviews been described as problematic due to cultural diversities and the difference in the nature of the tasks of the agencies (Mayall 2004; Trott 2005; Russell 2005; Palmer 2005).

The British administrative practice at its best is thus one of close informal relationships between officials regardless of which government is in power. The centralized political system, in combination with an intricate interagency system of permanent and ad hoc committees, provides for strong government control as well as a smoothly running civil–military interface. The committee system enables civil servants from the different relevant departments to have regular contact through which they develop mutual understanding for each other. The theoretical sections on trust and command and control taught us the importance of these informal relationships and their resulting interpersonal trust building as facilitators of effective command structures. Another positive aspect of a well-developed interagency structure and working culture is that personality problems are minimized. Instead of letting bad personal relations inhibit the co-operation between ministries, departments and agencies, a well-oiled interagency system finds alternative routes to useful discussions and common positions, thereby, bypassing discordant personal relations. Being part of the interagency system also makes it easier for everyone involved to see themselves within a larger picture. How does my work relate to larger government aims?

Significantly, interagency co-operation – albeit far from perfect – is in interviews with British officials described as a cultural feature of the political system rather than something imposed from the political leadership. It is not something that is particular in the field of defence or foreign affairs, 'It is the way we do government in this country' (Russell 2005; Palmer 2005).

The Ministry of Defence

The role of the Ministry of Defence (MoD) in crisis management situations is to function both as a Department of State and as a military headquarters. The dual function of the ministry is reflected in a unified and integrated civil–military structure, as these functions are not only considered complementary, but also cannot be carried out separately. The MoD's framework text states that 'experience has confirmed that this integrated approach is both more efficient and more effective than the previous approach of "parallel hierarchies"' (UK MoD 2005: 4). One of the main features of the British MoD is, therefore, the integration of military and civilian personnel. Ministers are supported by the top management of the MoD, headed jointly by the Chief of Defence Staff (CDS) and the Permanent Under Secretary of State for Defence (PUS). They share responsibility for much of the Department's business and, in the words of the MoD website 'About the MoD', 'their roles reflect the importance of both military and civilian advice on political, financial, administrative and operational matters'. The principal military advisor, the CDS, who, besides being the military adviser to both the Defence Secretary and the Government, is also the professional head of the armed forces. An interesting cultural feature of the MoD is that everybody wears civilian clothing, and that the departments within the ministry are built as open planning office landscapes, thereby, emphasizing openness and co-operation.

The management of defence is rightly described by the MoD as a 'complex business'. To effectively provide direction of this business, a number of senior committees underpin the management of defence. The four defence ministers and ten senior officials (six military and four civilian) provide, in different groupings, the membership of these committees. The Defence Council and the Defence Management Board are considered the most important committees within the ministry. The Defence Council is the senior departmental committee, chaired by the Secretary of State. It provides the formal legal basis for the conduct of defence. The Defence Management Board is the highest, non-ministerial committee, which is described as the MoD's 'corporate board'. It provides senior-level leadership and strategic management of defence to maximize the achievement of the UK's defence vision (UK MoD n.d.b).

The Chief of the Defence Staff plays the role of military adviser to the Government by attending Cabinet meetings or one of its relevant sub-committees. The CDS, in turn, draws on the advice provided by the single Service Chiefs of Staff and senior civil servants through the forum of the Chiefs of Staff Committee. These committee meetings are attended by the Permanent Under Secretary, as senior advisor on defence policy, as does a senior official from the Foreign and Commonwealth Office to ensure proper co-ordination between these key ministries. Attending the meetings are also the policy director and a number of military men, such as the Deputy Chief of the Defence Staff, Chief Joint Op CJO, etc. (JDCC 2004a: 1–5). The Chiefs of Staff Committee is in itself not only inherently civil–military in its nature, it also provides the CDS with an interagency perspective on all matters. This means that the Cabinet, the Defence Secretary, or committees that require the CDS's advice and input will get a very broad perspective from the top military adviser.

The functions of the MoD headquarters in London are carried out as one organization as opposed to the Pentagon which includes a sharp distinction between the Office of the Secretary of Defense and the staff of the Chairman of the Joint Chiefs of Staff. In the central areas of the ministry there is widespread civil–military mixed management of the different divisions. Where the head is a military officer the deputy is often civilian and vice versa (JDCC 2004a: 33). Brigadier Simon Mayall argues that the integrated organization of the ministry leads to greater civilian advice on political matters, better civilian understanding of military matters, as well as a better understanding of political concerns within the military (Mayall 2004). The close working relationships mean mutual trust and understanding, which is a precondition for effective civil–military leadership during operations. An important positive aspect of the British MoD, as well as of the government in general, is noted by Lieutenant Colonel Tim Russell, namely the small size relative to their US counterparts. Within the ministry people develop personal relationships far beyond the limits of their own units and departments, and, therefore, develop mutual understanding as well as interpersonal trust. In terms of the interagency relationships the small physical and conceptual distances between the ministries and agencies of Whitehall mean that it is very easy to walk between the different ministries for a quick chat and discussions with different counterparts (Russell 2005).

Significantly, MoD respondents find it difficult to explain where the most important interaction between the civilian and military sections of the ministry takes place. The integrated structure of the ministry means that such interaction takes place at all levels and at all times. However, one respondent did highlight some problem areas in the civil–military interface. Ben Palmer claims that civil–military integration works very well within the MoD in London, but the farther away from the headquarters you are the more problematic it becomes. An example is the Permanent Joint Headquarters (PJHQ), located at Northwood outside London, which is essentially a military headquarters between the operational and strategic levels. Both Palmer (2005) and Russell (2005) see room for improvement at this level and expressed worries regarding the civil–military integration within or around the PJHQ.

Command of operations is provided by the Permanent Joint Headquarters and the MoD acting together within what is called the Defence Crisis Management Organization (DCMO). DCMO is a virtual organization, which combines the MoD departments, the PJHQ, as well as the single service commands. It exists in order to provide the Government with military advice and, in return, receive political direction as the basis for a military operation (JDCC 2004b: 1–4). The MoD is supposed to provide policy guidance and strategic direction, while the PJHQ's function is to provide politically aware military advice, produce contingency plans and exercise operational command of forces committed to operations. During operations, all deployed UK personnel outside NATO are under the command of the Joint Commander at the PJHQ. This function is supposed to help bridge the gap between the operational and the strategic levels of command (JDCC 2004b). Government policy is thus translated by the Ministry of Defence through the Permanent Joint Headquarters and the Joint Commander into the criteria for the Joint Task Force Commander (JTFC) to develop and execute a campaign plan in order to achieve the political aims (JDCC 2004a).

Another important aspect of the MoD structure is the strong and highly professional civil service which is based on the principle of impartiality, meaning that civil servants are servants of the Crown, and thus ideally responsible to a higher purpose than that reflected by the government of the day. The principle of impartiality also means that, in theory at least, promotion is based on professional competence and not on political grounds. There is little influence of outsiders coming in at top levels (Jones and Kavanagh 2003: 186–187). The professional civilian elements of the ministry not only add a better grounding in public finance and diplomacy, but perhaps even more importantly, an ability to work closely with officials from the other government departments (Hopkinson

2000b: 37). The civil service, thereby, provides a useful buffer between the political leadership and the military commanders within the MoD. Its political impartiality, coupled with experience and understanding of military matters as well as policy imperatives, makes them the ideal mediators in the civil–military interface of the department (Mayall 2004). The civil service also provides permanence and institutional memory within the government ministries. On average, ministers remain in their departments for about two years. The politicians, therefore, rely on the permanence and experience of the civil service for advice (Jones and Kavanagh 2003: 189).

Conclusions

British military professionalism and military culture were formed under close scrutiny of the British Government during the imperial era of colonial policing. This meant that the British military was forced to develop political sensitivity not only to handle the essentially civil–military operations in the colonies. The political leadership's effective control over military administration, promotions and appointments also forced the commanders in the field to be more sensitive to the Cabinet's preferences.

The British patterns of civil–military relations can be summarized as integrated, according to the model outlined in Chapter 2. Civilians and servicemen are deeply integrated both structurally and culturally within the MoD, just as the ministry is integrated into the government administration as a whole. At the interagency level, there is an extensive and somewhat intricate web of committees, which aims to make government policy informed by all the relevant departments. It also means that there is a culture of co-operating and working towards common goals across Whitehall. However, despite the relatively extensive interagency structure, there are turf wars between the different departments and agencies, and much work is done in departmental stovepipes. The committee system as a form for interdepartmental integration is also problematic as it is sometimes considered too slow for the complexity and fast moving pace of contemporary military operations.

Within the MoD, the integrated structures are more noticeable. In the everyday workings of the ministry as well as in the command of operations, there is a joint civil–military structure that ensures military understanding of government policy as well as politically informed military advice. The ministry's integrated structure also leads to a common culture of mutual understanding and trust among military and civilian personnel. Another important aspect of the British system is the highly professional civil service. Its apolitical nature and the fact that it holds positions at the very top of the ministries provide for high levels of political and military understanding, as well as institutional memory of crisis management that the more fleeting political and military leaderships can never provide.

In recent years an increasing strain in the civil–military relationship is obvious as senior officers speak out against government policy regarding the operations in Iraq as well as concerning everyday management of the British armed forces. Increased political micro-management and operational stress are two causes of this strain. This has caused a debate regarding the Military Covenant in Britain, also fuelled by the fact that many among the lower ranks feel that their interests are not well defended by the senior military leadership or the civilian officials within the MoD.

With reference to the theoretical discussion on trust, the British case of integration provides interpersonal trust within the MoD as well as, to a more limited extent, within the interagency structure. The common background and close working relationships even provide what sociologists call thick interpersonal trust. Zucker (1986) argues that this form of trust is based on social similarities and shared moral codes – personal characteristics like gender, ethnicity and cultural background. Narrow social recruitment, close working relationships across the civil–military divide, and the small size of the ministry support this process. Frequent personal contact across some departmental and ministerial boundaries also develops thin interpersonal trust within the civil–military interface and the interagency structures. Although these contacts do not develop close personal relationships they provide familiarity and trust in other organizations through the process of reciprocity.

On the whole, the British structure and culture at the civil–military interface emphasize integration and mutual understanding. To use Bland's terminology, there is a high-level of shared responsibility in the British case. The British pattern of civil–military relations also involves low cost civilian monitoring of the armed forces, which in turn perceive shirking as being costly as it historically means sackings or replacing military dissidents. However, the recent criticism by the current and former head of the army may imply that the cost of monitoring is increasing. At any rate, British officers are relatively politically attuned and more easily adapted to different forms of conflict. Interestingly, in terms of Janowitz's view of integrated civil–military relations, the British armed forces also resemble the constabulary force concept that Janowitz (1960) introduced in the 1960s.

While the US case presented an almost perfect real world example of the divided approach to civil–military relations as outlined in Chapter 2, the British case is slightly more ambiguous. It clearly leans in the direction of the integrated approach, but the culture and structure of the interagency structure, would ideally be more integrated to provide a perfect case. Let us nevertheless take a closer look at the British way of war.

7   The British way of war

The British patterns of civil–military relations involve relatively well-integrated structures at the interagency level, and even more so in the civil–military interface at the Ministry of Defence (MoD). The political leadership has enjoyed low costs of civilian monitoring of the armed forces, which has meant civilian ownership of the military's functional imperative. The hypothesis of this book argues that these patterns of civil–military relations have an effect on the conduct of operations by affecting the organization, culture and doctrine of the armed forces. This chapter, therefore, mirrors Chapter 4 by analysing these features of the British case. An important aspect of the chapter is to investigate to which functional imperative the structure and culture of the armed forces are adjusted, and to relate that to the literature review on the nature of contemporary conflict. In other words, are the British armed forces fit for purpose in the contemporary strategic context? Emphasis is placed on the cultural and doctrinal aspects of the British armed forces.

In 1932, British strategist Basil Henry Liddell Hart described the British way of war as that of the indirect approach, which in its ideal form 'creates conditions in which the enemy is forced to the inescapable conclusion that defeat has become inevitable before battle has been joined'. He arrived at this conclusion, or normative argument, from a disdain for the massive and suicidal frontal attacks of the First World War, and a romantic view of Britain's businesslike colonial tradition of war, which had at its heart 'economic pressure exercised through sea-power' (Hart cited in Freedman 1993). The British Army's nineteenth century experience of colonial wars influenced British military culture into the twentieth century. 'The British way of war, as embodied in the campaigns of Victorian heroes Garnet Wolseley, Frederick Roberts, and Horatio Kitchener, reflected essentially all the British people knew of war' (Cassidy 2004). Since the formation of the British Army and for the greater part of its history, the principal mission was to acquire and then to police imperial possessions (Thornton 2004b). Thus, in the search for a British way of war, it is in the counter-insurgency type of operations of colonial policing we shall place our focus.

The functional imperative and British strategic culture

While US military culture is a strong and inflexible feature that is maintained through doctrine and socialization at the military academies, British military culture is better described as an intuitive approach from past operations, an empirical, pragmatic military tradition, with a naval focus. While US professionalism and military culture were formed in relative isolation, their British counterparts were formed out of managing a complex range of issues in the vast territories of the British Empire. As noted in the previous chapter, the British political leadership closely supervised the military's professionalization. The unified civilian control and oversight of the British military simply did not allow the military to define its own raison d'être. Instead, the military's tasks were defined by the political leadership and thus reflected political needs in the strategic context of imperial management. Thus, military leaders with interest in and capability of meeting the diverse nature of the British military tasks in the colonies were rewarded, which meant that adaptability and flexibility became central characteristics of the British military profession (Avant 1994). In essence, the context in which the British military operated came to form its organizational culture and structure.

British counter-insurgency doctrine is based on the three pillars of minimum force, flexibility and civil–military co-operation. As noted in the previous chapter, these principles can be traced well into the nineteenth century and the combination of pragmatic lessons from colonial policing and the societal influence of Victorian values (Thornton 2004a). Let us, nevertheless, take a closer look at the specific features of the British way of war.

The colonial experience meant that the British military came to emphasize small-scale instead of large-scale operations (Cassidy 2004). In the colonies, the British Army was forced to manage conflicts with limited resources. Moreover, the wide range of tasks in imperial policing as well as the many different geographical and cultural conditions encountered created a constant need to adapt responses to fit local circumstances (Pimlott 1985). It is notable that in the second half of the nineteenth century, the UK had a professional army of about 200,000 men that policed the enormous territories of the British Empire. Without at least some level of consent it would have been impossible to rule such vast numbers of people. As an example, the Army of British India had a huge span of control, operating in the current territories of India, Pakistan and Bangladesh with a relatively small number of British officers and soldiers (Heathcote 2003).

A broad principle of British counter-insurgency operations is the emphasis on close civil–military co-operation. The committee system of British political and administrative structures facilitates this co-operation from the local level to the national level. It is a bottom-up approach that starts with co-operation at the very lowest levels, which means that soldiers are essentially forced to adapt to the need of the civilians on the ground (Mockaitis 1999). Close co-operation between the military, the colonial administrators who implemented reform, and the police who maintained order was essential to the British approach to counter-insurgency. Civilian officials most often remained in control of emergencies and were responsible for the broader political strategy. The military, therefore, operated under close civilian control and accepted the requirement of employing minimum force. Moreover, the British military became highly flexible, adapting to meet local circumstances and switching to small-unit operations with decentralized control when necessary (Cassidy 2004).

Sir Robert Thompson, a British counter-insurgency expert and Permanent Secretary of Defence for Malaya in the 1950s, argued that military plans must be devised in co-ordination with civilian counterparts and activities in order to achieve lasting success. The policies and operational plans created should then be implemented by the various departments and headquarters involved, with regular committee meetings at the local level of colonial administration to ensure co-ordination among the local actors (Thompson 1966).

General Sir Gerald Templer, who was the High Commissioner and Director of Operations in Malaya at the height of the insurgency, was a strong advocate of hearts and minds policies. When he was asked if he had sufficient troops General Templer responded emphatically that he certainly had, and added: 'The answer lies not in pouring more soldiers into the jungle but rests in the hearts and minds of the Malayan people' (cited in Bulloch 1996). However, it should also be noted that there will always be a breaking point where the appropriate behaviour is impossible because of limitations on the number of troops. The lessons from the colonial era in general, and Malaya in particular, led Frank Kitson (1971) to stress the importance of hearts and minds approaches and the principle of minimum use of force. In the wider goal of winning hearts and minds, Kitson noted the negative impact of excessive force. It tended to drive the population away from the administration and towards extremist positions. Similarly, in the 1930s, Major-General Sir Charles Gwynn argued:

> Excessive severity may antagonize the neutral or loyal element, add to the number of rebels, and leave a lasting feeling of resentment and bitterness. On the other hand, the power and resolution of the government forces must be displayed. Not only did certain tribes or groups occasionally need to be cowed with force, but the peoples who had put their security into the hands of the British also had to be assured of British strength.
>
> (Cited in Thornton 2004a: 96)

The principle of minimum use of force emerged as a result of the fact that British colonial administrators were bound by the common law principle of minimum force and the legal concept of military 'aid to the civil power' that governed the responses to unrest (Mockaitis 1999: 133). Using a quote from a 1923 British Army manual, *Duties in Aid of Civil Power*, Thomas Mockaitis points out that British soldiers have constantly been reminded that what is important is 'not the annihilation of an enemy but the suppression of a temporary disorder, and, therefore, the degree of force to be employed must be directed to that which is necessary to restore order and must never exceed it' (1990: 18). The same restraints in the use of force had to be used regardless if the army was dealing with strikes in Britain or riots in the colonies. This tradition remains very much alive in the application of rules of engagement (interview with Lowe 2004). The simple, yet flexible, tradition has thus continued to this day. However, it should also be noted that each operation of the British armed forces is preceded by theatre relevant training involving cultural understanding, language, as well as specific tasks beyond basic training, such as riot control or peacekeeping. Although important lessons may be learned on the streets of Belfast there are clear limits to how applicable they are in other theatres. However, through theatre specific training, units have a chance to practice applying the appropriate lessons of past operations to new contexts.

Significantly, the principle of minimum use of force refers back to the imperative of political understanding and sensitivity. It is, therefore, based on an understanding of the overall political objectives with the operation and how they relate to the actions of soldiers at all levels of command. The minimum use of force principle, thereby, stems from a pragmatic belief in the importance of winning the hearts and minds of the local population, rather than defeating the enemy insurgents. The vast territories of the Empire and the limited resources of the colonial army forced the British to apply a softer approach. Mockaitis (1990: 64) suggests that 'the British, like all successful imperialists, had long realized that the key to maintaining an empire lay in making the yoke of foreign rule as light as possible'. Consent and legitimacy were as essential then as they are now and the 'carrot and stick' strategies had to be balanced with extreme caution and political finesse. Violence used too broadly could lead to the loss of consent and legitimacy which are moreover essential in the gathering of intelligence. The balance was achieved by the application of an offensive force posture, often achieved by having a presence and showing that force was there to be used if necessary. Or, as Richard Caniglia puts it: 'the British have long practised persuasion based on an iron fist in a velvet glove' (2001: 80).

It should, nevertheless, be underscored that the British strategic and military culture has not been a guarantor for minimum use of force. There are numerous examples in British colonial history of severe brutality in the application of tactics. The Boer War, the Amritsar massacre in India, and the response to the Mau-Mau rebellion in Kenya are but a few examples. Interestingly though, these instances also caused great upset among the civilian population and the political leadership in Britain, as well as other parts of the army. It was clearly not considered acceptable behaviour in the pursuit of the political aims.

Another interesting feature of the British way of war is the informal and improvised approach to operations. The pragmatic British tradition highlights the fact that all personnel engaged in counter-insurgency must be able to routinely adapt, improvise, and innovate in order to meet the unique challenges as well as the sheer complexity and unpredictability of such operations (Garfield 2006). The improvised approach is derived from the idea that each operation and theatre is so different that it requires its own doctrine and policy – something which creates greater flexibility and adaptability in the theatre (Nagl 2002). The idea is that template solutions are usually inappropriate, not least because the enemy will quickly exploit weaknesses and adapt to previous behaviour and doctrine. Based on a study of British operations in Malaya, John Nagl describes the British military as a 'learning organization'. He argues that when conventional methods and tactics failed in Malaya the British military had few problems in identifying the problems and changing its strategy to a more politically focused counter-insurgency campaign. The innovative and creative past had created an organizational culture that was open to changes in strategy as well as in organization (Nagl 2002: 216). British military culture also values individuality and what Garfield (2006) describes as 'a healthy questioning of authority', which serve to strengthen the culture of flexibility and innovation. Another aspect that fosters innovation within the organizational culture of the British armed forces is an acceptance of error and even failure. Officers are supposed to think for themselves, to question their superiors and to try new and innovative ideas of solving problems – something which is emphasized in the recruitment and training of British officers.

As argued in the previous chapter, the British emphasis on flexibility and adaptability is not just a tradition from colonial warfare, but also a result of the British pattern of civil–military relations. The low cost of monitoring the armed forces, and more precisely, the ease with which the political leadership has been able to replace officers, created an officer corps and a military culture that quickly adapted to the political leadership's wishes. This is what Samuel Huntington (1957) described as subjective civilian control, which would lead to decreased military effectiveness.

Significantly, the cultural features of flexibility and political sensitivity have been well maintained and further developed in the contemporary military culture. During 30 years of counter-insurgency in Northern Ireland, British troops have not only reinforced the understanding of minimum force, civil–military co-operation, and flexibility, they have also learned to work under the close scrutiny of the law and of the media. Working closely with the political leadership is also a tradition that remains in the British case and that is seen as a requirement in all operations. According to Brigadier Simon Mayall (2004), former commander of the British-led Multinational Brigade in Kosovo, political oversight and leadership are not a problem within the British chain of command. There are political advisors for all commanders, normally down to brigade level, who keep a line open to London on the political–military side, and who ensure that the commanders understand the background of the operation. This is not perceived as political meddling as the advisors are considered a resource for the commanders and not as tools for control. The British commanders are normally left to do their job as they please and instead refer back to London if they feel the need for further political guidance. Other commanders argue that the problem is often the reverse. There is too little political direction and clarity regarding the aims during operations, leaving commanders to make difficult political interpretations and decisions (interview with Lowe 2004; see also Rose 1999: 367). However, as noted in the previous chapter, the technological advancements, in combination with the political sensitivity of operations, have created an incentive for the political leadership to micro-manage operations. To a larger extent than before, responsible ministers are, therefore, seeking to influence the outcomes of day-to-day operations, for which they will be held accountable (Dandeker 2006; Forster 2006b).

The organizational culture that underscores flexibility, adaptability and an ad hoc approach to operations has also created a level of forgetfulness. While the flexible feature of British culture allows for early adjustment to operational specifics, lessons from past operations have often been forgotten or ignored centrally in the organization. As an example, the Second World War created a distinct bias towards conventional large-scale warfare, and that it took about a decade, a failure in Palestine and a very shaky start to the counter-insurgency operations in Malaya before the British would readjust their strategic culture to effectively deal with counter-insurgency contexts (Hoffman 2004). Equally, in the wake of the World Wars, the operations in India in 1919 and again in Palestine in 1946 were failures because the army had been insufficiently politicized. It had lost its sense of understanding of the political objectives and the importance to work with civilian agencies. The army failed to recognize that in the pursuit of political aims its tools were not restricted to force (Strachan 2003). It is, in other words, possible to see a trade-off between flexibility and forgetfulness. Neither in the Boer War, nor in the Malayan emergency, did the British adapt before the operations began. Instead, after a rocky start, the British quickly adapted doctrine and tactics during the conflict. Adaptability and flexibility sometimes come at the expense of the failed institutionalization of successful behaviour, or of peacetime innovation to foresee problems. The lack of doctrine, or other formal means of structured debate on warfare, means that operational experience has often remained compartmentalized within the military's various groupings, and innovation was largely left to coincidence, or to the individual officers (Mäder 2004: 22). Therefore, the British way of war is often described as 'muddling through' as problems emerge.

The imperial experience of the British armed forces has also created a limited reliance on technology that stems from the hearts and minds approach and the fact that the British military has often been forced to make do with limited resources. The British seem to have struck a healthy balance between the human and material factors. Another feature of the British way of war is that people were only somewhat averse to the idea of casualties. The British approach to casualties is described as a 'stiff upper lip' attitude, created by a history of numerous, yet limited, casualties in remote places for reasons not directly related to national security. This does not mean that the British are not trying to avoid casualties, only that they do not seem to be averse to them (Cassidy 2004).

An important organizational feature of the British armed forces is the regimental system, which is often contrasted with the continental European system in which the division is the central unit around which the training and administration of soldiers revolve. In a regimental system each regiment is responsible for recruitment, training and administration of its personnel, and units are maintained permanently. Therefore, the regiment will develop unique unit cohesion due to its history, traditions and functions. An important aspect of the British regimental system is that the regiment or the battalion of about 500–1,000 men has been the key tactical building block, and not the division, as within the continental system. This is another heritage from the colonial period, when battalions were widely dispersed and virtually autonomous.

David French (2005) has created a more nuanced view of the British regimental system than the overly positive as well as critical voices have previously provided. While the system has certainly helped create good relations with the local community, and created unmatched loyalties between soldiers and towards the regiment, French notes that the regimental traditions have often changed, and also meant less to soldiers than generally thought. Officers came from certain elements of a national elite and soldiers were often recruited from large areas rather than from the local community. The more mythological descriptions of the system are, thereby, downgraded somewhat. Moreover, in times of war on the continent, the local regimental system virtually collapsed and proved incapable of adjusting to the increased need for soldier recruitment and training. Other weaknesses have been the failure to prepare properly for combined arms operations, as the regiments of different arms have generally trained separately (French 2005).

While there are both advantages and disadvantages to the regimental system, it is considered particularly useful in the context of complex peace operations. One positive aspect is that soldiers and officers tend to stay with their regiment for most of their military careers. This provides for good unit cohesion and trust among colleagues and subordinates. This trust and unit cohesion allow for the use of mission command tactics, the delegation of authority, and, consequently, the effective use of small units in large operational areas (Mockaitis 1990). Although the turnover of soldiers is usually very high, the regimental system ensures the retention of experience thanks to its non-commissioned officers who usually serve together for up to 15 years. Through the NCOs, both collective and personal experience is retained, as well as interpersonal trust created. The regimental system, therefore, not only increases interpersonal trust through personal reciprocity and close friendship, but also institutional trust through the unique esprit de corps and traditions of the regiment.

The regimental emphasis on small units is also suitable for irregular warfare. Most tactical actions of counter-insurgency operations are inherently small-scale activities. They are conducted at the squad, platoon and company levels, which means that great trust and delegation of authority from higher command levels to junior officers and NCOs in the field. This is particularly salient with regard to the close media scrutiny and the political sensitivity of contemporary conflict. However, a negative aspect of the regimental system is that the familiar spirit can create a parochial system which perpetuates procedures and complicates organizational change (Cassidy 2004). It should be noted that in recent years the British regimental system has been reformed. Essentially, the reforms are organizing the British infantry in larger multi-battalion regiments, compared to the many single-battalion regiments of the past. While the effects of these reforms are yet to be seen, the reforms can cause a rift in the close relationships between the regiments and their local communities, and that soldiers moved around or part of larger units will not know each other as well as they did when they go into combat – something that may influence the effectiveness of units.

This chapter has made frequent references to the historical past of colonial policing and counter-insurgency operations, arguing that this is what has created the British way of war. But to what extent have the British armed forces managed to accommodate and adjust to the requirements of both conventional and unconventional warfare? British officers are, despite the obvious emphasis on expeditionary operations, keen to express the fact that conventional warfare is the foundation and core of British military training and culture. As an example, Brigadier Simon Mayall, Director of Army Resources and Plans at the British MoD, contends that the British train for conventional war, while constantly staying ready for different forms of peace operations. Conventional warfare is thus, the foundation of British military training and culture, but, on top of that foundation, much training goes into, and great pride is taken, in building a capacity for the wars that the armed forces are more likely to fight – complex peace operations and counter-insurgencies (Mayall 2004). This also means an acknowledgement of the fact that peace operations are no less important or less demanding than conventional warfare. As General Sir Charles Guthrie (2001) has put it:

> Being a 'force for good' is not about helping little old ladies across the road. It is about maintaining international stability through a willingness to deploy rapidly, anywhere in the world, credible combat forces capable of making a real difference.

However, the coexistence of the conventional warfighting ethos and the small wars ethos in the British military is not entirely unproblematic. The historical overview of the previous chapter mentioned the conceptual struggles between the 'Continentalist' officers of the British armed forces, since 1945, often serving in the British Army of the Rhine, and those officers focusing on the imperial defence mission, counter-insurgency and, most recently, peace support operations. The tensions between these two camps have never been quite resolved, sometimes resulting in extreme positions and limited effectiveness. Examples are the extremely offensive tactics of the First World War which led to enormous casualties and the failure to remember the counter-insurgency lessons of the colonial past after the Second World War. There are, in other words, good reasons to further discuss this aspect of British military culture in the chapter on British operations in Iraq.

British military doctrine

As argued in the corresponding chapter on the American way of war, doctrine constitutes a potentially important variable in the causal chain between certain patterns of civil–military relations and the conduct of operations in complex peace operations. It is sometimes used as an independent variable in its own right for explaining operational conduct. However, this book treats doctrine as an indicator of organizational and strategic culture, as well as of the weight of history and past operational experience. The purpose of this section is, thereby, to analyse doctrine in order to further trace and understand the British way of war. A second aim is to evaluate the importance of doctrine as a variable, thereby helping trace the causal mechanisms of the hypothesis.

Historically, the emphasis on flexibility has meant that doctrine never played a big role within the British armed forces. Instead, the tradition has involved informally developed doctrine that was spread by word of mouth and through the unofficial writings of the participants in different campaigns (Nagl 1999). Thornton (2000) even argues that a long-held belief within the British Army is that doctrine is something to be treated with a degree of indifference that even borders on disdain. Similarly, Brian Holden-Reid suggests that there is a

> fundamental and instinctive reality in the British Army – a widespread reluctance to formulate scientific, doctrinal statements; a preference upheld by the pragmatic and empirical tradition to review and resolve each problem as it occurs on its own terms free from any system.
>
> (Holden-Reid 1998: 12)

The introduction to the *British Defence Doctrine* conveys a message about the tone and nature of the British approach to military activity at all levels. The doctrine argues that the British approach must be flexible and pragmatic, attributes that are considered essential for the effective application of the manoeuvrist approach to operations. Doctrine is not, therefore, mandatory dogma to be applied in all circumstances; 'that is simply not the British Armed Forces' way of doing business'. Instead, 'doctrine is the distilled experience of many years – indeed generations – of making strategy and of mounting and conducting military operations' (JDCC 2001: iii). However, the *British Defence Doctrine* further states that it should not merely be viewed as a record of past practice. Doctrine is instead the assessment of the best approach based on a sound understanding of current imperatives and lessons learned from past successes and failures. It is, however, dangerous, in the words of the *British Defence Doctrine*, 'to assume that past success necessarily provides the best route for the future. Indeed, successful past practice may contain the seeds of future disaster if applied too rigidly in different circumstances.' British commanders are, therefore, encouraged to remain flexible in their thinking (JDCC 2001: 3–1).

A reason for the wariness of doctrine has been the political skill of British commanders at all levels. The armed forces were comfortable with the political dictates and overall strategic aims and gave senior officers confidence to delegate responsibility to the very lowest levels of command, thereby encouraging displays of flexibility and initiative, and discouraging doctrinal solutions. British soldiers knew what was expected of them without the restricting framework of doctrine (Thornton 2000). However, despite the weariness of doctrinal thinking, doctrines have been published with an increasing rate since the end of the Cold War. Significantly, the introduction of doctrine was primarily promoted by the British Army of the Rhine and the continental officers of the British armed forces. The section below reviews a number of doctrinal publications that are relevant to the British approach to complex peace operations.

Contents of British doctrine

'The Defence Vision' is the starting point for everything that the MoD does. It states that the common purpose of all the military and civilians who work in defence is the defence of the United Kingdom and its interests, as well as strengthening international peace and stability, all under the catchphrase: 'A force for good in the world' (UK MoD n.d.a). The *British Defence Doctrine* firmly establishes the political nature of military operations. It argues that the key to successful conduct of external relations and the essence of grand strategy is the use of the most appropriate mix of the diplomatic, economic and military instruments of the state. For the military to be an effective instrument of grand strategy, it must be developed in a manner 'consistent with the demands that are likely to be placed upon it'. Thus, with the given strategic context, the doctrine argues that the British military will never operate in isolation but only as part of 'a fully co-ordinated grand strategy in which diplomatic and economic instruments will be as important in their ways as the military forces and the military strategy supporting them' (JDCC 2001: 2–5).

An important observation is that British doctrine argues that neither peace nor war exists in extreme form. 'Perfect peace is the stuff of utopian dreams; absolute war the unlimited thermonuclear construct of one's worst nightmares' (JDCC 2001: 6–1). Conflict is instead described as existing along a continuum between these extreme forms. According to doctrine: 'The spectrum of conflict provides an environment in which predominant campaign themes change over time, indicating priorities allocated to multiple types of operations that may be conducted simultaneously' (UK Army 2005: 11). British soldiers must, therefore, be able to conduct operations along the entire spectrum of conflict simultaneously. However, combat, which is defined as 'the application of armed violence against a responsive enemy', is considered the most demanding task. British troops must, therefore, primarily be prepared for high-intensity conflict. That ability then produces a wide variety of other activities, including humanitarian assistance, peace support and assisting in the rebuilding of failed states (UK Army 2005: 11).

The significance attached to conventional warfare is exemplified by the doctrinal emphasis on six themes that represent the core of the British approach to operations, and that are supposed to permeate down through the entire organization and 'be reflected in all aspects of training and preparation'. The principles include the warfighting ethos, the manoeuvrist approach, and the importance of the principles of war which, according to doctrine, are as applicable at the strategic level as they are at the tactical level, and which are considered as relevant to PSOs as they are to warfighting (JDCC 2001: 3–9). Doctrine further argues that the fighting skills of the armed forces must remain the key to their credibility and effectiveness:

> By preparing for war and developing to the full all three components of fighting power – Conceptual, Moral and Physical – the Armed Forces will retain the physical and mental ability and agility to apply themselves to a wide range of challenges.
>
> (JDCC 2001: iii)

Another observation, therefore, is that British doctrine stresses high-intensity conflict as the foundation for training and structuring the military organization. The emphasis on fighting skills, the warrior ethos and principles of war does not reflect the British way of war as described in the previous sections.

However, British doctrines on operations other than war paint a more familiar picture. Doctrine acknowledges that in counter-insurgency operations the strategic centre of gravity will be the support of the mass of the people, which means a struggle for the hearts and minds of the local population (UK Army Field Manual 2001: B-2-4). It also argues that the British armed forces should place due emphasis on the intellectual and psychological aspects of operations, not simply the material. It emphasizes the focus on people and ideas, not only on ground taken. As in warfighting, force should be applied selectively, and 'its use is carefully measured and controlled: destruction is a means not an end ... a subtle approach to a subtle problem' (UK Army 2001: B-2-4). Significantly, with reference to peace support operations, the concept of sensitized action is developed.

> Military forces should understand the law, religion, customs and culture of the elements of the population with whom they deal. Such understanding is necessary to predict the psychological effect of physical action. It will determine the plans and responses of the peace support force. Intelligence, education, training and experience all contribute to the required sensitivity.
>
> (UK Army 2005: 25)

British doctrine is ambiguous and, thereby, reflects the uneasy coexistence of the warfighting ethos and the small wars ethos in the British military. A number of observations are in any case worth repeating. First, in general terms, doctrine is not very authoritative in the British armed forces. More emphasis is placed on flexibility than the ability to apply different doctrinal principles. As an example, Gavin Bulloch argues that 'despite long experience in counter-insurgency, the British have not developed any set methods of dealing with the problem of insurgency; indeed it is probably unwise to attempt this because every situation is different' (1996: 4). Second, current counter-insurgency doctrine resonates well with the British way of war and past principles of colonial policing and counter-insurgency. However, the foundation of British doctrine is that of high-intensity combat. The stated raison d'être of the armed forces is 'to engage in combat of war in defence of the nation'. There is a distinct hierarchy of British doctrine which places high-intensity combat as the foundation of doctrine and training, with doctrines on operations other than war as add-ons, perhaps reflecting the preferences of the British Army of the Rhine more than the traditional British approach. Third, instead of a divide between war and operations other than war, British doctrine describes conflict as existing along a continuum between the extremes of war and peace. It is expected of British soldiers to be able to conduct operations along the entire spectrum within the same operational arena and within a short period of time.

Conclusions

The British way of war is mainly informed by the historical legacy of the British Empire. Low costs of civilian monitoring during the process of professionalization have led to a functional imperative essentially defined by the political leadership, informed by the strategic context of imperial policing and counter-insurgency operations. These tasks have defined the British way of war. Pragmatism and adaptability were necessary features in order to effectively adjust to the multitude of different tasks involved in policing the Empire, as well as to perform effectively within essentially different contexts and cultures. Other features of the British way of war include the wholehearted acceptance of 'hearts and minds' approaches, cultural understanding and restraint in its application of force. Close co-operation between the civilian and military aspects of national power is another feature inherited from past operations. These features of the British way of war have been effectively maintained to the present day through the operations in Northern Ireland, as well as the peace operations of the 1990s. Thus, the British still have a cultural preference for counter-insurgency type operations.

A negative aspect of the British way of war is the failure to perpetuate past experiences and lessons learned. The counter-insurgency operations in the aftermath of the Second World War as well as in Malaya and Northern Ireland all began in a troubling manner because of lacking doctrine and procedures, which could have been established from passed lessons.

While the cultural and structural aspects of the British way of war emphasize small wars and counter-insurgency, British doctrine clearly stresses the warfighting ethos and high-intensity combat. This is interesting as conventional warfare has been a limited part of British military experience since the end of the Second World War, and may, therefore, reflect the importance of the officers of the British Army of the Rhine in the process of formalizing doctrine. The emphasis on warfighting capabilities is nevertheless interesting and may imply that if given autonomy from the political leadership the British military would define its functional imperative more narrowly. There is clearly a somewhat uneasy co-existence of the two separate military cultures of the traditional British approach that emphasizes the colonial heritage, and the continentalists of the British Army of the Rhine. However, political primacy prevails in the UK and the British way of war still reflects the needs of the political leadership and the contemporary strategic context of complex peace operations.

Thus, in terms of theory, the patterns of civil–military relations have in the British case led to an untraditional definition of the functional imperative and the creation of a strategic culture that can be summarized as pragmatic and flexible, with emphasis on civil–military co-operation and the minimum use of force. The British way of war is theoretically well adjusted to the contemporary strategic context of complex peace operations. As the Assistant Under Secretary (programmes) said to the Defence Committee in the House of Commons in 1991: 'We have structured our forces precisely to deal with the unexpected' (cited in Grove 1996: 10). Phrasing it in the language of this book, the indirect effect of integrated civil–military relations and low costs of civilian monitoring of the armed forces has in the British case provided the flexibility and learning capability that keep the military well adjusted to changes in the functional imperative. At the same time, the small defence budgets mean that the British armed forces are comparatively limited in terms of troop numbers and technological acquisitions – especially in relation to the ambitious political aims of the British armed forces. This has become a serious concern since 2003, as the British military has been forced to fight two highly complex campaigns in Afghanistan and Iraq. The hypothesis argues that this is likely to have consequences in the conduct and effectiveness of operations in complex peace operations. The next chapter conducts the empirical study of British operations in Iraq from 2003.

8 Civil–military aspects of British operations in Iraq

This chapter examines the total outcome of the British patterns of civil–military relations, as seen in the context of the war in Iraq from 2003, or what the British call 'Operation Telic'. The analysis, thereby, functions as an empirical test of the hypothesis in relation to the British case, and also adds some insights to the literature on British operations in Iraq, mainly by adding the civil–military perspective to the analysis. The empirical test involves tracing the causal chain to the dependent variable of operational conduct in complex peace operations and includes both the direct and indirect effects of civil–military relations. The chapter, therefore, does not provide a comprehensive analysis of British operations in Iraq, but instead focuses on three thematic discussions that are relevant to the hypothesis of this book. They involve the British approach to operations in Iraq, the level of civil–military co-operation and co-ordination, and the tactical conduct of operations. The first thematic discussion seeks to answer how the operation was interpreted and conceptualized by the military and civilian leadership in the UK, as well as how this was translated into political aims and operational plans. The discussion of civil–military co-operation and co-ordination involves two sub-categories in the civil–military aspects of the planning process and of the command and control structures. Finally, the discussion on tactical behaviour studies the conduct of tactical operations with reference to the hearts and minds approach, minimum use of force, cultural understanding and adaptability.

The main research questions for the chapter are: how have the patterns of civil–military relations affected post-conflict planning, and how have they functioned as a link in the chain of command? To what extent is the British way of war reflected in their operations in Iraq?

British military operations in Iraq

As the junior partner in the coalition that invaded Iraq, the British armed forces received the separate task of securing the south of Iraq, most importantly the city of Basra. The first test of the British troops was the early task to seize the Al Faw Peninsula during the initial invasion, and to secure southern Iraq's oil infrastructure. As the first conventional ground force action of the war, the Al Faw operation had great strategic significance. The operation was, moreover, necessary in order to open the sea route to Umm Qasr, which needed to be seized simultaneously. As Iraq's only deep-water port, Umm Qasr was planned to be the essential hub for delivery of humanitarian aid. The objective to seize the oil infrastructure on Iraq's Al Faw Peninsula was also crucial to the coalition's overall campaign plan. Failure could have enabled Iraqis to carry out sabotage, leading rapidly to a major environmental disaster in the northern Gulf. Moreover, the oilfields were also considered crucial to the subsequent reconstruction of the Iraqi economy (UK MoD 2003a).

The British Commando Brigade's operation was completely successful. The level of resistance put up by the Iraqi defence proved to be less than expected, to a large extent because of the surprise caused by the speed and force of the initial assault on the peninsula. The Iraqi forces were, thereby, unable to put together a co-ordinated defence although they attempted a number of counterattacks. The result of the operation was that four days into the campaign the Iraqi 51st Division had been removed from its defence of the oilfields, and 3rd Commando Brigade held the critical oil infrastructure at Al Faw and the port of Umm Qasr (UK MoD 2003a).

The more difficult test of British strength did not come until Basra, a city with a population of about 1.25 million. The British faced heavy resistance from the city and the advance came to a halt. According to the British command, an immediate attack on the city was likely to result in unnecessary military and civilian casualties as well as considerable material damage (UK MoD 2003a). Therefore, the British forces did not hasten to crack the nut, and instead commenced a siege of the city by creating a loosely formed cordon around it. Between 23 and 31 March, the siege of Basra almost took the form of a stand-off. The British waited and watched, gathered information and infiltrated the city with small units of Special Forces (Murray and Scales 2003; Keegan 2004). It was the Iraqi troops, led by Ali Hassan al-Majid, 'Chemical Ali', who lost their patience first and sought to provoke a British attack by launching completely unsuccessful sorties out of the city with tanks and armed vehicles, as well as by mortaring the British positions. After 31 March, the British commander nevertheless thought he had a clear enough intelligence picture to start infiltrating larger units into Basra. During the first few days of April the British raided Basra with Warrior fighting vehicles, very much like the Americans were doing in Baghdad with tanks. They destroyed Baathist positions, added to the division's stock of intelligence, and managed to infiltrate more sniper teams into the city (Murray and Scales 2003: 149).

Finally, on 6 April, after 15 days of siege and information gathering, the British launched a full-scale assault on Basra from essentially every direction. By utilizing 'battle groups', smaller improvised formations of troops suited for the particular task, the British made their presence known all over the city. By the evening of 6 April, the British were largely in control of the city. The following day the remnants of the Baathist regime in Basra as well as the remaining Fedayeen fighters were chased out of the area by a battalion from the Parachute Regiment (Keegan 2004: 180–182). During this day, an interesting and indicative episode took place. As the Parachute Regiment withdrew from the city, Shia crowds began throwing rocks at British tanks and armoured personnel carriers. Instead of withdrawing to safety or firing warning shots, a British battle group commander ordered the armoured personnel carrier crews as well as the infantry to 'get out of the vehicles, take off their helmets, stow most of their weapons on their vehicles and walk out into the agitated crowd' (Murray and Scales 2003: 152). This first 'social patrol' was conducted in a firm but friendly manner that clearly signalled to the people of Basra that the British were there to stay, and that the Shiite population would not be abandoned like in 1991.

The British commanders' cautious approach in Basra was criticized by US officers at the time, as quicker results were sought after during the final push to Baghdad. The patience nevertheless allowed the British troops to eventually enter a city that was relatively intact and where there had been few casualties (Thornton 2005). This initially led to less local hostility and more consent once troops moved into Basra. It was this level of consent that allowed the British troops to conduct foot patrolling without the use of body armour and helmets. Theoretically, such behaviour creates the impression of normality and a diminished threat for the local population. It also reduces the sense of distance between soldier and civilian by making the soldiers seem more accessible and less threatening to the local population – something which is of great importance when soldiers have to take on the job of policing, as they did in Basra (Thornton 2005). However, the positive feedback from the local population did not last – an issue that is further discussed below.

British objectives in Iraq

The UK was the junior partner in the coalition in Iraq, and a central question is the extent to which the British interpretation and approach to the campaign in Iraq mirrored that of the US. It is, therefore, relevant to examine the British political and military aims and planning approaches.

On 7 January 2003, ten weeks before the war, Foreign Secretary Jack Straw stated that the policy objectives in Iraq were 'to ensure Iraq complies with its obligations under relevant United Nations Security Council Resolutions (UNSCRs), including by giving up its weapons of mass destruction'. There is, in other words, an emphasis on the UN Security Council resolution that was not quite as obvious in the US case. The Foreign Secretary went on to give a more detailed view of the UK Government's objectives on Iraq:

> Our prime objective is to rid Iraq of its weapons of mass destruction (WMD) and their associated programmes and means of delivery, including prohibited ballistic missiles (BM), as set out in UNSCRs. This would reduce Iraq's ability to threaten its neighbours and the region, and prevent Iraq using WMD against our own people. UNSCRs also require Iraq to renounce terrorism.
>
> (Straw 2003)

In March 2003, it was clear to the British Government that Iraq was not comply-
ing with its disarmament obligations and that military action was necessary to
remove Saddam Hussein's regime in order to enforce Iraqi compliance (UK
MoD 2003c). At the Azores Summit on 17 March 2003, Tony Blair announced
the UK's *Vision for Iraq and the Iraqi People*, a document that outlined the
future end-state of Iraq as

> a stable, united and law-abiding state within its present borders, co-operating
> with the international community, no longer posing a threat to its neigh-
> bours or to international security, abiding by all its international obligations
> and providing effective and representative government for its own people.
>
> (UK MoD 2003d)

An unarticulated political aim in Iraq was to support the US and, thereby,
strengthen the position as its greatest friend and ally. Another aim was to provide
security to the UK by fighting terrorism well away from the shores of Britain
(*The Economist* 2008).

On 20 March 2003, the Defence Secretary announced in Parliament the
British objectives for the military campaign in Iraq:

- Overcome the resistance of Iraqi security forces.
- Deny the Iraqi regime the use of weapons of mass destruction now and in
  the future.
- Remove the Iraqi regime, given its clear and unyielding refusal to comply
  with the UN Security Council's demands.
- Identify and secure the sites where weapons of mass destruction and their
  means of delivery are located.
- Secure essential economic infrastructure, including for utilities and trans-
  port, from sabotage and wilful destruction by Iraq.
- Deter wider conflict both inside Iraq and in the region.

> (UK MoD 2003c)

The MoD also issued a number of wider political objectives in support of the
military campaign that would demonstrate goodwill towards the Iraqi people,
work with the UN to lift sanctions, sustain the widest possible international and
regional coalition in support of military action, preserve regional security, help
create conditions for a future, stable and law-abiding government of Iraq, and to
further the British policy of eliminating terrorism as a force in international
affairs (UK MoD 2003c).

To determine the British interpretation of the campaign these objectives are
later discussed in relation to the post-conflict planning process and the conduct
of operations in Iraq.

Civil–military co-ordination and co-operation: a comprehensive approach?

The previous chapter described a British approach to complex peace operations that involves close civil–military co-operation in the field as well as within the civil–military interface at the strategic level. This section investigates the extent to which this principle was adhered to in the context of Iraq. The section, therefore, involves two thematic discussions: post-conflict planning and the command and control structures.

Post-conflict planning

The main issue of this section is the fact that the UK was the junior partner in a coalition in which the senior partner clearly did not provide enough planning of the post-conflict phase. Obviously, the UK was part of the coalition that went to Iraq without a complete strategy for post-conflict operations, but what role did the British play in the planning process? How did they seek to influence the senior coalition partner?

A MoD report on the War in Iraq described the detailed planning for the post-conflict phase as taking place in parallel with the contingency planning for combat operations. 'Indeed, the military campaign was designed specifically with the coalition's post-conflict objectives in mind: for example, offensive operations were carefully targeted to ensure they had the least possible impact on Iraq's civil infrastructure' (UK MoD 2003a). This was perhaps most apparent in the patient attack on Basra during the invasion phase. However, the importance of giving the impression that conflict was not inevitable during the run up to the launch of the operation led to certain planning problems. Contingency planning for a post-conflict Iraq was very sensitive, as it had to start from the assumption that an invasion would eventually take place. A consequence was that involvement in the initial stages of the post-conflict planning was restricted to a relatively small group within the British Government. The Cabinet Office initially took the lead in co-ordinating work on post-conflict planning and reconstruction, but as the work grew this responsibility was increasingly transferred to the Foreign and Commonwealth Office (FCO) (UK MoD 2003a). More specifically, British planning for the post-conflict phase was centralized in the Iraq Planning Unit (IPU), based in the FCO. The IPU was led by a senior Foreign Office official and worked closely with the Government's central co-ordinating machinery in the Cabinet Office. It included an interagency group of MoD military and civilian staff as well as the FCO, Department for International Development and Treasury officials (UK MoD 2003d).

However, the *Review of Intelligence on Weapons of Mass Destruction* (2004), more commonly known as 'the Butler Report', noted that the traditional committee system had been bypassed. The report argued that Prime Minister Blair used a smaller group of people for policy-making, which confirms his presidential style of leadership, as discussed in the chapter on the British pattern of civil–military relations. The Butler Report expressed concern that 'the informality and circumscribed character of the Government's procedures which we saw in the context of policy-making towards Iraq risks reducing the scope for informed collective political judgement' (*Review of Intelligence on Weapons of Mass Destruction* 2004: 160). The presidential style of Prime Minister Blair, resulting in limited committee work, was enhanced by the need for secrecy in the run-up to the war. In essence, the traditional approach to planning and operations, involving interagency co-operation and co-ordination through the committee system, may, therefore, have been circumvented in the case of Iraq.

Peter Hennessy has a more nuanced view of this problem. He notes that 'the Prime Minister's "morning meetings" or the "War Cabinet" were in fact proper Cabinet Committee meetings, although in ad hoc form and more limited in scope' (Hennessy 2005: 5). In other words, the committee system was not bypassed, but limited. The question that must be raised is how limited the committee system can be and still deserve the title of committee system? Nevertheless, Hennessy goes on to argue that the mistakes of intelligence interpretation and policy-making in the run-up to the war were hardly the faults of centralization of the government structure and the exclusion of Cabinet Committees from the planning process. Instead, the system failure occurred at formal Cabinet meetings. 'If the full Cabinet will not take on a dominant Prime Minister in full cry – even in the last days before hostilities begin – there is no other part of the system of government that can compensate for such supineness' (Hennessy 2005: 9, 11). There are two possible explanations for this supineness in the British case. First, the presidential leadership style of Prime Minister Blair may not only have demanded stricter agreement regarding policy within the Cabinet, it may also have led to the recruitment of Cabinet ministers who were generally considered compliant. Second, because the work of Cabinet Committees was limited, the multitude of different information and ideas generally produced within committees may have been limited, thereby, failing to produce alternative views to the Cabinet ministers. In the final analysis, the British committee system of interagency co-operation was not employed to its fullest capacity in the planning process of the war in Iraq.

The coalition's lack of pre-war planning of post-conflict operations has been covered in the chapter on the US in Iraq, and it seems the British were, at an early stage, concerned about the lack of planning on the other side of the Atlantic. The British complained internally in a memo written in advance of a Cabinet meeting on Iraq held on 23 July 2002. The memo noted that 'military planning for action against Iraq is proceeding apace', but adds that 'little thought' has been given to 'the aftermath and how to shape it'. The memo warned that 'a post-war occupation of Iraq could lead to a protracted and costly nation-building exercise.... As already made clear, the U.S. military plans are virtually silent on this point' (Pincus 2005).

In contrast with the US administration, the British MoD also published a post-conflict strategy at the onset of the campaign. This stated that in the wake of hostilities, the immediate military priorities for the coalition were to:

a provide for the security of friendly forces;
b contribute to the creation of a secure environment so that normal life can be restored;
c work in support of humanitarian organizations to mitigate the consequences of hostilities and, in the absence of such civilian humanitarian capacity, provide relief where it is needed;
d work with UNMOVIC/IAEA to rid Iraq of its weapons of mass destruction and their means of delivery;
e facilitate remedial action where environmental damage has occurred;
f enable reconstruction and recommissioning of essential infrastructure for the political and economic benefit of the Iraqi people; and
g lay plans for the reform of Iraq's security forces.

(UK MoD 2003c)

The extent to which the early concerns and the later plans and objectives were expressed to those across the Atlantic is unclear. The former British Ambassador in Washington, Christopher Meyer, argued in his memoirs that Prime Minister Blair had been very weak in the discussions with President Bush before the war. The British, as the only major coalition partner, had much more leverage than what was used before the start of the campaign (cited in Jordan 2005).

A House of Commons Defence Committee report (2005) argues the obvious: 'The post-conflict situation with which the coalition was faced did not match the pre-conflict expectations'. The report made this argument despite the fact that advisors from the academic world had warned of the difficulties and complexities of post-conflict operations in the context of Iraq, among them professor Lawrence Freedman (Dandeker 2007). The committee listed five key planning misjudgements: first, instead of the grateful, amenable population, which the coalition had apparently hoped to find, many Iraqis sought actively to take advantage of the power vacuum that followed the combat phase. Second, and perhaps most importantly, the coalition underestimated the insurgency – or, at least, its potential. Third, the coalition seemed to be unable to decide what to do about the Iraqi military and security forces. Fourth, the coalition did not appear to plan adequately for the scope of the reconstruction task that lay before it nor did it seem to realize how quickly it would be expected to act to ameliorate the situation. Finally, the coalition underestimated the number of troops required to meet the challenges of Iraq's post-conflict transition (House of Commons Defence Committee 2005).

The Defence Committee's critique, which talks of the Coalition Provisional Authority in Baghdad as a complicating factor for the British, implies that the co-operation with the American partners was part of the problem. 'This has also been one of the first times in recent history that the UK has had to take on the obligations of an occupying power, and operated as a junior partner in a counter-insurgency' (House of Commons Defence Committee 2005). With what right can the UK as the junior partner in a coalition fall back on the fact that it was not solely, or even mainly, responsible for the misjudgements in the pre-war planning process?

It is clear that the British were concerned about the lack of US planning for the post-conflict phase, and that the MoD went somewhat further than its coalition partner in the post-conflict planning process. However, the British administration did not push its coalition partner very far. In reply to a question from the House of Commons Defence Committee regarding the level of involvement the MoD had in the US planning and conduct of post-conflict and counter-insurgency operations outside the British area of responsibility, the government made no attempt to hide behind the fact that it is a junior partner in coalition with a superpower. Instead, the British Government argued that it had been extensively involved in the coalition planning of post-conflict operations. The UK had significant representation in the US-led headquarters. Embedded British officers also contributed to the development of the coalition's campaign plan. There has also been extensive exchange of information between the countries regarding counter-insurgency experience and doctrine (House of Commons Defence Committee 2005).

Not only was the British Government part of the planning process, it also shared many of the miscalculations before the war. The House of Commons Defence Committee asked the British Government about the estimates on the size and scope of a possible insurgency before the end of major combat operations. The reply was that 'the prospects for a major insurgency were not the main focus of the MoD's attention at the time and there was very limited relevant intelligence'. The administration, nevertheless, recognized that, after a brief honeymoon period, significant elements of civil society could become anti-occupation and that caution needed to be taken considering the reduced Sunni role in the running of Iraq. 'However, an insurgency on the scale that subsequently developed was not foreseen before the end of major combat operations' (House of Commons Defence Committee 2005).

The Defence Committee also questioned the level of guidance given before March 2003 to British commanders on re-building the Iraqi Security Forces. The government's reply indicates the planning consequences the assumption of limited insurgency in the post-conflict phase would have.

> Formal guidance to British Commanders on the conduct of Operation TELIC [Iraq] was issued in the form of an Executive Directive from CDS [Chief of the Defence Staff] to the Joint Commander for Op TELIC, dated 18 March 2003. This stated that one of the tasks of the commander was 'if directed, be prepared to contribute to the reform of Iraq's security forces'. At this stage, however, formal guidance was mainly concerned with combat operations.
>
> (House of Commons Defence Committee 2005)

The combat phase was, in other words, the main concern of pre-war planning on both sides of the Atlantic, and post-conflict operations were treated as a contingency to be dealt with at a later stage. This could possibly be explained given the British military's culture of flexibility and muddling through. However, the magnitude of the post-conflict task would make such an approach in the Iraqi case rather futile.

The British Chief of the Defence Staff, General Sir Michael Walker, has stressed that 'if the Chiefs of Staff and I had doubted that we were on the right strategy, we would not hold back from saying so' (Walker 2005: 25). Even with the political considerations and the lack of influence in an unequal partnership considered, the British did accept the campaign plan by remaining a coalition partner, and did not force changes in the planning by exerting real pressure as the only serious coalition partner. In the final analysis, there are few extenuating circumstances for the British as the junior partner within the coalition.

British command and control structures

The previous section noted that the British committee system was not utilized to its fullest potential. The MoD report on first reflections of the war in Iraq nevertheless argued that, at the top levels of strategic command, inter-departmental consultation was ensured through the creation of special committees led by the Cabinet Office. Moreover, within the MoD, the Defence Secretary normally met twice daily with the CDS and others in the direct chain of command for the operation. The Permanent Secretary advised regularly on policy issues. The Chiefs of Staff also met most days, including with officials from other relevant departments and agencies, to assist the Chief of the Defence Staff (UK MoD 2003d). However, as noted above, the Butler Report showed that the level of interagency co-operation and committee deliberation in the run-up to the war was less than usual in the case of Iraq. A number of consequences are discussed later in this chapter.

The military command and control structures for the operations in Iraq were in accordance with British doctrine. The Chief of Joint Operations (CJO), General Sir John Reith was appointed as Joint Force Commander. He was responsible to the Chief of the Defence Staff for the conduct of operations, and exercised operational command over all British forces assigned to the operations in Iraq. The CJO exercised his responsibilities through the Permanent Headquarters to the UK Contingent Commanders in theatre, Air Chief Marshal Sir Brian Burridge. This form of national command did not mirror the US command structure and, therefore, led to a degree of complexity at the operational and tactical levels. However, the specifically British structure of command also ensured that UK forces would only undertake missions approved by British commanders (UK MoD 2003a). In the field the three UK Contingent Commanders (Maritime, Land and Air) operated under the tactical control of their respective US Component Commanders. This reflected years of interaction and co-operation between the two countries in the Gulf region. A defence report suggests that 1(UK) Armoured Division worked exceptionally well under US command thanks to the strong professional links already established between the two countries' armed forces (UK MoD 2003a).

Regarding the civil–military co-operation and co-ordination in the field the House of Commons Defence Committee noted in 2005 that British forces carried out their reconstruction-related tasks admirably, but remained concerned about the level of support offered by other departments and organizations. The MoD responded by contending that the security situation restricted the freedom of movement of DFID and FCO personnel (House of Commons Defence Committee 2005). Regarding the NGOs the security situation was so severe that they have not been able to operate in southern Iraq at all.

These concerns are confirmed by Captain Louise Heywood who worked as a Civil–military Co-ordination Officer in Iraq. Captain Heywood argues: 'I am very critical of interagency co-operation because it does not exist on the ground'. She noted that there was very little joint planning between the different agencies involved, and that the result was loss of unity of effort. The military emphasized traditionally well-understood and well-defined functions, such as Security Sector Reform (SSR). However, Heywood notes that while SSR was of great importance in Iraq, the narrow focus of the military as well as the lack of civilian organizations in the region meant that civil–military integration of the British intervention was largely set aside, particularly in the early phases of the Peace Support Operation (Heywood 2006).

Lack of civil–military integration and the severe security situation meant that the traditionally civilian aspects of post-conflict operations, such as political reform, capacity building and economic reconstruction, were forgot in the early post-conflict operations. In the end, the military was involved in post-conflict activities for which it clearly was not trained for, such as governance capacity building. The main reason was that the security situation did not allow other agencies to handle them. Lack of training as well as lack of interagency planning and instructions meant that the military would do things that were detrimental to the activities of DFID, causing further rifts and even more lack of communication and information sharing between the agencies. Most seriously, according to Heywood, was the fact that as late as 2006, there was 'no overarching plan' for post-conflict reconstruction, and, therefore, no continuity in reconstruction activities. Instead, military commanders were allowed to rotate every six months with a new set of objectives they wanted to achieve – objectives that included civilian aspects, such as governance. As a consequence there was little interaction between DFID and the MoD in the field. The interaction between the Foreign Office and the MoD was slightly better, mainly thanks to the political advisors within divisional and brigade headquarters. However, they were not involved with civil–military co-ordination or co-operation (Heywood 2006).

In conclusion, neither the interagency integration at the strategic level, nor the civil–military co-operation and co-ordination of operations in the field was as well developed as would be expected of the British approach to complex peace operations. The planning process did not utilize the full capacity of the interagency committee system, and, in the field, the level of civil–military co-operation and co-ordination was not enough to address the full range of post-conflict issues. The British failure to apply the Comprehensive Approach in practice has also been obvious in the context of the Helmand Province in Afghanistan (Docherty 2007). It seems the British conceptualization of the campaign in Iraq was more or less made in conventional terms. The British approach to complex peace operations was at the strategic level violated in several respects, and focus was placed on the invasion phase of the campaign. The strategic-level misinterpretation of the campaign in Iraq is bound to have had consequences for the tactical conduct of operations, which is the topic of the following section.

Tactical behaviour of British troops

The analysis of British conduct of tactical operations in Iraq has produced slightly contradictory results. The findings are presented in three thematic discussions. First, the hearts and minds approach is analysed with reference to the use of force as well as force protection policy. Second, the cultural understanding and adaptability of British troops are discussed. Finally, this section looks at the outcome and effectiveness of British conduct.

The hearts and minds approach

British Defence Secretary Geoff Hoon declared at the onset of the campaign that

> [o]ur focus on the minimum use of force makes sense militarily, as well as being consistent with our obligations under international law. In particular, for this campaign, we not only have an eye to overcoming resistance to our forces, but also to the very real need to enable the rapid reconstruction of Iraq in the wake of hostilities.
>
> (UK MoD 2003e)

The idea of minimum use of force is really a standing operating procedure for the British forces and, therefore, nothing exceptional in the case of Iraq. However, it is still worth highlighting as it stands in stark contrast to the American way of war. The Defence Secretary's statement also showed that at least some level of mental preparation for the post-conflict phase of the campaign existed during the invasion phase. The patient attack and the quick transition to firm but friendly patrolling of the streets in Basra have already been described as two examples of the British hearts and minds approach. However, the British way of war became more evident in the post-conflict phase.

Instead of the expected humanitarian crisis the most immediate and visible post-conflict challenge was the period of looting that followed the fall of Saddam Hussein's regime. Looting was not completely unexpected, according to a MoD report on Iraq, but the scale of the problem was greater than envisaged and particularly difficult for forces to address while they were still committed to combat operations (UK MoD 2003a).

However, through 'Quick Impact Projects' (QIPs), the British forces were able to make a relatively quick positive impact for the population in southern Iraq. The funding for QIPs was made available as a direct result of lessons learned from Afghanistan and proved very useful in Iraq. According to the

British administration, QIPs have helped gain the consent of the Iraqi people by providing early security, education and health activities. Moreover, British forces quickly began to work with senior police figures in Basra to encourage the Iraqi police back to work. Joint UK/Iraqi police patrols commenced on 13 April 2003, only a few days after the fall of Basra. In December 2003, there were already around 2,000 Iraqi police back at work in the city. Similar initiatives took place in towns across the British area of responsibility, with the result that Basra and the Maysan provinces were quickly declared permissive environments by the Humanitarian Operations Centre (UK MoD 2003d). The initial results were increased security and normality in the UK area of responsibility (UK MoD 2003a). The levels of looting and destruction by early insurgent attacks were also much more limited in the British area of responsibility. This was partly due to the larger support from the Shia-dominated population in the south than from the Hussein supporting Sunni population in the American area of responsibility, and partly due to the effective takeover of British troops in Basra, which quickly established a greater sense of security than in the bigger and more complex city of Baghdad.

However, the British conduct of operations as well as the long-term consequences of British behaviour, have been seriously questioned as the security situation in the British area of operations deteriorated after the relative calm of the initial honeymoon period. Before becoming involved in that discussion, let us take a closer look at some examples of British conduct of tactical-level operations.

On 2 August 2004 the US forces launched a major offensive in Najaf against the Mehdi Army, led by Shia cleric Moqtada al-Sadr. The attacks on Najaf also involved a threat to attack al-Sadr's forces in the holy mosque of Imam Ali. The offensive and the threat against the mosque caused much anger in southern Iraq and led to widespread unrest in the British area of responsibility. The unrest in Basra led to a number of British casualties over a short period. A number of British bases were besieged and battles were fought with much greater intensity than anything experienced during the invasion phase of the campaign. During these battles the British showed restraint by taking heavy fire without resorting to indiscriminate weaponry, such as artillery, fast-jet air strikes or helicopter gunships (Thornton 2005: 144). However, as a result of the increased insurgent activity, the British decreased the patrolling of the streets of Basra, and instead chose to remain passive within their bases. During this time the British only patrolled within a perimeter of 100 yards from base. The resulting security vacuum was quickly filled by forces loyal to al-Sadr. The British troops, nevertheless, had Special Forces operating in the city, and enough intelligence on the key leaders of the estimated 400 insurgents to 'take them out if we want to'. The British commanders insisted that their strategy of waiting out the barrage was preferable to attacking Sadr's militia. Such an attack would, according to the commanders, have led to an escalation of violence and the increased risk of civilian casualties (Harding 2004). Innocent casualties and collateral damage were thus kept to a minimum, and despite heavy casualties among insurgents, overall consent, therefore, still remained among the local population. Against US orders, negotiations were also held with the insurgents to help reduce the tense situation (Thornton 2005).

An interesting and contrasting event was the forced liberation of two British Special Forces soldiers from an Iraqi jail in Basra in September 2005. Relations between the British and Iraqis had turned sour during the summer of 2005, following a series of incidents, including the release of film footage showing British troops beating up Iraqi youths. As the Basra police refused to release the Special Forces detainees, the British used armoured vehicles, supported by attack helicopters to smash the walls of the prison in an attempt to forcibly release them. In the event, an angry mob attacked two armoured vehicles with rocks and petrol bombs (*The Times* 2005). The incident caused a break-off of contacts between the Iraqi authorities and the British troops. The governor of Basra, Mohammed Walli, called the British assault 'barbaric, savage and irresponsible' (Knickmeyer and Finer 2005). The day before this incident about 200 members of the Mahdi Army staged a show of force in the city, blocking roads in the city centre and demanding the release of a local commander who had previously been arrested by British and Iraqi security forces. After a stand-off lasting several hours, the militiamen withdrew after negotiations between an al-Sadr representative and the Iraqi police and the British forces (*The Times* 2005). A day of stand-off and negotiation with the militia was, in other words, followed by use of force on both sides.

A similar event took place in May 2006, when British soldiers clashed with local insurgents after a UK helicopter crash in Basra. When reinforcements were sent to secure the area, they came under attack by live fire from small arms as well as petrol bombs and stones. Several armoured vehicles caught fire and the British forces were forced to open fire during the unrest that in the end killed five people. Just as worrying as the unrest was the fact that crowds of Iraqis cheered and celebrated at the site of the helicopter crash as the wreckage burned. The BBC's Andrew North (2006) claimed that the event marked a 'dramatic change in attitude' towards the British presence in southern Iraq, and that the event would make it increasingly difficult for British troops to control the streets of Basra.

However, the day after the helicopter crash and the subsequent riots, the Basra battle group commander, Lieutenant Colonel Johnny Bowren, took his men patrolling in soft hats. The patrol was described as a deliberate attempt to convey the army's view that the displays of hatred and triumphalism at British casualties did not represent the majority of Basra's opinion. While the patrol was attacked by rocks in certain areas, it received a warmer welcome in others (Wood 2006).

Arguably, the most debated episode of the British post-conflict campaign was the November 2004 redeployment of the Black Watch Regiment to an American-controlled area close to Baghdad. The redeployment was made in support of the American operations in Fallujah and relieved the US Marines that normally patrolled the area. The fact that the British troops were subordinate to US commanders in what was considered a more dangerous area, created great debate in the UK. Lieutenant Colonel James Cowan, the regiment's commanding officer, was in the end promised total control over the way his men operated. The British also negotiated an agreement with the Americans that laid down what missions and tasks the British troops would undertake, and that they would be carried out under British Army rules of engagement (Smith 2004). Although the British conducted their operations in full combat gear, the hearts and minds approach was, thereby, exported to the redeployment area.

An early setback proved that the area was as dangerous as expected. On 4 November 2005, 11 soldiers were caught in a suicide bomb blast at a checkpoint. Three of them, as well as their civilian interpreter, died instantly while the other eight were injured. This could be interpreted as a failure of the British approach, but while the event certainly raised the guard of the Black Watch, the hearts and minds campaign continued. In fact, less than 24 hours after the attack, troops were out on foot patrols again. Lieutenant Richard Holmes, the patrol commander, argued that 'we've got to get out, get the intelligence, and get feet on the ground, otherwise we'll never get anywhere' (Lloyd Parry 2005).

In the aftermath of these attacks, the Black Watch conducted a large search operation named 'Operation Tobruk' that possibly shows a different mindset of the Black Watch in the more volatile area south of Baghdad. Soldiers stormed what was considered an insurgent stronghold by bursting into houses and arresting a large number of people. The emotional stress of the British troops was evident in the comments of a sergeant before the operation: 'It's payback time. We have been looking forward to getting out there and stopping these people attacking us' (Harrison 2004). The operation stands out as 'unBritish', and was clearly not a typical hearts and minds operation. Walls were knocked down, doors smashed and stun grenades thrown. More than 700 soldiers in over 100 vehicles, including 42 Warrior armoured assault vehicles, took part in the operation that lasted for 12 hours. Interestingly, despite the sense of 'payback time' and the unusually brutal tactics that led to the arrest of more than 100 men, only a handful of shots were fired, leading to no casualties on either side (Harrison 2004). It seems that, even under emotional stress, the principle of minimum use of force was adhered to by officers and soldiers alike. It is also clear that the British approach to force protection, involving close contact with the local population, emphasis on human intelligence and hearts and minds approaches, was maintained despite increased violence and risk.

Cultural understanding and adaptability

A joint UK MoD and US DoD report on British approaches to low-intensity operations notes that the British forces in Iraq benefited from their ability to 'engage with the local population, escalate force rapidly, and then re-engage with the local population almost immediately'. This ability to 'smile, shoot, smile' was further described as a classic component of the British hearts and minds approach and dedication to this principle was more intuitive than doctrinal. In essence, doctrine was not considered as a tool used to determine actions. Instead, good training and experience from previous operations was cited as engendering tactical flexibility (US DoD 2007: 88).

While this account resonates well with the British way of war as described in the previous chapter, it should be noted that the British troops in Iraq initially displayed serious shortcomings in terms of cultural understanding. Christopher Varhola contends that the British had even less recent institutional experience in the Middle East than the US military, and that no civil–military assets within the British armed forces were specifically trained for the Middle East at the onset of operations. The lack of experience from the region, combined with too much emphasis on the tactical and operational lessons from Northern Ireland, resulted in poor understanding of local culture, which was reflected in the frequent riots in Basra and the negative attitudes of Iraqis towards British forces in southern Iraq. As an example, early in the campaign, British soldiers looking for weapons conducted house searches with dogs. In the Muslim faith the dog is an unclean animal, and the use of dogs in Arab homes was perceived as an insulting act meant to demonstrate British dominance. Local leaders, clerics and residents, therefore, complained that British soldiers were not sensitive to the local customs (Varhola 2004).

This view is confirmed by Andrew Garfield (2006) who maintains that the cultural awareness of British soldiers who participated in the invasion phase of the operation was surprisingly poor. However, he also notes that this shortcoming was quickly rectified by adding lengthy cultural training of subsequent troop rotations. In a training city, modified to look like a typical Iraqi city, British soldiers were trained in interpreting situations as well as interacting with the local population. Garfield, thereby, argues that the British showed excellent adaptability when faced with difficulties and initial shortcomings. However, the fact that British soldiers were not well prepared for the context of Iraq shows the importance of understanding that each conflict presents a unique set of challenges, and that there are limits to the benefits of experience from Northern Ireland and other conflicts (Bulloch 1996). The cultural challenges of operating in the context of Iraq were clearly underestimated before the invasion.

As previously argued, the British culture of minimum use of force and political sensitivity also does not provide a guarantee against abuse. The case in which three British soldiers were charged and later jailed and dismissed from the army in disgrace over the abuse of Iraqi detainees in Basra highlights this fact (BBC News 2006b). Such events underline the lack of understanding of the political and strategic consequences of tactical mistakes. However, the British armed forces generally have a good understanding of the importance of the strategic narrative and of making the right impression on the local population and leaders. As an example, British Brigadier Nick Carter argued in 2004 that maintaining the goodwill of local Shia Muslim leader, Sayid Ali al-Safi al-Musawi, was vital. 'The moment that Sayid Ali says, "We don't want the Coalition here," we might as well go home' (Kite and Thomson 2004). To keep up to date with public opinion the British Operational Analysis section at Division Headquarters, therefore, conducted continuous surveys administered by locally hired Iraqis throughout the whole of its sector (Varhola 2004).

The outcome of British operations in Iraq

Initial reports from the British area of operations mostly contained positive contrasts with the American sector. The House of Commons Defence Committee (2005) argues that the considerable success that had been achieved in the UK-controlled areas can be traced to the British forces' ability to adapt to changing circumstances. 'Suppleness and pragmatism are at the heart of the British forces' professionalism.' However, the early gains in terms of security and reconstruction efforts were quickly replaced by increasing security problems and growing insurgent activity in and around Basra. As noted, the effectiveness of the British approach in Iraq has, therefore, been questioned. However, before discussing the soundness of British tactics, it should be observed that the number of UK military personnel deployed in Iraq decreased substantially after the initial invasion phase. The peak during major combat operations involved 46,000 British troops, a number that in May 2003 was down to 18,000. In May 2004, only 8,600 soldiers remained to control the south of Iraq (UK MoD n.d.b). With only 8,000 troops overseeing security in the Shia heartland, British troops had no option but to apply a 'softly-softly approach', keeping a low profile and handing over much responsibility to the local authorities. However, reports from early 2006 indicated that many Basrans were disappointed by the British military's hands-off approach that allowed hard-line groups to take control of the city (Hider 2006). Similarly, an anonymous senior British Army officer who has served in Basra claims that the brigade-sized force employed to secure the British area of responsibility is 'farcically small' for the task. 'We've done some bloody good things, but the truth is that we've also had to turn a blind eye to an awful lot of iffy behaviour from the militias – assassinations, graft, vote-fixing and so on' (cited in Royle 2005).

Human Rights Watch (2003) has presented a bleak view of British post-conflict operations in the Basra area. The report reveals that extensive looting and civil unrest took place in the immediate aftermath of the fall of Basra. It further argues that 'the extent of looting in the first week, and British failure to respond to it, convinced many residents of Basra that their security was not a priority for British forces'. The report is significant as it implies that what the British considered an acceptable level of disorder and violence in the aftermath of the fall of Basra was, in the eyes of the local population, not enough to provide the sense of individual security that was necessary to create or maintain support for the occupation (Hills 2003).

This can be put in relation to the British emphasis on security sector reform in the area. While violence was kept at what the British considered an acceptable level, they successfully trained Iraqi troops that have been able to take over responsibility for security in all four provinces in the British area of responsibility. From that perspective, not only were there enough British troops in Iraq, but also operations were going according to plan. However, the emphasis on SSR meant that the many other aspects of post-conflict reconstruction were forgotten or impossible to execute. The fact is that the security situation did not allow the Foreign Office, DFID personnel, or NGOs to operate in the area, resulting in limited successes in reconstruction and political reform. The hands-off approach to operations and the limited amount of soldiers in the British area of responsibility were not adequate to achieve the more far-reaching political aims of the campaign in Iraq.

Meanwhile, 'Operation Sinbad', a jointly executed operation by the Iraqi Security Forces and the British, conducted between September 2006 and March 2007, did regain some initiative by rooting out corruption in the police force and by conducting extensive reconstruction projects in Basra. It has also proved the worth of the Iraqi Security Forces trained by the British. The Iraqi 10th Division is from the spring of 2007 in charge of planning and leading security operations in Basra with minimal or no coalition support. However, the operations also highlighted the difficulty of shaping events in Iraq, and the lack of available troops. Toby Dodge argues that 'Britain has never had the forces [in Iraq] needed to make a sustained difference to law and order, and meaningful reconstruction is almost non-existent' (cited in the *Independent* 2006). The improvements during Operation Sinbad seem to have been temporary as reports coming out of Basra during the spring speak of increased attacks on British troops, as well as a quick return to a militia-led anarchy on the streets. The police are again completely run by militia groups, as are large parts of the Iraqi Army (Abdul-Ahad 2007).

As junior partner in the coalition that occupies Iraq, the British forces seem to have opted for a limited approach that keeps the security situation at an acceptable level while conducting security sector reform in the British area of responsibility. The approach means that British troops are leaving the country and that the responsibility for security is transferred to the Iraqi security forces. However, for the local population, the operations have not been enough as the security situation has been severe for civilians, and as the civilian aspects of post-conflict operations – such as economic reconstruction and improved governance – have been sacrificed. This has also failed to meet the requirements of the political aims of the campaign in Iraq.

Despite the hearts and minds operations of the British forces, the lack of security as well as the failure to conduct the civilian aspect of post-conflict reconstruction meant that the local community's consent was never secured. This view is confirmed by Lieutenant General Sir Robert Fry, Deputy Commander of Multinational Force Iraq, who has argued that one of the greatest problems in Iraq was the failure to translate tactical behaviour into operational effect in the pursuit of strategic goals (Fry 2005). There is, in other words, a disconnection between the strategic-level aims and the tactical work in the field. Despite British tactical behaviour that, to a large extent, mirrors the lessons learned of past expeditionary operations and existing counter-insurgency doctrine, the intended operational effects of stabilization and reconstruction are painfully absent. Heywood maintains that she experiences 'a worrying lack of willingness among Government agencies to work together effectively' (Heywood 2006: 40).

Despite the deteriorating security situation after the initial honeymoon period, the British have, in fact, handed over responsibility for their four provinces, with the Basra province last to be handed over in December 2007. The security sector reform has, in some respects, been successful, producing a number of reliable Iraqi military units. A positive view comes from Andrew Garfield (2006):

> Notwithstanding the fact that the UK's area of responsibility is less hostile than many of the areas occupied by U.S. forces, informed opinion suggests that the British approach to S&R [stability and reconstruction], which differs significantly from that of the U.S., has achieved some success in Iraq, ensuring greater stability, fewer casualties, less alienation, and more rapid reconstruction.

In October 2008, the British commander of UK forces in Iraq, General Salmon, argued that the security situation in the British area of responsibility was greatly improved – not least thanks to the increasing number of British-trained security forces. 'There are 30,000 ISF [Iraqi Security Forces] on the streets of Basra and Basra is secure' (cited in MoD Defence News 2008). Garfield credits the British organizational culture, the effective adaptation of existing doctrine for complex peace operations, and a much more integrated national approach to stability and reconstruction operations. The findings of this chapter, nevertheless, suggest a more nuanced view of British operations in Iraq. Moreover, in the final analysis, the outcome of operations in Iraq can really only be measured in terms of coalition success on a national scale, and the British have in this regard done little beyond damage control and providing for their own exit strategy.

Anthony Cordesman (2007) argues that the problem in the southern provinces was that the British essentially gave up. The British lost control after the election in 2005 and 2006 as different Shiite groups came to power. 'Once they came under control, the Shiites firmly were in charge of virtually the entire area and there was little the British could do about it'. Other analysts contend that the soft approach of the British was the very reason Basra slipped out of their grasp in 2005. The determination not to inflame the local populace and the failure to project power meant that the British military all but invited an external challenge.

> With Basra civilians cowed and the levers of civic power increasingly coming under the domination of fractious religious parties, it has become tragically apparent that, for all intents and purposes, British forces have been relegated to the role of mere spectators.
>
> (Devenny and McLean 2005)

In June 2007, the situation in Basra was described as completely out of control. Different militia groups controlled the oil production, the ports and borders, as well as the police and large parts of the military (Abdul-Ahad 2007). Serving British soldiers have told the media that they feel like 'just sitting ducks', constantly being mortared in their camps, and shot at during every patrol (Judd 2007).

In December 2007, the British forces, nevertheless, handed over the responsibility for Basra to the Iraqi Security Forces, and, thereby, reduced their own role to mentoring and training Iraqi forces and reconstruction through the Provincial Reconstruction Team (PRT). The withdrawal was at the time described as 'not graceful' and possibly creating a security vacuum in southern Iraq (Beaumont 2007; Dagher 2007; *The Economist* 2007). Interestingly, the opposite has happened as security has greatly improved since the British withdrew to Basra airport and the Iraqi Security Forces have been in control. However, the improved security situation in Basra should also be seen in the light of the national level of stabilization created by the American surge.

The British inability or unwillingness to seriously engage the insurgents in Basra may have had serious consequences in the fight for the hearts and minds of the local population. General David Richards, ISAF commander in Afghanistan, made an interesting observation regarding hearts and minds operations and legitimacy in the Helmand province of Afghanistan:

> If you are an Afghan who has spent thirty years fighting, you have learned not to put faith in the wrong side, because it comes back to haunt you. Until we demonstrated that we had the resolve and the capability to beat the Taliban decisively, we were not going to be able to win the 'hearts and minds'. We like to think that the concept of 'hearts and minds' is all about soft power – humanitarian aid, development projects – but in the Afghan context there is a hard edge to it. First you have to convince people that you are going to win, militarily.
>
> (RUSI 2007)

In certain contexts, the military capability can never be replaced by soft power. In Iraq, the combination of the soft approach and very limited numbers of troops clearly failed to establish what Rupert Smith calls a 'condition in which the political objective can be achieved by other means and in other ways' (2005: 270).

What is the long-term impact of the war in Iraq on the UK? *The Economist* (2008) argues that the schismatic nature of the pre-war debate, as well as the poor results displayed since, 'has made eerily little difference to Britain'. However, in grand strategic terms 'Iraq has unquestionably made the terrorist threat worse. It has thus also contributed to the sense of permanent emergency that has crept into politics and policing.' Moreover, the special relationship with the US does not seem more special than before the war (*The Economist* 2008).

Conclusion

The British ability to adjust from war to peacekeeping is a familiar phenomenon, witnessed in Bosnia, Kosovo, Sierra Leone and Afghanistan. Few commentators were, therefore, surprised by the professionalism and flexibility displayed by the British in Iraq. However, during the initial invasion phase the British also showed that it is possible to wage war with the more far-reaching political aims of democratization and post-conflict reconstruction in mind. The siege and fall of Basra showed well-developed political understanding of the British armed forces and restraint in the use of force even in open battle. The patience and respect for civilian lives and property during the battle for Basra serve as an example of what Lawrence Freedman (2006) calls 'liberal warfare'.

In important ways, the British have adhered to their way of war and the principles of complex peace operations. Tactically, British forces conducted hearts and minds operations involving the minimum use of force, good political understanding, and force protection through foot patrolling and interaction with the local community. The British troops, moreover, displayed an ability to be tactically flexible. Not only did they have the capability to adjust from the invasion phase to the post-conflict reconstruction tasks, they also displayed the same flexibility when being exposed to different levels of threat like during the Black Watch operations south of Baghdad in support of the US operations in Fallujah. Several instances in which escalation would seem normal were, in fact, de-escalated by the British.

At the same time, a number of principles of complex peace operations were violated. Most importantly, the British failed to draw upon the complete set of national instruments of power. At the strategic level the interagency committee system was not utilized to its full potential, creating strategic-level planning of the operations in Iraq that were of low quality as it seriously underestimated the post-conflict phase of the campaign and consequently did not produce an effective Phase IV plan. This can partly be explained by the fact that the British were the junior partner in the coalition, and, therefore, not solely responsible for strategy and operational planning in Iraq. However, as the analysis above has shown, the British did have leverage in the operational planning and also chose to accept the Pentagon's plans. At the tactical level, the principles of civil–military coordination and co-operation, as well as unity of command and effort, were also violated. The co-operation between different agencies involved in the British operations was substantially more limited than expected from the British approach.

As discussed above, the consequences of the hands-off approach of the British forces are contested by academics and US practitioners alike. While substantial results have been achieved in terms of security sector reform and handover of responsibilities to Iraqi authorities, the British have failed to provide security for the Iraqi population, as well as for civilian organizations that have not been able to operate in the south of Iraq. The small number of troops is a significant factor as the British from 2004 have operated with about 8,000 troops in a vast area of operations. In an imperial policing fashion, the British seem to have found what they feel is an acceptable level of violence without wasting too many resources and without creating too much of an imprint on Iraqi society. The result is that the British approach in Iraq has secured its own early withdrawal of troops, but has simultaneously failed to establish a condition from which to achieve the more far-reaching political aims of the operations by political and diplomatic means. In strategic terms, this means increased insecurity in the UK, continued regional instability in the Middle East, and a relationship with the US that is not more special than it was before the joint invasion of Iraq.

The two cases have, to a large extent, supported the hypothesis of this book. However, two significant questions in terms of the theoretical framework of this book have surfaced. First, why have the US armed forces, at least seemingly, started adjusting to complex peace operations, despite only minor changes in the civil–military interface? Second, why did the British not adhere to their way of war in the context of Iraq? The general findings of the two cases – compared and contrasted in relation to the hypothesis – as well as these important contradictions are discussed in the following chapter.

Part IV
Comparative analysis

9 Evaluating the hypothesis

The cases compared and contrasted

The case studies of US and UK patterns of civil–military relations, their ways of war, and their operations in Iraq have until this point been considered separately in order to trace the causal processes of each case. In this chapter, the more important findings from the case studies are used to evaluate the theoretical framework as well as to assess and further expand on the hypothesis constructed from the theoretical framework. This is achieved by comparing and contrasting the observations and conclusions of the cases with reference to the theoretical framework of the book. The discussion in this chapter also provides an opportunity to examine and discuss the sometimes contradictory observations of the case studies.

A recapitulation of the theoretical framework and the hypothesis

The theoretical framework for analysis, created in Chapter 2 by a critical review of the existing literature, argued that different patterns of civil–military relations affect the conduct of operations in two important ways: *directly*, as the level in the chain of command where strategic aims are created and translated into operational plans and activities, thereby affecting the planning and implementation of operations, and; *indirectly*, by being the arena in which funding, doctrine and direction for the military organization is decided, thereby determining the structure and culture of the armed forces. The direct causality of certain patterns of civil–military relations was partly derived from lessons learned and best practice in complex peace operations. Lessons from past operations stress the importance of comprehensive civil–military approaches, involving integration and joint planning at the strategic and operational levels and co-operation and co-ordination at the tactical level, to achieve unity of command and effort. The direct causality was also derived from mission command theory and the discussion on organizational culture and trust. Effective command and control in complex operations requires certain levels of trust in order to use mission type orders. At all levels of command, the structural set-up should, therefore, strive towards increased trust and mutual understanding across departmental and agency boundaries. The indirect causality is essentially about having civil–military structures that produce armed forces fit for purpose – size, training, doctrine, equipment and culture that are useful for whatever purpose the political leadership intends to use them, or what we call the functional imperative of the armed forces. Perhaps the most important mechanism of the indirect causality is the definition of the functional imperative, and the adjustment of the armed forces to those tasks. In other words, how, and by whom, is the functional imperative defined, and to what extent are the armed forces adjusted to it?

The hypothesis that was derived from the theoretical framework argued that the complex nature of contemporary peace operations means that integrated civil–military approaches are necessary for effectiveness in achieving the often far-reaching political aims of democratization and economic development. Such integrated, or comprehensive, approaches to operations also require integrated institutions at the national strategic level, and at the international organizational level in cases of multinational operations within different organizational frameworks. Two main reasons were highlighted as explanation of why integrated civil–military structures at the strategic level are likely to provide better results in complex peace operations. First, the indirect impact means that integrated structures provide more accurate and up-to-date interpretations and adjustment to the functional imperative of the armed forces. This leads to instruments of national power, not least the military instrument, that are better suited for the contemporary strategic context. Second, the direct impact of integrated structures is that they provide more inclusive command and control structures at the strategic level, which means that all relevant actors in complex operations are co-ordinated through integrated planning and execution of operations – providing a so-called comprehensive approach.

The starting point for the evaluation and discussion of the theoretical framework and the hypothesis is the independent variables of the two cases – the patterns of civil–military relations in the US and the UK.

Civil–military relations in the US and the UK

The analyses in Chapters 3 and 5 made it clear that British and US civil–military relations are poles apart. At the surface the differences are not entirely obvious. The British centralized system of government displays an intricate web of committees that ensures at least some level of formal interagency co-operation and involvement of all relevant government ministries in security-related policy-making. The US government structure also involves a system of interagency working groups and committees, albeit less extensive and at higher levels of the government hierarchy. Where the British system has the Cabinet committees for high-level policy-making, the US system has the National Security Council with its staff. However, a closer look at the two systems, especially of the cultural aspects, reveals greater differences in terms of civil–military relations.

The British parliamentary political system has – at least in relative terms – a tradition of cross-government co-operation. The work of interagency committees is considered an important tool for successful and comprehensive consideration of issues, especially related to security. Historically, the pragmatic lessons of imperial management developed strong links between the Foreign Office and the Ministry of Defence, as all operations were conducted in close co-operation between the different agencies and ministries involved. At its best the British committee system ensures that expertise is drawn from all relevant ministries and agencies when planning and executing complex peace operations. However, as noted in the analysis of the British case, the integration and co-operation across Whitehall are limited by departmental turf wars. Moreover, Prime Minister Tony Blair's presidential style of leadership had centralized governmental decision-making and further limited the status and importance of interagency co-operation in committees. A problem with the committee system of interagency co-operation is that it takes time and that it is often too slow for the effective implementation of contemporary military operations that require quick decision-making by the political leadership. In the UK, there are calls, therefore, for stronger formal structures at the interagency level.

In the US case, the interagency system is caught in the political system of checks and balances, in which distrust and competition are considered virtues and upholders of democracy. Regardless of the democratic virtues of checks and balances, the system has reduced the importance of the work done in interagency committees. While the interagency structures are rather well-established, the executive authority and status of these committees and working groups are minimal. An example is the National Security Council that, despite its inclusion of all the major players involved in national security matters, has virtually no mandate beyond an advisory function. The meetings of interagency working groups are moreover described as information sharing procedures, during which the different representatives describe their own views on different issues. Negotiations, discussions, modifications of positions or mutual decisions rarely take place.

The cultural differences are important because of the consequences thereof. A positive consequence of the British integrated system is that it creates trust at the institutional as well as the interpersonal level. By working together with colleagues from other agencies and departments, British civil servants develop mutual trust and understanding across Whitehall. Successful co-operation also means that they develop a sense of trust in, and respect for, the system or the institutions for which they are working. The British system of collective cabinet responsibility is unmatched in the US presidential system. In the US system the most important decisions can be made by the President without, and even against, the advice of the cabinet. Furthermore, the absence of a tradition of interagency co-operation in the US case means that issues are, to a larger extent than in the British case, dealt with by single departments, resulting in stovepipes. At best other relevant departments and agencies are informed of decisions and plans. The process of post-conflict planning for Iraq is an obvious case in point, in which the DoD was given the responsibility for planning and, thereafter, failed to include the expertise and resources from other relevant departments and agencies.

By comparing the defence ministries in the two cases, the structural and cultural differences become greater. While the British MoD includes a well-developed integration of military and civilian staff at all levels, the US DoD is divided into a military and a civilian side of the Pentagon. However, it should be noted that the US DoD also involves a more limited integration of its civilian and military staffs, even at the heart of the Joint Staff. Nevertheless, while the British emphasize civil–military interaction and integration at all levels of the ministerial hierarchy, the divide between the civilian and military sides of the US DoD creates more limited areas of meaningful interaction. In the central areas of the British Ministry of Defence there is widespread civil–military mixed management of the different divisions. An example is that where the head is a military officer, the deputy is often civilian and vice versa (Hopkinson 2000a). As noted in Chapter 3, the level where meaningful civil–military interaction and co-ordination in the US case take place is at the very top levels – often at the level of the Secretary of Defense, who receives separate policy and military advice from the two sides of the department.

The MoD's functions are carried out as one organization as opposed to the Pentagon which includes a sharp divide between the Office of the Secretary of Defense and the staff of the Chairman of the Joint Chiefs of Staff. The limits on serious civil–military interaction at the highest levels of the department create few 'buffer zones' in which differences of opinion can be sorted out and reconciled at lower levels. It also creates an exaggerated reliance on the individuals at the top levels. Moreover, at the higher levels of the DoD, there are very few career civil servants who, with extensive knowledge of both military and political matters, can function as a buffer and mediator in the civil–military interface. A possible benefit of the US system is that it provides the political leadership with both purely military and political advice, while the British system always provides military advice with the political aspects already included and vice versa. This could, according to the divided approach to civil–military relations, lead to the politicization of the armed forces and a loss of professionalism. However, the value of military advice without consideration of the political aspect can be questioned in a context of politically sensitive operations under global surveillance. The integrated approach to civil–military relations instead emphasizes the ability to understand both political and military aspects of security affairs as an important part of military professionalism.

Culturally, the British Ministry of Defence's system of integration of civil servants, officers and political appointees creates a higher level of mutual trust, respect and understanding than within the more limited co-operative culture of the interagency arena, and that stands out in stark contrast to its US counterpart. Civil–military integration in the British case ensures that both military and political expertise is heard, and more importantly, that the civilian and military advice is adapted and compromised when issues reach the top levels of the ministry. Pure military and political advice, as emphasized in the US, is not considered as important in the UK. Great care is taken to include the political aspects of military planning and operations at the Permanent Joint Headquarters as well. This is meant to provide for civil–military co-operation and co-ordination in the planning and execution of complex operations as well as the inclusion of all actors or instruments of power available to the state. However, as noted, this was not achieved in the case of Iraq.

Another factor worth highlighting in the British case is the importance of professional civil servants who provide extensive expertise, institutional memory and continuity across administrations as well as seasoned perspectives on policies and programmes. As such, the corps of professional civil servants has the potential not only to provide a broader civil–military perspective and act as a buffer between the political and military leaderships. They can also maintain the personal relationships and trust across agencies and departments that are essential for inter-office interaction as well as for interagency co-operation. Several US commentators, therefore, argue that it is time to start reversing the trend that increases the number of political appointees in order to increase the effectiveness and to retain the best and the brightest within the organization (Grissom 2005; White 2004; Murdock 2004: 57).

In sum, the US case is very clear the adaptation of the divided approach, which is not surprising as the US case is what Huntington sought to describe and explain in his seminal work. The British case, instead, provides an example of integrated Janowitzean type civil–military relations, although not quite as clear cut as the US case. By contrasting the two cases it also becomes clear that where the US system stresses civil–military division and the importance of pure policy advice and pure professional military advice to the top-level policy makers, the British system emphasizes integration and reconciliation between policy matters and military matters at all levels for joint civil–military advice to the leadership. The British do not separate policy from military matters, neither conceptually nor practically.

According to the theoretical framework of this book, the contrasting cases of civil–military relations should cause conflicting outcomes in the conduct of operations in complex peace missions. The following section, therefore, examines the direct and indirect impacts that the different patterns of civil–military relations in the two cases have on operational effectiveness.

The indirect effect of civil–military relations

The different patterns of civil–military relations indirectly affect the conduct and effectiveness of operations by determining the structure, doctrine, equipment and culture of the armed forces. These factors have, in this book, been brought together and described as the US and British ways of war and their approaches to complex peace operations.

The US and British ways of war

The British way of war, as described in Chapter 7, has developed as a combination of pragmatic lessons from imperial policing and counter-insurgency operations on the one hand, and the civil–military conditions of low-cost civilian monitoring of the armed forces during the period of military professionalization on the other. The British armed forces professionalized as a political tool in the colonies, making them highly sensitive to the wills of the political leadership. The functional imperative to which the armed forces had to adjust its structure and culture was defined by the political leadership as a result of the strategic context, and the varied demands of colonial policing and administration.

The UK has, therefore, developed a strategic culture with preference for small wars, involving the armed forces in a supporting role to achieve political aims. Political primacy has been a key pattern in British civil–military relations. Flexibility and adaptability were other necessary features of the British approach in order to effectively adjust to the multitude of different tasks involved in policing the Empire, as well as to perform effectively within very different contexts and cultures. Another aspect of the British approach to complex peace operations derived from pragmatic lessons of colonial policing is close co-operation between the civilian and military leaderships. By producing soldiers and officers with flexible and adaptable mindsets, and by nurturing sound civil–military relations, the British armed forces have a well-established capability of quickly adjusting to different levels of conflict. The British military also learned the importance of restraint in its application of force and has wholeheartedly accepted the hearts and minds philosophy involving the minimum use of force. The emphasis on flexibility has further meant that, until recently, doctrine has not been of great importance.

The structure of the British armed forces supports the culture by being built around the regimental system, which produces trust and decentralized command in operations. The British military stresses the importance of small unit operations and conducts its operations with the battalion as the most important building block. This suits complex peace operations well by allowing for mission command and trust in the lower levels of the command chain, where the important decisions are made on a daily basis. Regarding the contents of doctrine, the findings are, however, slightly ambiguous. An emphasis on warrior values and the core function of fighting wars are underscored to an extent that does not quite reflect the British way of war. However, as Brigadier Simon Mayall (2004) argues, while the British train for war, they mentally prepare for small wars and counter-insurgency. In other words, while the foundation of British training and doctrine is traditional warfare, the fine-tuning is for complex peace operations, invoking the strategic and cultural approach of the armed forces in general, and the regiments in particular. Flexibility, hearts and minds approaches and cultural understanding are not the contents of basic training or doctrine, but are instead invoked by the history and traditions of the organization. Significantly, the British armed forces are also considered one of few military organizations capable of performing both types of tasks to a high standard. However, the British military has also included an uneasy co-existence of two separate strategic cultures in the traditional British approach, emphasizing the colonial heritage of counter-insurgency operations, and the more conventional thinking of the continentalists of the British Army of the Rhine. This duality is also reflected in British doctrine publications.

These features of the British way of war have been maintained and refined to this day through the operations in Northern Ireland as well as the peace operations of the 1990s. With reference to the theoretical framework of this book, the British structure and culture of civil–military relations have via the functional imperative had an indirect impact on the conduct and effectiveness of the British military by providing for a military and interagency structure and culture emphasizing complex peace operations. In relation to the principles of best practice in complex peace operations, the British patterns of civil–military relations, thereby, produce a strategic culture that should be more effective in such operations. The British armed forces are conceptually and morally 'fit for purpose'. However, a negative aspect is that the strong civilian control of the armed forces has failed to secure enough funding to maintain armed forces with the size and equipment necessary to fulfil their roles in national and international security. The British, therefore, have limited capability in the physical sense, and have come to rely on the US as an ally in the defence of the nation as well as in the projection of British interests internationally. The peace operations in Bosnia and Kosovo are obvious examples in which the British and the rest of the European armed forces proved incapable of addressing the problems without the help of their American ally.

In contrast with British military professionalization under close political scrutiny, US military professionalism was developed in complete isolation from the political leadership. Moreover, the Huntingtonian divide between political and military leaders as well as the cost of political monitoring and control of the armed forces have led the US military to define its functional imperative without interference from the political leadership. Based on a misreading of classical Prussian texts the US military has therefore come to focus on large wars of annihilation, fought quickly, and at minimum cost, employing high technology, maximal firepower and overwhelming force. The US approach to all types of military operations begins with an anti-Clausewitzian conceptual division between war and peace, and the separation of political aims and military implementation. The dualistic conceptualization of war and peace is reflected in the US civil–military bureaucracies that are also clearly divided in a department that has monopoly on the conduct of war, while the others lead in times of peace. The US military strives to be apolitical in peace as well as in war and has, therefore, a poorly developed understanding of how to translate military victories into desired political aims as well as to adjust military activity in relation to different political aims.

The US military is structured to suit the American way of war, using the division as the most important building block for operations as well as training. The strategic culture for conventional warfare largely applies to US involvement in complex peace operations as well. The limited, or complex, political aims of such operations as well as the fact that the US military do not see such operations as part of their functional imperative mean that a low tolerance for casualties is added to the list as an American way of peacekeeping. US doctrine largely reflects the cultural bias of the organization and emphasizes the warrior ethos for fighting conventional wars. However, it also contains many of the best practices discussed in the introductory chapter of this book. US army doctrine on stability and support operations, as well as the recently published doctrines on counter-insurgency operations, are well up to date with the principles of complex peace operations. As argued in the chapter on the US way of war, this diversity is a result of an ongoing debate regarding the functional imperative of the armed forces. While operations other than war are clearly gaining in importance within the doctrinal studies and publication, they have not had the same impact on US military culture or the American way of war. Thus, US operations in the context of complex peace operations still reflect the American way of war and the traditional principles of conventional warfare as displayed in Vietnam as well as in Somalia. This was also confirmed within the scope of the study of US operations in Iraq. The cultural preferences of the US military take precedence over the choice of doctrine when it comes to the planning and implementation of operations – regardless of the actual nature of the conflict.

We can explain this outcome by noting that there are at least two different cultural narratives within the US military – a dominant and a subordinate. The narrative of conventional warfare and the traditional American way of war has a deeper cultural foundation than the more recent and secondary tasks of stability and support operations, counter-insurgency and post-conflict type operations. In the language of the multi-layered model of culture, the emphasis of the outer layer of artefacts and products, in this case the language and content of doctrine, is easier to change than the deeper cultural layers of norms and values, as well as the basic assumptions of the organization. As long as the basic assumptions and the norms and values of the organization are focused on traditional understandings of warfare, it will remain the dominant cultural narrative. As noted in Iraq, the subordinate cultural narrative of complex peace operations, as articulated in recent doctrines and tactical adjustments, is therefore likely to continue to have limited effects on behaviour. The essentials and significance of the conceptual, doctrinal and structural changes since 2003 is, nevertheless, further discussed in the final section of this chapter.

The patterns of US civil–military relations influence the conduct of operations indirectly by promoting a strategic and organizational military culture that narrowly defines the functional imperative as that of conventional warfighting. As noted in the theoretical section of this book, left to themselves, bureaucracies tend to pursue goals that reinforce their organizational essence, and that bureaucracies also tend to value autonomy even more than expanding tasks into other areas (Lord 1998). Thus, allowing the armed forces to define their own functional imperative, risks having armed forces not fit for purpose in relation to the political leadership's wishes and needs. One should, therefore, not be surprised by the fact that the US military has come to underscore its cultural essence of conventional warfare to the extent it has. However, the failure to apply the principles of complex peace operations, in contexts where they are needed, limits the effectiveness of the US armed forces in such operations. With a political leadership that utilized the US military pre-emptively on an expeditionary basis in order to provide stability and democratization, the US military is clearly not fit for purpose. It is, however, equally clear that the US patterns of civil–military relations provide excellent forces for conventional large-scale warfare.

In conclusion, the UK and the US cases confirm a causal link between different patterns of civil–military relations and strategic culture. The causal mechanisms identified between the two variables are the cost of monitoring and controlling the armed forces as well as the related mechanism of who decides the nature of the functional imperative. The following section compares the findings of the studies of US and UK operations in Iraq in order to complete the indirect causal chain between certain patterns of civil–military relations and the conduct and effectiveness of operations in complex peace operations.

The dependent variable: the conduct and effectiveness of operations in Iraq

The nature of civil–military relations affects the tactical behaviour in Iraq, both directly and indirectly. Mission interpretation, strategic planning, rules of engagement and direct orders are examples of direct influence from the civil–military interface. However, the conduct of operations of US and British troops is more a result of tradition, culture and training – to some extent indirectly influenced by the nature of civil–military relations as described above.

The British forces in Iraq effectively adjusted their tactical behaviour to the context of complex peace operations, as that is the cultural preference of the British military. With speed and relative ease the British troops transitioned from the invasion phase mode of operations into a post-conflict mode. On a positive note, the hearts and minds approach, minimum use of force, and the firm, but friendly, foot patrolling in Basra contributed to an early level of trust among the local population. Moreover, during the combat phase, as well as during the more violent episodes of the post-conflict phase, the British armed forces also successfully applied tactics with the larger political aims in mind, employed the hearts and minds approach of minimum use of force, and, thereby, minimized unnecessary casualties and damage to civilian property.

However, a number of negative aspects also emerged in the analysis. At the tactical level the principles of civil–military co-operation and unity of effort were violated. A surprisingly low level of cultural understanding was also displayed early in the campaign. The British military also focused on security sector reform during the post-conflict phase and neglected the traditional civilian aspects of governance and economic reconstruction. By disregarding these aspects of post-conflict operations, the British failed to produce notable improvements in the daily lives of ordinary Iraqis. Thus, the British occupation never gained legitimacy, and the hearts and minds of the local population were never won. The analysis showed that there was no joint civil–military planning to address these issues, resulting in a rift between the different agencies involved. At the strategic level, the British interagency system was weakened by the presidential-style leadership of Prime Minister Blair, and by the need for secrecy in the planning process, which led to a smaller circle of involved people and committees than normally. This was a factor in the serious underestimation of the security situation in post-war Iraq, and the corresponding limits of post-conflict planning and operations.

A report by Human Rights Watch (2003) noted that the level of post-conflict policing in Basra was not extensive enough, and that the early consent for British operations, gained by professional tactical behaviour, was quickly lost. The impact of British troops was too limited to create adequate security for the local population, or for civilian organizations that should have been involved in the rebuilding of the political and economic functions of Iraq. Neither the operational effects of security and stability nor the political aims of democratization and economic reconstruction have, therefore, been achieved four years into the campaign.

In sum, the British misinterpreted the requirements of the campaign in Iraq and initially focused most energy and resources on a conventional operation, despite the normal conceptualization of war and peace as a gradual scale in different shades of grey, and the cultural preference for small wars and counter-insurgency. After the invasion phase, the British military nevertheless quickly reinterpreted and readjusted its operations and alleviated the problems in cultural understanding. However, the initial misinterpretation of the campaign in Iraq may be a reason why the British violated their principle of close civil–military co-operation at the national strategic level as well as in the field.

There was also a missing link between the tactical operations on the ground and the operational and strategic effects that were sought to be achieved. The quick troop reduction from 46,000 during major combat operations to 8,600 at the end of May 2004 exacerbated this problem. The troop reductions, in the face of a deteriorating security situation, have highlighted a limited interest in, or understanding of, the political aims of the operation as well as the limited physical capabilities of the British armed forces. There are simply not enough troops to maintain rotations of more than 40,000 soldiers over a longer period of time – the time that the achievement of the political aims in Iraq would involve. Especially not while being heavily involved in Afghanistan as well. The British patterns of civil–military relations, involving low-cost civilian monitoring and control of the armed forces, have, therefore, failed in this regard. Without the proper resources to achieve the strategic aims, it does not matter how well-adjusted the tactical behaviour is.

In the US military, the strategic context of complex peace operations has been treated as an irritating deviation from the kind of wars that it thinks it should be fighting. The US military has, therefore, found it difficult to adjust its tactics to post-conflict operations after the fall of Saddam Hussein's regime. The US troops were neither mentally prepared nor trained for complex peace operations. Instead, the US military resorted to a mixture of conventional warfare tactics based on firepower and technology, and the ineffective peacekeeping tactics, with emphasis on force protection, displayed several times during the 1990s. In short, the US patterns of civil–military relations have, in the context of Iraq, failed to provide armed forces with the appropriate structure, culture and doctrine for effective conduct of operations. Most of the principles of counter-insurgency and complex peace operations have been violated by the US troops in Iraq. Arguably, the most serious flaw was interpreting the campaign in conventional terms, thereby failing to prepare for the complex reality on the ground. The dualistic conceptualization of war and peace and the cultural preferences for conventional warfare meant that the most challenging tasks in Iraq – the stabilization, occupation and reconstruction of the country – were lost in the planning of the operations.

While a number of positive exceptions in US conduct of operations can be found, and while the US military has adapted well during the surge of 2007, the general verdict is that the US forces not only lack cultural sensitivity and understanding, but also have little appreciation of how the political aims of the operation must be reflected in their behaviour on the ground. Lack of cultural awareness, in combination with the US approach to maximize the use of force, often served to alienate much of the local population and, therefore, undermined the coalition's goals. While this is most obvious in the well-exposed incidences of criminal behaviour, such as the abuse in Iraqi prisons, the bigger concern is the heavy-handed and less known routine work of US forces, condoned by the chain of command (Varhola 2004). The failure to achieve the political aims of the campaign, the number of dead soldiers and civilians (on both sides) as well as recent changes in training and doctrine in order to overcome the worst problems in Iraq are testament to the fact that the US conduct of operations, as prescribed by US strategic culture, has not been effective. It is worth stressing that the US cultural problem in relation to complex peace operations is not confined to the military. The entire political system and security apparatus share the problem of analysing conflicts in traditional interstate terms of war and peace, defeat and victory as well as friends and enemies.

In conclusion, the patterns of civil–military relations, via different functional imperatives, and the American and British ways of war as intervening variables have had a significant impact on the two countries' conduct and effectiveness of operations in Iraq. The British have conducted their operation more in line with what is considered best practice in complex peace operations. British forces have adhered to the principle of hearts and minds operations, involving minimum use of force, firm, but friendly, foot patrolling and interaction with the local population. At the same time, the British violated the principles of civil–military cooperation as well as unity of effort and command. The US troops have used heavy-handed conventional tactics with emphasis on firepower and technology. Both countries misinterpreted the type of conflict they were getting involved in, and prepared for more or less conventional warfare, giving little thought to the post-conflict phase. While the British troops were quickly able to adjust tactics to the demands of post-conflict operations, it took the US military and administration a long time before they even acknowledged the insurgency – let alone adjusted the tactical behaviour of US troops in the field.

In relation to the theoretical framework of this book, the indirect impact of civil–military relations on the conduct and effectiveness of operations is, thereby, supported by the case studies. However, with respect to the hypothesis, arguing that integration should lead to effectiveness, some aspects of the British failure in Iraq as well as the positive adjustments of US behaviour in Iraq must be further explored. This is done in the concluding section of this chapter.

It should also be noted that the indirect effect is the more intangible of the two causal chains between the independent variables of civil–military relations and the dependent variable of certain conduct and effectiveness of operations. The amount of variables involved in determining the structure, training and culture of the armed forces – what this book grouped together under the concept of strategic culture – is numerous and the civil–military dimension is but one, albeit important, factor. However, the case studies have traced the causal processes and found a number of important causal mechanisms between the patterns of civil–military relations and the intervening variable of strategic culture. The most significant is the nature and strength of civilian monitoring and control of the armed forces, which determines who decides the functional imperative of the armed forces. The interpretation of and adjustment to the functional imperative is, thereafter, an important factor in determining a country's way of war.

The direct effect of civil–military relations

As argued above, the hypothesis of this book created a direct causal effect of certain patterns of civil–military relations on operational conduct and effectiveness, which was derived from lessons learned and principles of best practice in complex peace operations as well as from command and control theory. Two related strands of direct civil–military impact on the conduct of operations are evident from the findings of the two case studies. First, the patterns of civil–military relations will have an impact on the conduct of operations by providing the structure and culture of the arena in which strategic aims are set, conflicts are analysed, and operational planning made. Second, the civil–military interface is an important section of the command chain during operations, and must, therefore, function as frictionless as the rest of the chain of command in order to provide timely and accurate decisions. The sections below elaborate further on these arguments.

The civil–military interface as an arena for strategic and operational planning

It is worth repeating that the civil–military interface is the arena in which conflicts are analysed, strategies made and operational assessments and plans approved. In short, the civil–military interface is where the objectives, strategies, size, content and equipment of the forces sent to the theatre of operations are decided. The patterns of civil–military relations – cultural and structural – therefore, have an important impact on the conduct and effectiveness of operations. The section on best practices in complex peace operations emphasized the need for comprehensive approaches that included all aspects of national power, essentially requiring close civil–military co-operation and co-ordination in the planning process. This is, in other words, the first causal mechanism of the direct causal relationship between patterns of civil–military relations and the conduct of operations.

British civil–military relations, involving relatively well-established interagency structures and civil–military integration, should, according to the hypothesis of this book, create comprehensive strategies involving all aspects of national power. However, in the case of Iraq, British interagency structures proved to be weaker than expected. The presidential style of Prime Minister Blair as well as the need for secrecy in the planning process led the British Government to partially abandon the committee system for a more intimate group involved in the policy-making. The traditional British way of war at the strategic level was, thereby, abandoned. The *Review of Intelligence on Weapons of Mass Destruction* (2004) blamed this un-British way of conducting business for the misinterpretation of intelligence data and policy-making in the run-up to the war.

The British Government and armed forces were the junior partners in the campaign and had limited possibilities to influence the planning of post-conflict operations. However, the British shared many of the flawed planning assumptions regarding post-Saddam Iraq. The British Government has, moreover, continually argued that it did influence the Americans on several points and that it certainly took part in the campaign planning. The British Chief of the Defence Staff has also made it clear that he would have raised his voice if he had not believed in the strategy in Iraq (Walker 2005). However, the British expressed concerns regarding the post-conflict planning process as early as the summer of 2002. The British also planned the post-conflict phase further than the Pentagon and made some post-conflict goals public on the eve of battle. It is, therefore, reasonable to assume that the British would have placed more emphasis on the post-conflict phase, had they been the lead nation in this campaign. In the end, additional British post-conflict planning was of little use as the total British contribution to the campaign was so limited, as was the British area of responsibility. Further consequences of the failure to utilize the interagency system to its full potential are discussed below in the section on the civil–military interface in the chain of command.

In the US case, the patterns of civil–military relations involve weak interagency structures and a civil–military divide within the Department of Defense. The failure to provide a comprehensive approach to the campaign in Iraq is, therefore, less surprising than in the British case. Planning of post-conflict operations was based on a number of false assumptions about the level of consent from the Iraqi population and the level of violence after the fall of Saddam Hussein's regime. The complexity and difficulty of the post-conflict phase were, thereby, underestimated and the planning was inadequate. During the post-conflict planning process, there were, however, plenty of voices who raised appropriate concerns regarding the assumptions and planning of the post-conflict phase, but these voices were effectively left outside the planning process. The limited amount of input in operational planning, due to poor civil–military integration within the Pentagon, and poor interagency structures meant that a small number of military planners, with Defense Secretary Rumsfeld's blessing, were allowed to interpret and plan Operation Iraqi Freedom in strictly traditional military terms, essentially leaving the post-conflict phase aside. Nora Bensahel accurately argues that 'the fundamental problem was not the content of these particular assumptions, but the fact that a *single* set of assumptions drove US government planning efforts, and no contingency plans were developed in case that one scenario did not occur' (2006: 458). Not only was the result that the coalition had too few troops in Iraq to secure the country after the fall of the old regime, the American troops that were there were given little guidance or direction, and were, as the previous section noted, neither trained nor prepared for counter-insurgency-type operations.

The Presidential Directive that assigned responsibility for post-conflict operations to the Department of Defense was a key mistake as the DoD had neither the personnel nor the expertise that was required in order to lead civilian reconstruction programmes on its own (Bensahel 2006: 470; Zinni 2003). While the US Government contains substantial expertise on post-conflict operations, it showed in Iraq that it lacks an effective mechanism for combining that expertise into a comprehensive and coherent approach. The decision to put the DoD and the Office of the Secretary of Defense in charge of post-conflict operations was in accordance with the US political culture which tends to divide and assign issues into the departmental stovepipes. The decision was also made in order to create unity of command. However, the result was the opposite, with all other departments and agencies effectively shut out of the planning process. The decision, therefore, meant that the military strategic culture of conventional warfare was allowed to taint the entire planning process. The lack of experience in post-conflict operations within the DoD meant that it never occurred to the military planners that the post-conflict phase might be the only real test of US capability in Iraq. The lack of experience, the competitive political culture, the weak interagency structures, and the distrust between the Departments of State and Defense meant that the expertise that other departments and agencies could provide was effectively excluded from the planning process, and no interagency planning group with appropriate authority was created in order to ensure the inclusion of all relevant strands of information and expertise.

As discussed in the theory chapter, the lack of civil–military co-operation at the strategic level is often further exacerbated in the field of operations. In the US case, the failure to co-locate the military and civilian headquarters in Iraq reveals the limited culture of civil–military co-operation at the operational and tactical levels. This was done despite the fact that such co-location had recently been successfully tested in the context of Afghanistan (Parmly 2005). There was, in other words, a violation of the principle of unity of command. This caused unclear chains of command between the civilian and military aspects of the operation. Co-operation difficulties between the civilian and military agencies in Iraq also led to insufficient unity of effort between these actors. Thus, in the US case, the divided patterns of civil–military relations have created a stovepiped and sequenced planning and execution of operations – completely contrary to the comprehensive approach required for complex peace operations.

In both cases, the civil–military interface failed in its role as the arena for strategic and operational planning. Limited interagency integration and civil–military co-ordination led to poor decisions and incomprehensive plans.

The civil–military interface as an important link in the chain of command

The literature on command and control has emphasized the continued, even increased, relevance of mission command in the context of complex peace operations. However, for effective implementation of mission command there has to be a high level of trust and mutual understanding along the entire chain of command, not least in the civil–military interface, where political aims are translated into operational goals and activities in the field. This involves giving appropriate authority to whatever planning structures are in place. Thus, a civil–military interface that lacks the necessary mutual trust and understanding is unlikely to provide an effective headquarters during complex peace operations.

The British system combines a centralized political system with a high level of mission type command in the civil–military interface. The interagency committee system and the civil–military integration within the Ministry of Defence create interpersonal trust based on familiarity and reciprocity. Officials from the different departments learn to trust each other and develop a sense of understanding despite possible differences in standpoints and opinions. Finally, interpersonal trust is further enhanced by the fact that British officers and civil servants are traditionally recruited from the same social groups, even the same schools. They may know each other personally, share each other's values, or at least trust the background and schooling of their respective counterparts. The interagency structure of the British system normally provides for the inclusion of all relevant actors and fields of expertise. The political leadership can, therefore, rest assured that all aspects of operational planning are considered within the committee system, thereby minimizing the risk of political micro-management and interference.

However, in the case of Iraq, lack of trust in the interagency committee system led Prime Minister Blair to centralize and reduce the decision-making circle – thereby contributing to the failure to create a comprehensive civil–military approach to operations. The failure to activate the interagency apparatus at the strategic level also had consequences in the field. Civil–military co-ordination and co-operation in the field are difficult to achieve without a comprehensive approach and clear directives from top levels of the chain of command. Without the comprehensive approach and joint directives from the strategic level, operations were, as in the US case, instead controlled in the institutional stovepipes of the individual agencies. Therefore, in the British case, little joint civil–military planning took place in the field, and the different agencies found it difficult to co-operate and co-ordinate their activities. The British way of war, involving civil–military co-operation and unity of effort, was, thereby, disregarded. The lack of a comprehensive approach and of clear objectives also made it difficult for the British to translate tactical successes into operational and strategic effects. There was no clear overarching aim or strategy to refer to.

As previously noted, the US civil–military interface is based on the American political culture of checks and balances, competition and conflict. This structure is not conducive to the mutual trust and understanding of mission command. Individual character-based trust, formed out of social similarities and shared moral codes, is lacking as civilians and officers generally differ politically and culturally, and are recruited from different social groups. Process-based trust, founded on experiences of reciprocity, fails as the interagency structures and the civil–military integration within the DoD are not extensive enough to create trust based on positive experiences of working together. Moreover, the high number of political appointees within the government departments creates a higher turnaround of people than a professional civil service, thereby missing another possibility of positive personal reciprocity. Institutional trust, flowing from institutional arrangements that create and sustain trustworthy behaviours, is again lacking due to the political system of checks and balances. The institutions of the US system are constructed to promote competition and mutual distrust – they are simply not supposed to create trust.

The civil–military interface, therefore, functions poorly in relation to the principles of mission command. While the divided tradition of civil–military relations leads the political leadership to make mission type orders, the system does not include enough trust and understanding to delegate appropriate authority to subordinates. The results are micro-management and political interference in purely military areas of expertise. Further results involve military operations with limited understanding of the political aims of operations. In both cases, the outcome is decreased effectiveness of operations. Another aspect of effective command and control is the importance of clear objectives. In complex peace operations, these objectives should be the result of comprehensive approaches to the operation, which leads to overarching aims and strategies.

In Iraq, the US planning process was, as already discussed, seriously hampered by the weak interagency system and the divided civil–military relations within the Pentagon. Mistrust between the Departments of Defense and State effectively stovepiped the planning of post-conflict operations, leaving out most expertise outside the Pentagon. Moreover, according to the military leadership, Defense Secretary Rumsfeld micro-managed the planning process, and thereby effectively reduced the number of troops that were considered necessary for the operation (Woodward 2004). During the campaign, the top levels of the chain of command clearly did not trust the commanders in the field. Interference from the top levels of the Pentagon took place, both regarding the military operations in Fallujah as well as a number of issues regarding the civilian reconstruction handled by the Coalition Provisional Authority (Bremer and McConnell 2005;

Bensahel 2006). The US system thereby initially failed to provide adequate plans and directives for the post-conflict phase of operations, and when it did, it was in the form of direct rather than mission type command.

In conclusion, the findings of the two case studies support the hypothesis that the patterns of civil–military relations have a direct impact on the conduct and effectiveness of operations. The main causal mechanism is the level of interagency co-operation and civil–military integration within the defence ministries, creating a level of trust that affects the leadership quality of the civil–military interface, and thereby the quality of strategic assessment and planning. The US system of weak interagency structures and divided civil–military structures within the Defense Department does not produce sufficient levels of trust within the civil–military interface, nor down through the chain of command. The results include stovepiped decision-making, incomprehensive plans as well as micro-management by the top levels of command, which were also the results in the context of Iraq. The British structures of close interagency co-operation and integrated civil–military structures create high levels of trust. These normally lead to mission type command within the civil–military interface as well as close civil–military co-operation and unity of effort in the pursuit of the political aims. However, in the case of Iraq, the British administration failed to employ the interagency system and thereby violated a number of principles of complex peace operations, making many of the same mistakes as the US administration.

Concluding questions and challenges

The observations of the case studies have produced two important questions that, because of their potential inconsistency with theory, require further deliberation. First, why are recent changes taking place in US doctrine and operational conduct, despite a relatively constant pattern of civil–military relations? What is the significance of these changes? Second, why have the British failed to operate according to the principles of complex peace operations, despite their integrated pattern of civil–military relations and such warfare clearly being a central part of the British way of war? The discussion below seeks to explain these findings within the theoretical framework of this book. Finally, a number of methodological challenges are addressed in this section.

Explaining US improvements

US changes in doctrine and operational conduct began as early as 2004 and since the beginning of 2007 they have been profound. However, as already noted, the US military has historically often adapted successfully in the field but has then failed to institutionalize the lessons after the end of the operation (Weigley 1973: 36). While repeating the mistakes made in Iraq may seem intellectually impossible, the historical failures and the hesitant and unsettled manner, in which the Pentagon has so far engaged with counter-insurgency, beg the question whether the US military has really learned its lesson this time. Are the quick and innovative but still limited reforms in terms of doctrine, training and institutional changes comprehensive enough, and are they sustainable within an organizational culture that still emphasizes conventional warfare? Are we witnessing a cultural shift within the US armed forces or is it merely the logical reaction to operational and tactical challenges in the specific contexts of Iraq and Afghanistan?

David Ucko (2008) convincingly argues that in order to address this question and understand the significance of current processes, one must look beyond the mere structural innovations, doctrinal changes and tactical adjustments, and look at these changes within the wider institutional context of the Pentagon, and the traditional US way of war. 'The DoD is a highly conformist institution, complicating efforts to introduce a new way of thinking, particularly one that goes against the organization's prevailing logic and culture' (Ucko 2008: 308). As noted in the analysis of the American way of war, the US military's institutional orthodoxy emphasizes conventional large-scale warfare over small wars, counter-insurgency and what are called 'operations other than war'. 'Any attempt to displace this orthodoxy has to occur with the consent of the senior brass, who would thereby devalue their own experience and standing' (Ucko 2008: 308). Indeed, Fred Kaplan noted in August 2007 that 'six years into this war, the armed forces – not just the Army, but also the Air Force, Navy and Marines – have changed almost nothing about the way their promotional systems and their entire bureaucracies operate' (Kaplan 2007).

It is premature to say with any confidence whether the US military has gone through a major cultural change and whether counter-insurgency will become a central priority in the future. While an impressive learning process has been driven by a group of officers within the DoD, they have also faced much resistance from within the military and the DoD. In the words of Ucko:

> Whether through inertia or conviction, large swathes of the DoD continue to view all 'operations other than war' as an afterthought to the US military's primary mission: major combat operations – and this in spite of the threat of terrorism, the US military's involvement in Afghanistan and Iraq and the significant difficulties faced in these campaigns.
>
> (2008: 299)

The fact is that the US military remains structured for conventional war, and that serious efforts to change the force structure or budgetary priorities have not been made (Ucko 2008: 310). Moreover, the US military's capability to learn and institutionalize counter-insurgency warfare is far from the only factor when increasing US capabilities in complex peace operations. Arguably, the more pressing challenge is the lack of integrated capability and capacity of the civilian agencies involved in complex peace operations (Gates 2007: i). Again, attempts to seriously increase civilian capacity for the planning and implementation of post-conflict type operations, for example, within the Office of the Coordinator for Reconstruction and Stabilization, have not been supported by the necessary legislation and funding from Congress.

In conclusion, the strong cultural preferences for conventional large-scale battles, in combination with the historical failures to institutionalize lessons beyond these preferences, make a major shift in US military culture questionable despite impressive adjustments in Iraq. This view is strengthened by the hesitant changes within the DoD, and the failure to support the strengthening of the necessary civilian capacities, and to seriously restructure the armed forces for different types of complex peace operations. This book would also add that a true cultural and operational shift should be reflected in changes in the structure and culture of civil–military relations in the US.

However, we should also explore the possibility that the changes from 2007 do signify a long-term shift in the American way of war. How can such a possible shift be explained within the theoretical framework of this book? One explanation is found in the strategic interaction within the civil–military interface regarding the functional imperative. Recent operations in Afghanistan and Iraq have highlighted that the military's traditional definition of the functional imperative as well as the continued adaptations of the military to that imperative are increasingly outdated. The US military has had to face a number of upsets in the field. Therefore, a tipping point in the strategic interaction between the civil and military leaderships should be expected when it is beyond doubt that the American way of war is flawed in the contemporary strategic context and when the organizational status of the armed forces decreases as a result.

With the competence, structure and training of the armed forces seriously questioned by the political leadership, by younger members of the military establishment, and most importantly, by public opinion, the cost of civilian monitoring is likely to decrease and the civilian interpretation of the functional imperative may prevail in the negotiations. At that point serious reconsideration of the American way of war will take place. As noted in the analysis of US doctrine, the increased importance of operations beyond the traditional functional imperative is starting to show within doctrine. As of yet, the contents of doctrines on operations other than war have nevertheless not had an impact on the American way of war, signalling a continued shirking of the military. It should also be noted that, in Vietnam, the same type and scope of failure and the same limited instances of successful adaptation in the field towards the end of the campaign did not produce any cultural or structural changes in the long run.

Another aspect of current changes within the US national security apparatus towards irregular warfare and operations other than war are structural changes in the civil–military interface at the strategic level. Increased interagency structures are sought, but still of limited scale and effect. An example beyond the already mentioned Office of the Coordinator for Reconstruction and Stabilization (S/CRS) is the debate regarding the need for a 'war czar' – a high-powered advisor to the President who oversees and co-ordinates the wars in Iraq and Afghanistan. However, if we were to see the development of a new definition or construction of the functional imperative, and a simultaneous increase in interagency co-operation and civil–military integration within the DoD, it would certainly support the theoretical framework of this book.

Explaining British failure in Iraq

In Iraq, the British not only failed to conceptualize the campaign accurately, they also violated a number of principles of complex peace operations and what in this book has been described as the British way of war. With relatively well-integrated civil–military structures, and with a strategic culture geared towards counter-insurgency warfare, why did the British fail in Iraq? First, it should be noted that failure in counter-insurgency is not uncommon in the history of the British military. The British often get it wrong, adapt and muddle through. To some extent the same has happened in Iraq. However, what has in the past been the British strength is the quick strategic and tactical adaptation to different realities on the ground. In Iraq, important aspects of adaptation, most importantly regarding the lack of a comprehensive approach of civil–military co-operation and co-ordination, never took place.

The fact that the British were the junior partner in a coalition is certainly part of the answer to this contradiction. As the junior partner the British were not mainly responsible for strategy and, therefore, had to subscribe to the US approach. However, an operation that contradicts the very foundation of the British way of war should have raised more debate had it not been supported by the political and military leaders in the UK. The junior partner theory is, therefore, not sufficient as an explanation. Instead, the hypothesis of this book, as well as the empirical findings, argue that the failure to integrate the civil–military and interagency structures at the strategic level has consequences throughout the entire chain of command. In the case of Iraq, the presidential-style leadership of Prime Minister Blair, as well as the need for secrecy in the run-up to the war, led to the circumscription of the interagency committee system. The result was an un-British approach to the planning and execution of operations. The circumscription created weak strategic direction, failed to produce a comprehensive plan, and led to the violation of tactical principles in the field. The section on mission command theory emphasized the importance of mutual trust as well as clear intent. Thus, without clear and comprehensive direction from London, the normal level of institutional trust throughout the interagency chain of command also suffered. In sum, the British integrated form of civil–military relations was violated, changing the independent variable of the causal chain. British interagency structures are simply no longer as integrated as described in Chapter 6, and perhaps the structures described in that chapter are also inadequate in the contemporary context. The high level of structural changes in the interagency arena since the beginning of the war in Iraq implies that this is indeed the view in Britain. At any rate, the outcome of the changed patterns of civil–military relations in the context of Iraq has been decreased effectiveness in the field of operations.

The failure of the British in Iraq also shows the dangers in over-relying on institutional theory. Despite what can be described as relatively good institutional set-ups for complex peace operations, other factors, such as the complex strategic realities in Iraq, as well as the sheer lack of British troops in the southern parts of Iraq, meant that the expected outcome was not reached. A number of positive aspects in the British operations in Iraq, such as the accurate tactical behaviour of British troops, still support the hypothesis of the book – integration leads to effectiveness.

Methodological challenges

To what extent have the case studies of US and British operations in Iraq been effective in testing the hypothesis of this book? The case studies, as well as the comparative analysis, have led to a number of interesting observations and conclusions in the support of the hypothesis. However, what is the explanatory power that can be expected of the choice of methodology in this book? Ideal case comparison requires identification of two cases that are similar in all but one independent variable and that differ in the outcome. This is called 'controlled comparison' and allows the researcher to employ experimental logic in making a causal inference regarding the impact that the variable has on the outcome (George and Bennett 2004). However, as with most case comparisons in the field of social science, the cases of US and British operations in Iraq are far less than ideal. Three specific challenges to the choice of cases were identified in the theory chapter: the different operational contexts of the US and British forces in Iraq; the fact that the British were the junior partner in the coalition as well as the fact that unfinished operations nullified the important variable of outcome in the evaluation of operational effectiveness. These challenges had the potential to weaken the explanatory power of the research design and, therefore, deserve further deliberation in hindsight of the case studies.

The first challenge is derived from the fact that British and American troops operate within quite different contexts in Iraq. The Shia-dominated British area of responsibility in the south of the country is considered less threatening than the Sunni-dominated areas in the American area of responsibility. Can the different conduct and effectiveness of operations in Iraq be the result of contextual differences rather than the civil–military aspect used in this book? It is certainly possible, but a glance at the literature on the performance of US and British troops in past complex peace operations supports the argument of this book. US troops, whether in the difficult conditions of Vietnam and Somalia, or the more benign contexts of Bosnia and Kosovo, have operated in a similar manner, as that exhibited in Iraq. Equally, the British display of political understanding, minimum use of force and flexibility is a familiar phenomenon from the different contexts of Malaya, Northern Ireland, Kosovo and Sierra Leone. The studies of British and US performance in these disparate cases imply that the findings of this study cannot be explained by the different contexts in which the troops were operating. The US and British armed forces most often operate according to their respective ways of war, despite great variation in the contextual variables (Nagl 2002; Avant 1994; Cassidy 2004; McInnes 1996; Prins 2002).

The fact that the British military operated in Iraq as the junior partner in an American-led coalition constitutes the second challenge. It has, therefore, been difficult to analyse the effectiveness of British strategic thinking in the context of Iraq. An example is the intriguing question as to whether the planning and execution of the post-conflict phase would have been more comprehensive and effective had it been a British-led operation? Although we can never answer that question for sure, the effective and well co-ordinated British operations in Malaya and Sierra Leone would suggest such a possibility. This suggestion is further supported by the fact that the British, despite being the junior partner in the coalition, not only expressed concern about the limitation of US planning of the post-conflict phase, they also went further than the Americans did in the planning of post-conflict operations by creating a list of post-conflict objectives.

Finally, the third challenge is that the outcome of operations is an important variable in the analysis of effectiveness that has not been available in the analyses of US and British operations in Iraq. However, as previously argued, effectiveness – especially in relation to efficiency – is much more than outcome. Rather than focusing on the outcome of operations in Iraq, the conduct of operations has, therefore, been measured against what the literature on complex peace operations describes as a number of themes of best practice in terms of effectiveness. This approach has proved effective in that the thematic analyses have provided useful information and increased our understanding of effectiveness in Iraq. The findings have demonstrated that the British conduct of operations, although involving a number of violated principles of complex peace operations, has been more effective than the conventional approach applied by the Americans, and that some of the violations of these principles can be explained by the fact that the British interagency system was circumscribed in the case of Iraq. Looking briefly at the outcome of operations, and notwithstanding the fact that the British have operated within a less hostile context, the number of casualties, the early withdrawal of troops, security sector reform and the handover of responsibility to Iraqi authorities support these findings.

10 Conclusion

The aim of this book has been to contribute to a large body of literature that seeks to improve operational conduct and effectiveness of the military and other relevant agencies in the contemporary strategic context. More specifically, an original theoretical contribution has been made by studying the civil–military aspects of effectiveness and how different patterns of civil–military relations affect the operational conduct and effectiveness of states and their armed forces in the most likely and important operations of the contemporary strategic context – complex peace operations.

The theoretical framework developed in the book argues that the nature of civil–military relations affect the conduct and effectiveness of operations in at least two important ways: *directly*, by providing the highest levels in the chain of command – the level where strategic aims are set and operational plans made, and *indirectly* by being the arena in which decisions regarding size, culture, equipment and doctrine of the armed forces are made. The civil–military interface is not only a factor that contributes to determine the nature of the armed forces, it also determines the quality of strategic and operational leadership when these armed forces are deployed. The nature of civil–military relations is, thereby, an important factor, among many others, when seeking to understand military relations in contemporary warfare.

The main argument is that in the contemporary strategic context of complex peace operations, integrated civil–military approaches are necessary for effectiveness in achieving the often far-reaching political aims of democratization and economic development. Such integrated, or comprehensive, approaches to operations also require integrated institutions at the national strategic level, and at the international organizational level in cases of multinational operations within different organizational frameworks. There are two main reasons why integrated civil–military structures at the strategic level provide better results in complex peace operations. First, the indirect impact means that integrated structures provide more accurate and up-to-date interpretations of, and adjustment to, the functional imperative of the armed forces. This means that the instruments of national power, not least the military, are better suited to the tasks of the contemporary strategic context. Second, the direct impact of integrated structures is that they provide more inclusive command and control structures at the strategic level, which means that all relevant actors in complex operations are co-ordinated through integrated planning and execution of operations – providing a so-called comprehensive approach to operations. The practical application of civil–military relations in the operational chain of command is in the book interpreted as a form of mission command. A key feature of successful mission command is, according to command and control theory, mutual trust and understanding across the civil–military divide. Integrated structures are more likely to create such trust and understanding through experiences of reciprocity.

The book has tested the outcome of two different patterns of civil–military relations – the divided US approach and the more integrated British approach. A number of significant findings of these two cases were made.

The effectiveness of the divided and integrated patterns of civil–military relations

The US divided approach to civil–military relations fails to achieve effectiveness in the context of complex peace operations. The limited interagency structures and the civil–military divide within the Department of Defense do not produce armed forces 'fit for purpose'. The civil–military divide, and the high costs of civilian monitoring of the armed forces mean that the US military is still allowed to define its own raison d'être in fighting and winning the nation's major wars, and is essentially organized, trained and equipped for that purpose. The US military, therefore, has not adapted well to the contemporary strategic context of complex peace operations.

The civil–military divide of the US case has also failed to produce mutual trust and understanding within the civil–military interface, which is essential for effective command and control in the context of complex operations. The operational planning process is stovepiped and highly exclusive, and, thereby, fails to include important expertise and advice from all relevant departments and agencies. The lack of trust in the civil–military interface also means that the political leadership, when it exercises control, does so by micro-managing and interfering in strictly military affairs. These deficiencies were confirmed in the case of Iraq. It is interesting, however, that the current changes in doctrine and operational conduct in Iraq are also accompanied by structural changes in Washington, such as the creation of the Coordinator for Reconstruction and Stabilization whose mission is to lead, coordinate and institutionalize US Government civilian capacity to prevent or prepare for post-conflict situations.

The integrated form of civil–military relations employed in the British system has provided for armed forces that are better adjusted for complex peace operations. A key facilitator is the fact that the British patterns of civil–military relations involve low-cost civilian control and monitoring of the armed forces, which, in stark contrast to the US, has not only allowed the political leadership to define the functional imperative of the armed forces, but also forced the military to adjust structurally and culturally to that imperative. The British approach emphasizes flexibility, minimum use of force and civil–military co-operation –

which are all considered essentials for effective conduct of complex peace operations in the contemporary context. The relatively extensive level of interagency co-operation and co-ordination through the committee system includes most relevant actors in the planning and execution of operations. The British case nevertheless also involves some bureaucratic infighting and stove-piping at the interagency level. More impressive is that the far-reaching civil–military integration within the Ministry of Defence provides mutual trust and understanding in the chain of command, leading to the implementation of mission-type command at the strategic and operational levels of command.

This was, however, only partly confirmed by the case study of British operations in Iraq. The British did not operate in full accordance with the British way of war and the principles of complex peace operations. The circumscription of the interagency structures can be interpreted as a change in the independent variable, meaning that in the case of Iraq, the British system did not adhere to the integrated approach. Interestingly, of course, the change away from the integrated pattern of civil–military relations also caused a distinct decrease in the effectiveness of British operational conduct. Poor strategic assessment and limited civil–military co-ordination and co-operation in the field were some consequences. In essence, without the integrated patterns of civil–military relations, the British failed to operate according to the British way of war.

In sum, the context of complex peace operations, often involving insurgencies and terrorists seeking to destroy the legitimacy, as well as the gains of operations, and with global media broadcasting every action live into living rooms around the world, the cost of inaccurately applying deadly force may prove politically and militarily disastrous. Extensive and authoritative interagency structures as well as civil–military integration within the Department of Defence are likely to create more trust and mutual understanding in the civil–military interface. They are also more likely to create comprehensive civil–military approaches to, and structures for, the planning and execution of operations, thereby providing higher quality strategic assessment and planning. Integrated civil–military relations with relatively low costs of civilian monitoring are also likely to result in a mutual interpretation of the functional imperative, reflecting the strategic context as well as the immediate needs of the political leadership – armed forces fit for purpose.

Theoretical implications

There are a number of implications of this analysis for theory. First, strategic theory and research on military effectiveness must, to a larger extent than before, include the civil–military dimension. The civil–military dimension has the potential to influence the physical, the conceptual, and the moral factors of military effectiveness, and should, therefore, be part of any analysis of military effectiveness. It can even be asked as to what extent it is relevant to speak of military effectiveness, or 'fighting power', in a context where operations are inherently multidimensional, involving diplomatic, military and economic aspects. A comprehensive view of operational effectiveness is more useful, and the question should be whether a country's entire security apparatus is fit for purpose, and thereby measured against the ambitions of the political leadership's foreign and security policy. This is in stark contrasts to Huntington's view that military performance can only be evaluated in terms of independent military standards, defined by a given functional imperative in conventional warfare. Clearly, a state like the US, with national security depending on international stability and international terrorism, and with high ambitions for spreading democracy, cannot measure its capabilities in strictly military terms, as they are only one part of a larger equation.

Regarding the physical factor of combat power and effectiveness – the means – the findings of this book stress the importance of including civilian assets as well as military ones. The lack of civilian planning structures and civilian professionals capable and available for comprehensive operations is a serious deficiency in most states today. The conceptual factor of effectiveness is in the context of complex peace operations pointless without a comprehensive approach that includes all instruments of national power. Doctrine as well as strategic and operational planning must be adjusted accordingly. The strategic and operational levels of complex peace operations will never have a purely military element, and the political and economic aspects of operations must always be considered. Finally, the moral factor has two interesting civil–military aspects. First, moral strength and effectiveness should be analysed as that of society as a whole – military, political and civil society. When one or more of these three actors falter, the moral strength of the system as a whole diminishes. Second, with operations, where it is of great importance to win the hearts and minds of the local population as well as international society, the moral factor can be seen as a 'weapon' with which to transmit the winning strategic narrative and gain legitimacy for operations. In the age of instant media, and a networked global society, or what Shaw (2005) calls global surveillance, the ability to convey the right message may be more important than any traditional aspect of 'fighting power'.

A second implication for theory concerns the conceptualization of civil–military relations. Traditionally, civil–military relations theory deals with the relationship between the armed forces, the political leadership, and civil society. The practical and operational aspects of this relationship, or what this book calls the direct impact of civil–military relations, are a remarkably understudied area. However, at the same time, there is a field of study that deals with different aspects of civil–military relations in the field of operations, involving civil–military co-operation (CIMIC), disarmament, demobilization and repatriation (DDR) of ex-combatants, and security sector reform (SSR). These fields are inherently interrelated, and instead of two different fields of study, a more comprehensive view of civil–military relations is hereby advocated. When discussing the UN's different functions, a distinction is often drawn between the UN as an 'actor' and the UN as an 'arena' (Berdal 2003a). A similar view of the civil–military interface would be useful. Not only is the civil–military interface the arena in which decisions regarding the size and structure of the armed forces are made, it also needs to be an effective actor in the chain of command during operations.

The third implication for theory also deals with civil–military relations theory. The findings of this book dispute Huntington's notion that the functional imperative of the armed forces is a given and that professional armed forces will automatically adapt to that imperative if given autonomy by the political leadership. In fact, the starting point in the notion that military institutions are a function of the societal and functional imperatives is not very helpful. The functional imperative cannot be treated as a given to which a professional military will automatically be adapted. Instead, the functional imperative is the result of civil–military negotiation based on perceptions of the strategic context, the political ambition in international affairs, as well as the organizational culture of the armed forces.

Peter Feaver's principal agency theory of civil–military relations that treats civil–military relations as an 'ongoing game of strategic interaction' between civilian leaders and military agents is highly useful in analysing these negotiations (Feaver 2003). The US case provides us with an obvious example of the failure to adjust its organizational structure and culture as the functional imperative changes. The strong military culture and the high costs of civilian control of the armed forces mean that the military view of the functional imperative has prevailed despite an obviously changed strategic context that involves numerous new tasks and priorities for the military. Applying Feaver's agency theory helps explain that, in the strategic interaction between the political leadership and the military, the political leadership was not in a strong enough position and therefore failed to exert its power as the principal actor. The British case provides a contrasting example. The strength of the political leadership in relation to the military has meant that the former has been able to define the functional imperative in accordance with British foreign and security policy, and thereby created a civil–military interface and armed forces properly fit for purpose in the contemporary strategic context. However, the difficulty for the military leadership to exert influence has at the same time resulted in the paradox that the British military establishment is undersized and under-funded in relation to the tasks that are asked of it.

Finally, the findings of this book also dispute Huntington's conclusion that military strength and effectiveness are best maximized through objective control of the armed forces, involving a clear divide between the political and military leaderships. Instead, this book supports Janowitz's view of military effectiveness as the result of increased integration of civilian and military actors in order to create mutual trust and understanding. This is also supported by Dandeker's view that the inherent tensions of command and control structures in the contemporary strategic context 'can only be mitigated satisfactorily by trust- and confidence-building measures being installed at the political-military interface' (Dandeker 2006: 241).

Instead of seeing the civil–military problematique as a zero-sum game in which an ideal balance between military strength and democratic civilian control should be found, the field of civil–military relations should, in theory as well as in practice, seek synergetic effects that strengthen both military effectiveness and civilian control. The starting point should, as Feaver (2003) argues, be the ideal of civilian primacy. Thereafter, a mutual understanding of what the functional imperative constitutes is a necessary point of departure for the ongoing game of strategic interaction regarding the structure and culture of the armed forces and the civil–military interface for maximized effectiveness.

Future research directions

The cases explored by this book have been useful for the construction and first tests of an interesting hypothesis of the causal relationship between certain patterns of civil–military relations and military effectiveness in complex peace operations. To further test and refine the hypothesis and the theoretical framework a number of different case studies are of interest and importance. This book used two cases of civil–military relations perceived to be at the extreme ends of what is actually a continuum between divided and integrated structure and culture. Further cases of these extreme ends should be studied in order to test the hypothesis. Such case studies of extreme cases along the continuum of civil–military integration give an opportunity to change a number of variables that may either strengthen or weaken the hypothesis of this book. Studying countries like Sweden, with highly divided civil–military structures, yet a co-operative parliamentary political system and a different geo-strategic position as a small, neutral power, would, therefore, be of great interest for theory. A case study of France, with a relatively similar historical colonial background as the British, yet a very different political system, would also be interesting.

However, future studies should also seek to include cases along the middle sections of the continuum to provide a complete picture of the theoretical framework. The interesting question which can only be answered by looking at further cases is whether outcome – meaning effectiveness in complex peace operations – also follows a continuum as expected, or if there is a tipping point somewhere that creates more of a dualistic outcome – either you are effective or not. Obviously, looking at historical operations with actual outcomes in victory and defeat is beneficial in this respect.

Finally, there are also important methodological variations to be made. Creating a number of variables, such as civil–military integration and strength of civilian control of the armed forces, would provide an opportunity to test the hypothesis of this book with quantitative methods. While Western civil–military relations are generally well enough covered to be quickly included in statistical analyses, more background on civil–military relations in African and Asian cases is often needed.

Policy implications

The policy implications of this book are, to a large extent, derived from the argument that a particular pattern of civil–military relations produces more effective armed forces. The normative ideal in terms of effectiveness in complex peace operations stems from the literature and is supported in this book; operations planned and executed comprehensively with all stakeholders and instruments of national power involved; armed forces and civilian counterparts on the ground operating jointly with enough flexibility, as well as political and cultural understanding, to adjust activities in accordance with contextual peculiarities rather than doctrine and drilled exercises. This book argues that such conduct of complex peace operations requires civil–military relations involving strong enough civilian control to define the functional imperative of the armed forces, civil–military integration and mutual understanding in order to produce armed forces that are fit for purpose, extensive interagency co-operation in order to plan and execute operations effectively, and a culture of trust and mutual understanding required for effective command and control during operations. What can be done within the strategic-level civil–military interfaces of different countries in order to create the structural and cultural fundamentals that are needed in order to achieve such effectiveness?

Before discussing any implications in detail, it should be emphasized that all political systems are unique and that solutions in one country may not be applicable to other countries and systems. Clearly the political systems and cultures of the UK and the US are very different. Both are successful democratic systems, including certain strengths and weaknesses. Drawing policy implications that are not sensitive to the foundations of a nation's political system risks being futile and potentially dangerous. An example discussed several times within this study is the US system of checks and balances. While making interagency co-operation difficult, the system of checks and balances constitutes one of the most important fundamentals of US democracy, and should, therefore, be treated as a given. However, the fact that all political systems are different does not mean that lessons from other systems are impossible to implement, it simply means that lessons from across boarders must be adjusted and implemented in accordance with the cultural circumstances of the system. With a sound understanding of the fundamentals and peculiarities of each system, the lessons of this book may, therefore, well be implemented in very different contexts. The following section discusses some of the more important policy implications.

First, the multitude of tasks and the complexity of the political aims in contemporary irregular warfare mean that the different instruments of national power must be involved and co-ordinated for effective operations. This requires well-functioning interagency structures as well as a co-operative working culture of trust and mutual understanding. Many commentators advocate a new more powerful interagency structure that better co-ordinates policy and operational implementation across all departments of the government. General Zinni (2003) draws upon the lessons from Somalia and argues that all aspects of operations have to be co-ordinated.

I've seen the disasters in Somalia and elsewhere when coordination mechanisms fail. Those mechanisms for coordination have to be solid, they have to be established from the lowest remote points on the ground to the highest decisions that may be made.

Although the Goldwater–Nichols legislation successfully dealt with a number of problems in the 1980s, the DoD is, according to a CSIS report, more and more outdated in the changing security context. 'A Defense Department designed for a massive, industrial-era opponent is clearly not suited for combating covert, non-state actors in the Information Age' (Murdock 2004: 18).

Reforms are taking place on both sides of the Atlantic to build on strengths and remedy weaknesses. In both Britain and the US new interagency planning units have been set up in order to facilitate co-ordination between the military, the development agencies and the Foreign Office/State Department. Within the UK it is the Post-Conflict Reconstruction Unit (PCRU), and within the US it is called Office of the Co-ordinator for Reconstruction and Stabilization (S/CRS). For the British, the main problem has been the tardiness of the committee system rather than the need for increased interagency co-operation. Working in committees is often too slow for the effective implementation of contemporary military operations that often require quick decision-making by the political leadership. Calls for stronger formal structures are therefore made, and, as a response, the concepts of 'comprehensive approaches' and 'effects-based operations' have been created. These doctrinal developments seek to increase interagency co-ordination and co-operation within a strengthened permanent interagency and planning structure.

Within what is called 'the comprehensive approach', the British are seeking to make the structure more effective through structural measures, such as the post-conflict reconstruction unit and interagency planning teams (IAPTs), to balance the military nature of the Joint Task Force Headquarters (JTFHQ). The IAPTs are also intended to have representatives within the JTFHQ as well as within lower level military commands. While such structural changes serve to ensure interagency co-operation in a more timely fashion, they are still dwarfed by the military command structures. As an example, the IAPTs consist of about 12 people while their military counterpart in the JTFHQ has a staff of 200–300. Another problem is that the IAPT currently does not own the execution capabilities, which are, of course, often military, and, therefore, does not carry the same weight as its military counterparts (Russell 2005). It remains to be seen to what extent the new interagency structures can complement the old committee system and the co-operative working culture that has been created. This book has, however, noted that the violation of a number of important principles of the British way of war was partly caused by the presidential leadership of Prime Minister Blair and the partial nullification of the interagency committee system. A risk when constructing new permanent structures that will further streamline the planning process is, therefore, that the benefits of the broad committee system are lost, and the British way of war with it.

The US interagency system is in more pressing need of reform as it lacks both the structures and the culture to co-operate effectively. Obviously, the National

Security Council is a useful foundation for such a structure. One important step in the right direction was taken in July 2004 with the creation of the State Department's Office of the Coordinator for Reconstruction and Stabilization (S/CRS). This office serves to lead, co-ordinate and institutionalize US Government civilian capacity to prevent or prepare for post-conflict situations, and to help stabilize and reconstruct societies in transition from conflict or civil strife. The office develops interagency assessment tools and planning frameworks for reconstruction and stabilization, based on the US military planning tools. It is nevertheless problematic that the S/CRS only has a mandate to lead, co-ordinate and institutionalize US *civilian* capacity. As the office is placed within the State Department it remains unclear to what extent it will be able to co-ordinate with the military planning structures. It has also not been able to secure the necessary funding from Congress in order to substantially increase civilian capacity for the planning and implementation of multifunctional operations.

A problem in the US case is that structural changes mean little if the working culture does not support it. As noted, trust and mutual understanding are essential ingredients in effective civil–military relations during operations, and a facilitator of mission type command from the political leadership. However, trust and understanding across departmental and agency borders are more difficult to achieve than structural changes, as these features are not a part of the US political tradition of checks and balances. Nevertheless, extensive structural changes that force officials from different agencies and departments to work together on a more regular basis have the potential to create interpersonal trust based on reciprocity. Effective outcomes may also develop an increased institutional trust in the structures of the interagency system. Unless there is a cultural change, recognizing the importance of such structures, increasing its status, and giving them stronger mandates, new interagency working groups are not likely to be effective. The big question mark is the extent to which the US interagency system can change its culture *within* the current US political tradition. Can the political culture of checks and balances with a healthy level of interagency competition be combined with a higher level of mutual trust and understanding?

The limited reforms of the US military and the civil–military interface, despite numerous failures in complex peace operations, can be derived from the fact that the US military continues to see these types of operations as less important than the 'real' functional imperative of major warfare in the defence of the nation. A shift in US military culture and its approach to complex peace operations, therefore, require a shift in the patterns of civil–military relations. However, the entrenched results of long historical processes are not easily changed. The cost of civilian monitoring of the armed forces and the lack of influence in terms of the functional imperative will not be changed through structural alterations, or impose change in training. Instead, the military must reach a new level of political understanding that leads to changes from within. Increased integration and civil–military co-operation may lead to increased mutual trust and understanding through experiences of reciprocity and the development of personal contacts outside the profession. It is also possible that the struggle to overcome the challenges in Iraq, in combination with the significance of the operation, will function as an eye-opener for the US military, re-evaluating the functional imperative somewhat.

Another policy implication is derived from the finding that integrated civil–military structures within the defence ministries are more effective than divided structures, especially in the context of complex peace operations. The US dualistic view of war and peace as well as of military and civilian affairs has not served the country well in past operations. The divided civil–military approach employed in the US has emphasized the importance of pure and separated military and political advice. It is, however, time to acknowledge that the dualistic view of civil–military relations is no longer applicable in a context where there really is no such thing as a purely military operation other than at the tactical level. In modern conflict, the Clausewitzian idiom, that war is the continuation of policy, is more relevant than ever. More important than pure military advice is, therefore, military advice which understands the political context of the decisions that are to be made. The other side of the coin is the need for policy advice that is well-informed about military consequences and imperatives. Such mutual understanding is only achievable through integrated structures, in which civilians and the military meet on a daily basis to exchange ideas and knowledge. Therefore, the US DoD should consider integrating its military and civilian staff in order to provide comprehensive advice to the political leadership.

The importance of professional civil servants is another policy-related finding of this book. One of the recurring themes of the book has been the importance to establish structures that contribute to mutual trust and understanding in the civil–military interface. Professional civil servants, in a range of different departments, with extensive knowledge of both political and military affairs, can thereby provide not only extensive expertise, institutional memory and continuity across administrations, they also provide a buffer zone between the political and military leaderships as well as across government ministries. With the dual knowledge and long experience they can mediate between locked positions as well as maintain important personal relationships across department and agency boundaries. As noted, several commentators, therefore, argue that it is time to start reversing the trend that increases the number of political appointees in order to increase the effectiveness and to retain the best and the brightest within the organization (Grissom 2005; White 2004; Murdock 2004: 57). While this trend is more serious in the US case, where all higher level appointments within the DoD are political, the problem has also developed in the UK, not least under the government of Tony Blair.

Finally, the fact that both the US and the British operations in Iraq are, in the fall of 2008, nothing short of a major failure begs to echo the question so well discussed by General Sir Rupert Smith: what political aims can actually be achieved by military force? This book argues that certain structures of civil–military relations are more effective than others when force is applied to achieve complex political aims, such as democratization and economic development. However, the failures in Iraq as well as in a number of historical cases – such as the War in Vietnam, the Soviet campaign in Afghanistan, as well as the peace operations in Rwanda, Somalia and the Congo – show that an increased level of caution is needed in the more adventurous applications of force. However, regardless if we are seeking victory, some form of success or merely an acceptable condition, the complex peace operations of the future are likely to be joint civil–military enterprises. Well-adjusted structural and cultural integration or co-ordination of the different instruments of power is imperative for effectiveness. In short, multifunctional operations require integrated bureaucracies at the national and international strategic levels.

Appendix

Indicators of effectiveness in complex peace operations

The introduction of this book highlighted a number of principles of best practice, or indicators of effectiveness, that have also served as a check-list for the empirical chapters of this book. While these principles are relatively uncontroversial, they deserve more deliberation than what the introduction could offer. This is done by reviewing some strategic thinkers, as well as some doctrinal developments, within the field. As already noted, the bulk of the principles discussed within this section come from counter-insurgency doctrine, as that is often considered the actual nature of contemporary military operations (Mockaitis 2000).

As a reminder, the strategic-level factors mentioned in the Introduction were:

1　the importance of a clear and achievable political aim;
2　civil–military co-operation and co-ordination;
3　the importance of the strategic narrative.

The tactical level indicators somewhat overlap with the strategic level and include:

1　civil–military co-operation – unity of command and effort;
2　the hearts and minds approach – force protection and minimum use of force;
3　cultural understanding of the local environment;
4　adaptability and learning.

The starting point for successful complex operations is that of a clear political aim and purpose that can guide the actions of all involved actors. 'Without a clear political purpose it is not possible to have a military strategic objective' (Smith 2005: 291). Carl von Clausewitz famously argued that:

> No one starts a war – or rather, no one in his senses ought to do so – without first being clear in his mind what he intends to achieve by that war and how he intends to conduct it. The former is its political purpose; the latter its operational objective. This is the governing principle which will set its

course, prescribe the scale of means and effort which is required, and make its influence felt throughout down to the smallest operational detail.

(1989: 579)

A clear aim creates a common point of departure in the planning of operations and helps to drive the different involved actors towards a common purpose. However, in the contemporary context of complex peace operations the aims are changing. In industrial warfare the political objectives were achieved by applying military force of such significance that the enemy conformed to our will. In the contemporary strategic context Western forces 'intervene in, or even decide to escalate to, a conflict in order to establish a condition in which the political objectives can be achieved by other means and in other ways' (Smith 2005: 270; Dandeker and Gow 2000). In other words, the military operation merely sets the stage for the diplomatic, political and economic activity that will lead to such far-reaching aims as democracy, economic development and respect for human rights.

The objective to create an acceptable condition in which the outcome can be decided changes the nature of the relationship between political aims and strategic activity. An end state determined by the conflicting parties themselves cannot be clearly defined at the onset of operations, and the military activity generally takes place at the sub-strategic level. Although new thinking is clearly needed regarding the political direction of military and civilian activity in the field, it does not take away the importance of a clear political purpose to which the military as well as the other involved agencies and organizations may relate to in the planning of operations.

The literature is explicit regarding the fact that a clear and common aim must be informed by a joint civil–military, in-depth analysis of the conflict situation. Without sound understanding of all aspects of the conflict – such as the actors involved, the political climate, the local culture, the financial situation on the ground, etc. – it is most difficult to establish what objectives the military and civilian organizations should pursue in the quest for the political aim (Smith 2005: 374). Clear political purpose must also be accompanied by the principle of political primacy. Clausewitz, again, argued that war should never be thought of as something autonomous, but always as an instrument of policy. This implies that policy must always have primacy and Clausewitz goes on to claim that interpreting war as an instrument of policy is the only way of understanding how 'wars must vary with the nature of their motives and the situations which give rise to them'. He continues:

The first, the supreme, the most far-reaching act of judgment that the statesman and commander have to make is to establish … the kind of war on which they are embarking; neither mistaking it for, nor trying to turn it into, something that is alien to its nature

(Clausewitz 1989: 88)

Cohen *et al.* (2006: 50) similarly contend that 'all actions, kinetic and non-kinetic, must be planned and executed with the consideration of their contribution toward strengthening the host government's legitimacy and achieving the U.S. Government's political goals'. Therefore, the political objectives must be the dominant.

The second principle is that of civil–military co-operation and co-ordination. One of the undisputed lessons of past irregular operations is the need for comprehensive approaches that include all instruments of national power in the pursuit of political aims. This means comprehensive and inclusive planning as well as execution. As an example, General Anthony Zinni (2003) draws upon the lessons from Somalia and argues that all aspects of operations have to be co-ordinated.

> I've seen the disasters in Somalia and elsewhere when coordination mechanisms fail. Those mechanisms for coordination have to be solid; they have to be established from the lowest remote points on the ground to the highest decisions that may be made.

In other words, the efforts of all agencies involved in operations must be harnessed to a single purpose. There is a need to analyse, plan and direct operations as a whole, fusing political, economic and military actions into one concerted effort at all levels of command, from the political strategic level, through the theatre headquarters, to the lowest levels of administration and tactical operations (Smith 2005: 287, 197).

Co-operation and co-ordination between the involved actors in complex peace operations are the only way to achieve the principle of 'unity of effort'. This strategic principle is stressed by all analysts and defence professionals – yet, to somewhat different degrees. Commentators argue that the ideal would be the principle of 'unity of command' – placing all civilian and military actors within one chain of command, led by a single operational commander. However, the sheer number and cultural divergence of actors involved in complex, multinational operations generally make that highly unlikely and many analysts instead advocate the creation of structures for co-ordination and co-operation to achieve unity of effort (Cohen *et al.* 2006: 50).

A strategic concept that emphasizes the importance of civil–military integration for a successful operation is that of the 'comprehensive approach' (CA). The concept is under development in the UK in the light of experience in Afghanistan and Iraq. The CA stresses the need for integrated structures for planning and execution of operations. 'The CA should be reinforced by institutional familiarity, trust and transparency between Government Departments and through frequent personal contact, human networks and information sharing' … providing horizontal, vertical and diagonal collaboration between communities of interest at all levels, within and between departments (UK MoD 2006: 16).

The British identify four guiding principles of the comprehensive approach. First, a proactive cross-government approach should allow for co-ordination of Whitehall activity at both official and ministerial levels within the framework of a shared strategic objective. Second, shared understanding and analysis must be achieved of both the nature of the conflict and of the response. To achieve shared understanding, staff drawn from the different departments and agencies should provide for 'breadth, depth and resilience to analysis, planning, execution and assessment and contribute to a common baseline of understanding on which risk assessments, judgements and decisions can be made' (UK MoD 2006). Third, planning and activity by all departments should be outcome based and, therefore, judged on the achievement of progress towards the cross-government strategic objective. This implies consideration and constant review of all likely effects and outcomes in both the short, medium and longer terms. Fourth, the principle of collaborative working means that the comprehensive approach should be reinforced by institutional familiarity, trust and transparency between the involved departments and agencies, through frequent personal contact, networks and information sharing, meaning an integrated interdepartmental and civil–military structure (UK MoD 2006). In sum, identifying the solid mechanisms for civil–military co-operation and co-ordination that General Zinni advocates is an important task of this book.

The importance of the strategic narrative is the third and final principle in the strategic level discussion. Narratives are 'compelling story lines which can explain events', and are intentionally designed to structure 'responses of others to developing events' (Freedman 2006: 22). The strategic feature of narratives lies in the fact that they are not spontaneous, but 'deliberately constructed or reinforced out of the ideas and thoughts that are already current' (Freedman 2006: 22). In the struggle for the hearts and minds of the local population, the number of battlefield victories or reconstruction projects completed matter little if the local population and the wider audiences of international opinion think you are not winning, or visibly improving people's situation. Instead, the success is achieved by communicating with the people through the media and other outlets, getting the right narrative out there and changing perceptions (Smith 2005: 391).

However, in the global surveillance age of instant media coverage, the Internet and mobile phones, as described by Shaw (2005), controlling a story or a narrative is not easy. Insurgents have the inherent advantages of better cultural understanding and closer contacts with the local population. They are, therefore, in a strong position to present alternative narratives to events, and even turning tactical losses into victories of perception. Turning a counter-insurgency bombing or attack against an insurgent stronghold into an ungodly attack on a local school, killing women and children, has the potential of turning tactical losses into strategic victories for insurgents. 'In modern counter-insurgency, the side may win which best mobilizes and energizes its global, regional and local support base – and prevents its adversaries doing likewise' (Kilcullen 2006a: 121). Importantly, developing a narrative is not a strategy in itself, as a convincing narrative must be supported by actual events on the ground and a sound underlying strategy (Freedman 2006: 93). Constructing a strategic narrative is, therefore, never an alternative to appropriate actions, but should be seen as a necessary supplement to sound strategies and tactical activities.

At the tactical level of complex peace operations the nature of field activities merges into relatively similar activity regardless of operational type. In contemporary complex peace operations, stability and reconstruction operations, small wars, humanitarian interventions and counter-insurgency operations, the work of a soldier is more or less the same, although with varying levels of violence and legal constraints. As previously noted, scholars have come to describe the practical application of military force in complex operations as counter-insurgency-type operations (Mockaitis 2000). The theory and practice of counter-insurgency are, therefore, where this section has its emphasis.

The recent renaissance of counter-insurgency theory is, to a large extent, a rereading of old masters within a new context. Key theorists within the classical school of counter-insurgency include Robert Thompson, David Galula, Mao Zedong, Frank Kitson and T.E. Lawrence. A simple relearning of traditional theory may not be enough in a context which contains essentially different types of insurgencies than the wars of national liberation after the Second World War (Kilcullen 2006a: 111). Any application of traditional theory must, therefore, take place within the context of full appreciation of contemporary strategic challenges. This section covers the following principles of complex peace operations at the tactical level:

1   civil–military co-operation – unity of command and effort;
2   the hearts and minds approach – force protection and minimum use of force;
3   cultural understanding of the local environment;
4   adaptability and learning.

Civil–military co-ordination and co-operation, or what we can call multifunctional unity of command and effort is the first principle. The tactical-level application of this principle is of such importance that it merits a closer analysis despite its coverage in the discussion regarding the strategic level. Traditional theory stresses the importance of this principle, and Robert Thompson, a British counter-insurgency expert and Permanent Secretary of Defence for Malaya in the 1950s, advocated the committee structure and suggested structures, incorporating all relevant actors, to be used at the national and local levels to ensure co-ordination. At the national level, the committee should have the responsibility to develop clear operational plans and policies. Thompson also emphasized that military plans must be devised in co-ordination with civilian counterparts and activities in order to achieve lasting success. The policies and operational plans created should then be implemented by the various departments and headquarters involved, with regular committee meetings at the local level of colonial administration to ensure co-ordination among the local actors (Thompson 1966: 52, 55). The weaker modern day application of this principle is in Europe called CIMIC (Civil–military Co-ordination), and in the US, Civil Affairs. Unfortunately, CIMIC and Civil Affairs units are military-led forms of co-operation, with the purpose of achieving military objectives in the field. Not only does this fail to adhere to the principle of political primacy, it also deters civil and humanitarian organizations from co-operating. The humanitarian principles which govern the activities of most civilian organizations also make co-operation with the military difficult (Egnell 2008).

As noted in the previous section, unity of command is the ideal in counter-insurgency. However, this ideal is seldom achieved and the weaker principle of unity of effort often becomes the more practicable solution. To achieve unity of effort despite lacking unity of command, an important principle is the co-location of the military and civilian headquarters in the field. The co-location of the different actors allows for at least some level of joint analysis and planning.

The hearts and minds approach to operations is the second indicator of effectiveness in complex peace operations. Directly related to the strategic-level principle of political primacy is the idea of winning 'hearts and minds'. Robert Thompson (1966) explains this view by arguing that counter-insurgency forces and agencies must give priority to defeating the political subversion, not the guerrillas. Therefore, they achieve the most meaningful success by gaining popular support and legitimacy for the host government – winning hearts and minds – not by killing insurgents. While security is important, the lasting victory is likely to come from a vibrant economy, political participation, and restored hope. In Clausewitzian terminology, the centre of gravity in any complex operation is the people. The local population in the field of operations is at best ambivalent towards the intervening force. The most important component of counter-insurgency operations is, therefore, weaning the population away from the insurgents (Garfield 2006: 16). Defeating the political subversion conducted by insurgents requires making a difference in the lives of the local population as early as possible. This means

> significant efforts to ensure fair treatment, the creation of jobs, improvements in education and medical services (in the short term, getting an education and being treated is far more important than the construction of new schools and hospitals), providing a bearable standard of living, basic personal security, and some form of legitimate representative governance.

Military presence and activity are vital to establish the necessary level of security and for coercive purposes. However, military activity can only work in a support function to the civilian activities of political and economic reform (Garfield 2006: 16).

Translated into specific tactics, the hearts and minds approach involves two interrelated principles: the minimum use of force, and what this book calls 'soft force protection'. The lessons from the colonial era in general, and Malaya in particular, led Frank Kitson (1971) to stress the importance of using minimum force. In the wider goal of winning hearts and minds, he noted the negative impact of excessive force, and argued that such force tends to drive the population away from the administration and towards extremist positions. Some level of force is necessary to restore order and achieve a breathing space where positive inducements can have an effect, as well as to act as a deterrent (Kitson 1971: 84, 87). Significantly, the principle of minimum use of force should be based on an understanding of the overall political objectives with the operation and how they relate to the actions of soldiers at all levels of command. It goes back to the importance of political understanding and sensitivity.

The strategic aim of counter-insurgency operations always involves establishing some form of rule of law, and that tactical operations must consequently be conducted within the framework of the law in order not to attack one's own strategic interests (Smith 2005: 379). Equally, Cohen *et al.* (2006) assert that to establish legitimacy, all security operations must be treated as law enforcement rather than combat operations. This view has been more elaborately discussed by Lawrence Freedman (2006) who suggests that the political context of irregular wars, coupled with the fact that combat is integrated with civil society, means that both the purpose and the practice of all operations should be governed by liberal values. Freedman calls this 'liberal warfare'.

Force protection in operations 'among the people' is difficult, but can essentially be achieved in two different ways. Units can distance themselves from the local population by living in fortified camps, wearing full combat gear, and patrolling in armoured vehicles with guns pointed at all potential targets. However, force protection can also be achieved through 'soft effects', meaning the conduct of hearts and minds operations and reconstruction efforts rather than the application of force (Garfield 2006: 25). The idea is that small units patrolling and continuous contact with the local population will not only establish legitimacy for the operation, but also increase intelligence on insurgent activity. Force protection is, thereby, a paradox of counter-insurgency. 'The more you protect your force, the less secure you are.' Since the ultimate aim of operations is to win the hearts and minds of the local population and establish legitimacy for the local government, the counter-insurgent achieves success by protecting the population and not himself (Cohen *et al.* 2006: 52).

Force protection measures, such as living in remote fortified camps and limiting patrolling to armoured vehicles at high speed, or always wearing full combat gear when interacting with the local population are, therefore, likely to be counterproductive. Instead, the most fundamental rule of counter-insurgency is to 'be there'. Presence should be established by living in close proximity to the population, through frequent patrolling on foot, night patrolling and sleeping in local villages. This type of activity, though seemingly dangerous, will establish links with locals and increase human intelligence – thereby increasing the security of the counter-insurgents (Kilcullen 2006b: 105).

Cultural understanding is the third indicator of success. Counter-insurgency operations are about winning hearts and minds in the pursuit of legitimacy. To do so, every soldier must have an understanding of the demographics, history and culture of the local population, as well as the aims, ideologies, capabilities and approaches of all organizations and parties in the conflict. In the words of Cohen *et al.* (2006: 50): 'The interconnected politico-military nature of insurgency requires the counter-insurgent to immerse himself in the lives of the people in order to achieve victory.' The importance of cultural understanding is well-highlighted by the concept of the strategic corporal, a concept developed by US Marine Corps General, Charles Krulak (1999), to emphasize the dispersion of military authority towards the lower levels of command. The idea is that, in the age of global surveillance, actions and choices of corporals and soldiers may have strategic consequences. Thus, understanding local culture and having at least a very basic understanding of the language radically reduces the risk of making tactical-level mistakes that could have strategic consequences.

The fourth tactical level principle is that of adaptation and innovation. David Galula (1964) argues that no one approach can defeat an insurgency. Equally, Cohen *et al.* (2006: 52) state that '[i]f a tactic works this week, it will not work next week; if it worked in this province, it will not work in the next'. Each insurgency is different and presents a unique set of challenges for the counter-insurgents. The complexities involved, as well as the adaptive nature of the insurgent, mean that the counter-insurgent must be equally adaptable and innovative. This problem is best described by the concept of 'Three Block War'. Within a very limited area, and within a few hours' work, troops can be involved in high-intensity combat, low-intensity peacekeeping and humanitarian assistance (Krulak 1999). The complex challenges of counter-insurgency operations should, therefore, place premium on the selection, training, and empowerment of personnel at all levels who can 'adapt and overcome' (Garfield 2006: 30). In a highly useful analysis of the counter-insurgency campaigns in Malaya and Vietnam, John Nagl (2002) concludes that one of the most important factors of success in Malaya and failure in Vietnam was the ability to learn and adapt. This ability stems from an organizational culture that allows armed forces such learning and adaptation.

Bibliography

Books and academic articles

Abrahamsson, B. (1972) *Military Professionalism and Political Power*, Beverley Hills, CA: Sage.

—— (2006) 'Defeating David? Effects Based Operations: Challenges to Military Organization and Professionalism', in B. Abrahamsson, R. Egnell and K. Ydén (eds), *Effects Based Operations, Military Organization and Professionalization*, Stockholm: National Defence College.

Alberts, D.S. and Hayes, R.E. (2003) *Power to the Edge: Command ... Control ... in the Information Age*, Washington, DC: CCRP.

Alexandrou, A. (2004) 'Creating a Collective Representative Body for British Military Personnel Through European Community Law', *Defence Studies*, 4(1): 114–130.

Allen, G. (2001) *The Last Prime Minister: Being Honest About the UK Presidency*, London: House of Commons.

Allin, D. (2007) 'American Power and Allied Restraint: Lessons of Iraq', *Survival*, 49(1): 123–140.

Angstrom, J. and Duyvesteyn, I. (eds) (2007) *Understanding Victory and Defeat in Contemporary War*, London: Routledge.

Arreguin-Toft, I. (2005) *How the Weak Win Wars: A Theory of Asymmetric Conflict*, New York: Cambridge University Press.

Avant, D. (1994) *Political Institutions and Military Change: Lessons from Peripheral Wars*, London: Cornell University Press.

Aylwin-Foster, N. (2005) 'Changing the Army for Counter-Insurgency Operations', *Military Review*, November–December 2005.

Baram, A. (2005) *Who Are the Insurgents? Sunni Arab Rebels in Iraq*, United States Institute of Peace, Special Report No. 134. Available online at www.usip.org/pubs/specialreports/sr134.html (accessed 3 April 2007).

Barnett, C. (1972) *The Collapse of British Power*, New York: William Morrow.

Bartle, R. (2006) 'The British Armed Forces: No Trust, No Representation, No Change', in R. Bartle and L. Heinecken, *Military Unionism in the Post-Cold War Era: A Future Reality*, London: Routledge.

Barton, F.D. and Crocker, B. (2003) 'Winning the Peace in Iraq', *The Washington Quarterly*, 26(2): 7–22.

Becker, M.D. (1994) 'Strategic Culture and Ballistic Missile Defense: Russia and the United States', *Aerospace Power Journal*, Special Edition. Available online at www.airpower.maxwell.af.mil/airchronicles/apj/sum97/-spe94/becker.html (accessed 3 February 2005).

Bensahel, N. (2006) 'Mission Not Accomplished: What Went Wrong with Iraqi Reconstruction', *The Journal of Strategic Studies*, 29(3): 453–473.

Bensahel, N., Oliker, O., Crane, K., Brennan Jr, R.R., Gregg, H.S., Sullivan, T. and Rathmell, A. (2008) *After Saddam: Prewar Planning and the Occupation of Iraq*, Santa Monica, CA: RAND Corporation.

Berdal, M. (2003a) 'The UN Security Council: Ineffective, but Indispensable', *Survival*, 45(2): 7–30.

—— (2003b) 'How "New" Are "New Wars"? Global Economic Changes and the Study of Civil War', *Global Governance*, 9(4): 477–503.

Berg, B.L. (2001) *Qualitative Research Methods for the Social Sciences*, Boston, MA: Allyn and Bacon.

Betts, R. (1980) 'Comments on Mueller', *International Studies Quarterly*, 24(4): 520–524.

Biddle, S. (2004) *Military Power: Explaining Victory and Defeat in Modern Battle*, Princeton, NJ: Princeton University Press.

—— (2008) 'Stabilizing Iraq from the Bottom Up'. Statement by Dr Stephen Biddle before the Committee on Foreign Relations, US Senate, Second Session, 110th Congress, 2 April 2008.

Biddle, S., O'Hanlon, M.E. and Pollack, K.M. (2008) 'How to Leave a Stable Iraq: Building on Progress', *Foreign Affairs*, September/October 2008.

Bijlsma-Frankema, K. and Costa, A.C. (2005) 'Understanding the Trust-Control Nexus', *International Sociology*, 20(3): 259–282.

Birtle, A.J. (2001) *U.S. Army Counterinsurgency and Contingency Operations Doctrine 1860–1941*, Washington, DC: Center of Military History US Army.

Bland, D. (1999) 'A Unified Theory of Civil–Military Relations', *Armed Forces and Society*, 26(1): 7–26.

—— (2001) 'Patterns in Liberal Democratic Civil–Military Relations', *Armed Forces and Society*, 27(4): 525–540.

Boëne, B. (1990) 'How Unique Should the Military Be? A Review of Representative Literature and Outline of a Synthetic Formulation', *European Journal of Sociology*, 31(1): 3–59.

Boëne, B., Dandeker C., Kuhlmann, J. and van der Meulen, J. (2000) *Facing Uncertainty, Report No. 2: The Swedish Military in International Perspective*, Karlstad: Försvarshögskolan Acta D5, Ledarskapsinstitutionen.

Bogdanos, M.F. (2005) 'Joint Interagency Cooperation: The First Step', *Joint Force Quarterly*, (37): 10–18.

Bond, B. (1980) *British Military Policy Between the Two World Wars*, Oxford: Clarendon Press.

Boot, M. (2002) *The Savage Wars of Peace: Small Wars and the Rise of American Power*, New York: Basic Books.

—— (2003) 'The New American Way of War', *Foreign Affairs*, July/August 2003.

Booth, K. (1979) *Strategy and Ethnocentrism*, New York: Holmes & Meier Publishers.

Booth, K. and Vale, P. (1997) 'Critical Security Studies and Regional Insecurity: The Case of Southern Africa', in K. Krause and M.C. Williams (eds), *Critical Security Studies: Concepts and Cases*, Minneapolis, MN: University of Minnesota Press.

Booth, W.C., Colomb, G.G. and Williams, J.M. (2003) *The Craft of Research*, Chicago, IL: University of Chicago Press.

Bremer, P.L. and McConnell, M. (2005) *My Year in Iraq: The Struggle to Build a Future of Hope*, New York: Simon & Schuster.

Brooks, R.A. (2003) 'Making Military Might: Why Do States Fail and Succeed?', *International Security*, 28(2): 149–191.
—— (2008) *Shaping Strategy: The Civil–Military Politics of Strategic Assessment*, Princeton, NJ: Princeton University Press.
Bull, H. (1977) *The Anarchical Society: A Study of Order in World Politics*, Basingstoke: Palgrave.
Bulloch, G. (1996) 'Military Doctrine and Counterinsurgency: A British Perspective', *Parameters*, 26(2): 4–16.
Burk, J. (1999) 'Military Culture', in L. Kurtz and J.E. Turpin (eds), *Encyclopedia of Violence, Peace and Conflict*, San Diego, CA: Academic Press.
—— (2002) 'Theories of Democratic Civil–Military Relations', *Armed Forces and Society*, 29(1): 7–29.
Caniglia, R.R. (2001) 'US and British Approaches to Force Protection', *Military Review*, 73–81.
Carafano, J.J. (2003) 'Post-Conflict and Culture: Changing America's Military for 21st Century Missions', *Heritage Lecture*, No. 810, 22 October. Available online at www.heritage.org/Research/NationalSecurity/HL810.cfm (accessed 18 May 2004).
Cassidy, R.M. (2004) *Peacekeeping in the Abyss: British and American Peacekeeping Doctrine and Practice After the Cold War*, Westport, CT: Praeger.
—— (2005) 'The British Army and Counterinsurgency: The Salience of Military Culture', *Military Review*, May–June. Available online at www.army.mil/professionalwriting/volumes/volume3/november_2005/11_05_2.html#15 (accessed 30 August 2006).
Clark, W.K. (2001) *Waging Modern War: Bosnia, Kosovo, and the Future of Combat*, Oxford: Public Affairs Ltd.
Clausewitz, C. von (1989), *On War*, trans. by Michael Howard and Peter Paret. Princeton, NJ: Princeton University Press.
Cohen, E. (1986) 'Constraints on America's Conduct of Small Wars', in S.E. Miller (ed.), *Conventional Forces and American Defence Policy*, Princeton, NJ: Princeton University Press.
—— (1996) 'A Revolution in Warfare', *Foreign Affairs*, 75(2): 37–54.
—— (1997) 'Civil–Military Relations: Are U.S. Forces Overstretched?', *Orbis*, Spring 1997, 177–186.
—— (2000) 'Why the Gap Matters', *The National Interest*, Fall 2000, 38–48.
—— (2001) 'Kosovo and the New American Way of War', in E.A. Cohen and A.J. Bacevich (eds), *War Over Kosovo: Politics and Strategy in a Global Age*, New York: Columbia University Press.
—— (2002) *Supreme Command: Soldiers, Statesmen and Leadership in Wartime*, New York: The Free Press.
Cohen, E.A., Crane, C., Horvath, J. and Nagl, J. (2006) 'Principles, Imperatives, and Paradoxes of Counterinsurgency', *Military Review*, March–April 2006, 49–53.
Coker, C. (1997) 'How Wars End', *Millennium*, 26(3): 615–629.
—— (2001) *Humane Warfare*, London: Routledge.
Cordesman, A.H. (2003a) 'Iraq: Too Uncertain To Call', CSIS paper. Available online at www.csis.org/features/031114toouncertain.pdf (accessed 15 January 2005).
—— (2003b) *The Iraq War: Strategy, Tactics, and Military Lessons*, Westport, CT: Praeger.
—— (2007) 'The British Defeat in the South and the Uncertain Bush "Strategy" in Iraq: "Oil Spots", "Ink Blots", "White Space", or Pointlessness?', SCIS Report.
Crabb, C.V. and Holt, P.M. (1989) *Invitation to Struggle: Congress, the President, and Foreign Policy*, Washington, DC: CQ Press.

Creveld, M. van, (1991) *The Transformation of War*, New York: The Free Press.
Dandeker, C. (1999) *Facing Uncertainty: Flexible Forces for the Twenty-First Century*, Report No. 1, Karlstad: Försvarshögskolan Acta D5, Ledarskapsinstitutionen.
—— (2001) 'On the Need to be Different: Military Uniqueness and Civil–Military Relations in Modern Society', *RUSI Journal*, 146(3): 4–9.
—— (2002) 'Military and Society: The Problem, Challenges and Possible Answers', paper presented at the 5th International Security Forum, 14–16 October 2002.
—— (2006) 'Surveillance and Military Transformation: Organizational Trends in Twenty-First Century Armed Services', in K. Haggerty and R.V. Ericson (eds), *The New Politics of Surveillance and Visibility*, Toronto: University of Toronto Press.
Dandeker, C. and Gow, J. (2000) 'Military Culture and Strategic Peacekeeping', in Erwin A. Schmidl (ed.), *Peace Operations Between War and Peace*, London: Frank Cass.
Denscombe, M. (1998) *The Good Research Guide: For Small-Scale Social Research Projects*, Philadelphia, PA: Open University Press.
Derblom, M., Egnell, R. and Nilsson, C. (2007) *The Impact of Strategic Concepts and Approaches on the Effects-Based Approach to Operations – A Baseline Collective Assessment Report*, FOI-R–2394–SE, Stockholm: FOI 2007.
Desch, M.C. (1999) *Civilian Control of the Military: The Changing Security Environment*, Baltimore, MD: Johns Hopkins University Press.
—— (2001) 'Explaining the Gap: Vietnam, the Republicanization of the South, and the End of the Mass Army', in P.D. Feaver and R.H. Kohn (eds), *Soldiers and Civilians: The Civil–Military Gap and American National Security*, Cambridge, MA: MIT Press.
Delong, M. and Lukeman, N. (2004) *Inside CentCom: The Unvarnished Truth About the Wars in Afghanistan and Iraq*, Washington, DC: Regnery Publishing.
Dewar, M. (1990) *Brushfire Wars: Minor Campaigns of the British Army Since 1945*, London: Robert Hale.
Dewar, J., August, D. and Builder, C. (1996) *Army Culture and Planning in a Time of Great Change*, Santa Monica, CA: RAND.
Diamond, L. (2004) 'What Went Wrong in Iraq', *Foreign Affairs*, 83(5): 34–56.
—— (2005) *Squandered Victory: The American Occupation and the Bungled Effort to Bring Democracy to Iraq*, New York: Times Books.
Dobbins, J., McGinn, J.G., Crane, K., Jones, S.G. Lal, R., Rathmell, A., Swanger, R. and Timilsina, A. (2003) *America's Role in Nation-Building: From Germany to Iraq*, Washington, DC: RAND.
Docherty, L. (2007) *Desert of Death: A Soldier's Journey from Iraq to Afghanistan*, London: Faber and Faber.
Dodge, T. (2007) 'The Causes of Failures in Iraq', *Survival*, 49(1): 85–106.
Downie, R.D. (1998) *Learning from Conflict: The US Military in Vietnam, El Salvador, and the Drug War*, Westport, CT: Praeger.
Echevarria, A.J. (2004) 'Towards an American Way of War', Strategic Studies Institute Report.
—— (2005) *Fourth-Generation War and Other Myths*, Carlisle, PA: Strategic Studies Institute.
Egnell, R. (2005) 'Achieving Effect in Contemporary Operation: Network Enabled Capabilities in a Changing Strategic Context', in Karl Ydén (ed.), *Directions in Military Organizing*, Stockholm: Försvarshögskolan.
—— (2006) 'Squandered Victory: An Effects Based Analysis of the War in Iraq', in B. Abrahamsson, R. Egnell and K. Ydén (eds), *Effects Based Operations, Military Organization and Professionalization*, Stockholm: National Defence College.

—— (2008) 'Between Reluctance and Necessity: The Utility of Military Force in Humanitarian and Development Operations', *Small Wars and Insurgencies*, 29(6): 397–422.

Eisenhour, J.H. and Marks, E. (1999) 'Herding Cats: Overcoming Obstacles in Civil–Military Operations', *Joint Force Quarterly*, 22: 86–90.

Erdmann, A.P.N. (2002) 'The U.S. Presumption of Quick, Costless Wars', in J.F. Lehman and H. Sicherman (eds), *America the Vulnerable: Our Military Problems and How to Fix Them*, Philadelphia, PA: Foreign Policy Research Institute.

Essens, P., Vogelaar, A. Tanercan, E. and Winslow, D. (eds) (2004) *The Human in Command: Peace Support Operations*, Amsterdam: Mets & Schilt.

Fallows, J. (2004) 'Blind into Baghdad', *The Atlantic Monthly*, January/February. Available online at www.theatlantic.com/doc/prem/200401/fallows (accessed 4 April 2007).

Farrar-Hockley, A. (2003) 'The Post-War Army 1945–1963', in David Chandler and Ian Beckett (eds), *The Oxford History of the British Army*, 2nd edn, Oxford: Oxford University Press.

Farrell, T. and Terriff, T. (2002) *The Sources of Military Change: Culture, Politics, Technology*, London: Lynne Rienner Publishers.

Feaver, P.D. (1996) 'The Civil–Military Problematique: Huntington, Janowitz, and the Question of Civilian Control', *Armed Forces and Society*, 23(2): 149–178.

—— (2003) *Armed Servants: Agency Oversight, and Civil–Military Relations*, Cambridge, MA: Harvard University Press.

—— (2004) 'Civil–Military Relations', *Annual Review of Political Science*, 2: 211–241.

Feaver, P.D. and Kohn, R.H. (2001) *Soldiers and Civilians: The Civil–Military Gap and American National Security*, Cambridge, MA: MIT Press.

Finer, S.E. (1962) *The Man on Horseback: The Role of the Military in Politics*, London: Pall Mall Press.

Foley, M. (2000) *The British Presidency: Tony Blair and the Politics of Public Leadership*, Manchester: Manchester University Press.

—— (2004) 'Presidential Attribution as an Agency of Prime Ministerial Critique in a Parliamentary Democracy: The Case of Tony Blair', *British Journal of Politics and International Relations*, 6: 292–311.

Forster, A. (2000) 'New Civil–Military Relations and its Research Agendas', DCAF Working Paper. Available online at www.dcaf.ch/publications/Working_Papers/83.pdf (accessed 26 January 2003).

—— (2006a) *Armed Forces in Europe*, Basingstoke: Palgrave Macmillan.

—— (2006b) 'Breaking the Covenant: Governance of the British Army in the Twenty-First Century', *International Affairs*, 82(6): 1043–1057.

Franke, V.C. (1999) *Preparing for Peace: Military Identity, Value Orientations and Professional Military Education*, Westport, CT: Praeger.

Franks, T. (2004), *American Soldier*, New York: Regan Books.

Freedman, L. (1993) 'The Gulf Conflict and the British Way in Warfare', Annual Liddell Hart Centre for Military Archives Lecture. Available online at www.kcl.ac.uk/lhcma/info/lec93.htm (accessed 15 February 2005).

—— (1998) *The Revolution in Strategic Affairs*, Adelphi Paper, No. 319, Oxford: Oxford University Press for IISS.

—— (2002) 'Calling the Shots: Should Politicians or Generals Run Our Wars?', *Foreign Affairs*, 81(5): 188–193.

—— (2006) *The Transformation of Strategic Affairs*, Adelphi Paper, No. 379, London: Routledge.

French, D. (2005) *Military Identities: The Regimental System, the British Army, and the British People, c. 1870–2000*, Oxford: Oxford University Press.

Fromkin, D. and Chace, J. (1985) 'Vietnam: The Retrospect: What Are the Lessons of Vietnam?', *Foreign Affairs*, 63(4): 722–746.

Fry, R. (2005) 'Expeditionary Operations in the Modern Era', *RUSI Journal*, 150(6): 60–63.

Galula, D. (1964) *Counter-Insurgency Warfare: Theory and Practice*, New York: Fredrick A. Praeger.

—— (2005) *Counterinsurgency Warfare: Theory and Practice*, New York: Fredrick A. Praeger.

Garfield, A. (2006) *Succeeding in Phase IV: British Perspectives on the U.S. to Stabilize and Reconstruct Iraq*, Philadelphia, PA: Foreign Policy Research Institute.

Garnier, M. (1975) 'Technology, Organizational Culture and Recruitment in the British Military Academy', *Journal of Political and Military Sociology*, 3: 141–151.

Garofano, J. (2004) 'The United States in Bosnia-Herzegovina: Points of Tension and Learning for the U.S. Military', in J. Callaghan and M. Schönborn, *Warriors in Peacekeeping: Points of Tension in Complex Cultural Encounters*, Münster: Lit Verlag.

Garrison, J. (1997) 'The Political Dimension of Military Professionalism', in P.L. Hays, B.J. Vallance and A.R. van Tassel (eds), *American Defence Policy*, Baltimore, MD: Johns Hopkins University Press.

Geertz, C. (1973) 'Thick Description: Toward an Interpretive Theory of Culture', in *The Interpretation of Cultures: Selected Essays*, New York: Basic Books.

George, A.L. and Bennett, A. (2004) *Case Studies and Theory Development in the Social Sciences*, Cambridge, MA: MIT Press.

Gorman, M.J. and Krongard, A. (2005) 'A Goldwater–Nichols Act for the U.S. Government: Institutionalizing the Interagency Process', *Joint Forces Quarterly*, (39): 51–58.

Graff, J.K. (2004) *United States Counterinsurgency Doctrine and Implementation in Iraq*, MA thesis, Fort Leavenworth.

Gray, C.S. (1981) 'National Style in Strategy: The American Example', *International Security*, 6: 21–47.

—— (1984) 'Comparative Strategic Culture', *Parameters*, Winter 1984, 26–33.

—— (1986) *Nuclear Strategy and National Style*, Lanham, MD: Hamilton Press.

—— (1998) 'The Revolution in Military Affairs', in B. Bond and M. Mungo (eds), *The Nature of Future Conflict: Implications for Force Development*, Camberley, Surrey: SCSI.

—— (1999) 'Strategic Culture as Context: The First Generation of Theory Strikes Back', *Review of International Studies*, 25: 49–69.

—— (2005) *Another Bloody Century: Future Warfare*, London: Phoenix.

Grove, E. (1996) *The Army and British Security After the Cold War: Defence Planning for a New Era*, London: Strategic and Combat Studies Institute/HMSO.

Guthrie, C. (2001) 'The New British Way in Warfare', Annual Liddell Hart Centre for Military Archives Lecture. Available online at www.kcl.ac.uk/lhcma/info/lec01.htm (accessed 15 February 2005).

Gwynn, C.W. (1934) *Imperial Policing*, London: Macmillan and Company.

Gwynne Jones, A. (1966) 'Training and Doctrine in the British Army Since 1945', in M. Howard (ed.), *The Theory and Practice of War*, New York: Praeger.

Hamby, J.E. (2002) 'Civil–Military Operations: Joint Doctrine and the Malayan Emergency', *Joint Force Quarterly*, Autumn 2002, 54–61.

Hammes, T.X. (2004) *The Sling and the Stone: On War in the 21st Century*, St Paul, MN: Zenith Press.

Hanna, M.W. (2008). 'Still No Clear Path for Integrating "Sons of Iraq" into Iraqi Government', *World Politics Review,* 10 July. Available online at www.worldpoliticsreview. com/article.aspx?id=2412 (accessed 3 August 2008).

Hayes, M.D. and Weatley, G.F. (1996) *Interagency and Political–Military Dimensions of Peace Operations: Haiti – A Case Study*, Washington, DC: NDU Press Book.

Heathcote, T.A. (2003) 'The Army of British India', in D. Chandler and I. Beckett (eds), *Oxford History of the British Army,* Oxford: Oxford University Press.

Heffernan, R. (2005) 'Exploring (and Explaining) the British Prime Minister', *British Journal of Politics and International Relations*, 7: 605–620.

Hennessy, P. (2000) 'The Blair Style and the Requirements of Twenty-First Century Premiership', *Political Quarterly*, 71(4): 386–395.

—— (2005) 'Informality and Circumscription: The Blair Style of Government in War and Peace', *Political Quarterly*, 76(1): 3–11.

Heywood, L. (2006) 'CIMIC in Iraq', *RUSI Journal*, 151(6): 36–40.

Hillen, J. (2000) *Blue Helmets: The Strategy of UN Military Operations*, Washington, DC: Brassey's.

—— (2002) 'Must U.S. Military Culture Reform?', in J. Lehman and H. Sicherman (eds), *America the Vulnerable: Our Military Problems and How to Fix Them*, Philadelphia, PA: Foreign Policy Research Institute.

Hills, A. (2003) 'Basrah and the Referent Points of Twofold War', *Small Wars and Insurgencies*, 14(3): 23–44.

—— (2005) 'Something Old, Something New: Security Governance in Iraq', *Conflict, Security and Development*, 5(2): 183–202.

Hirst, P. (2001) *War and Power in the 21st Century*, Cambridge: Polity Press.

Hoffman, B. (2004) *Insurgency and Counterinsurgency in Iraq*, RAND paper. Available online at www.rand.org/publications/OP/OP127/ (accessed 3 January 2005).

Hoffman, F.G. (2006) 'Peace Support Operations: The Next Revolution in Military Affairs', *Orbis*, Summer 2006, 395–411.

Hoffpauir, C. (2005) 'First Cavalry's Chiarelli Shares Iraq Experiences with NDIA Symposium', Available online at www.jfcom.mil/newslink/storyarchive/2005/pa040705.htm (accessed 3 August 2005).

Holden-Reid, B. (1998) 'A Doctrinal Perspective, 1988–98', *SCSI Occasional Paper 33*, Camberley, Surrey: SCSI.

Holsti, O.R. (2001) 'Of Chasms and Convergences: Attitudes and Beliefs of Civilian and Military Elites at the Start of a New Millennium', in P.D. Feaver and R.H. Kohn (eds), *Soldiers and Civilians: The Civil–Military Gap and American National Security*, Cambridge, MA: MIT Press.

Hopkinson, W. (2000a) 'The Making of British Defence Policy', *RUSI Journal*, October 2000, 21–24.

—— (2000b) *The Making of British Defence Policy*, Norwich: The Stationary Office.

Human Rights Watch (2003) *Basrah: Crime and Insecurity under British Occupation.* Available online at www.hrw.org/reports/2003 (accessed 3 April 2006).

Huntington, S. (1957) *The Soldier and the State: The Theory and Politics of Civil–Military Relations*, Cambridge, MA: Harvard University Press.

International Crisis Group (ICG) (2008) *Iraq After the Surge II: The Need for a New Political Strategy*, Middle East Report No. 75, 30 April. Available online at www.crisisgroup.org/home/index.cfm?id=5418&l=1 (accessed 25 May 2008).

IISS (2007) 'Iraq under the surge: Implementing Plan B', *IISS Strategic Comments*, 13(2): 1–2.

—— (2008) 'Complex Irregular Warfare: The Face of Contemporary Conflict', *The Military Balance*, 105(1): 411–420.

Jackson, M. (2000) 'KFOR: The Inside Story', *RUSI Journal*, 145(1): 13–18.

Janowitz, M. (1960) *The Professional Soldier: A Social and Political Portrait*, New York: The Free Press.

Johnson, D. and Metz, S. (1995) 'American Civil–Military Relations: New Issues, Enduring Problems', Strategic Studies Institute Report. Available online at www.dtic.mil/doctrine/jel/research_pubs/amcivil.pdf (accessed 21 February 2005).

Johnston, A.I. (1995) 'Thinking About Strategic Culture', *International Security*, 19(4): 32–64.

Johnston, P. (2000) 'Doctrine Is Not Enough: The Effect of Doctrine on the Behavior of Armies', *Parameters*, 30 (Autumn): 30–39.

Jones, A. (1966) 'Training and Doctrine in the British Army Since 1945', in M. Howard (ed.), *The Theory and Practice of War*, New York: Praeger.

Jones, B. and Kavanagh, D. (2003) *British Politics Today*, 7th edn, Manchester: Manchester University Press.

Kagan, D. (2002) 'Roles and Missions', in J.F. Lehman and H. Sicherman (eds), *America the Vulnerable: Our Military Problems and How to Fix Them*, Philadelphia, PA: Foreign Policy Research Institute.

Kaldor, M. (1999) *New and Old Wars: Organized Violence in a Global Era*, Cambridge: Polity Press.

Katzenstein, P.J. (ed.) (1996) *The Culture of National Security: Norms and Identity in World Politics*, New York: Columbia University Press.

Keegan, J. (1993) *A History of Warfare*, New York: Knopf.

—— (2004) *The Iraq War*, London: Hutchinson.

Khodyakov, D. (2007) 'Trust as a Process: A Three-Dimensional Approach', *Sociology*, 41(1): 115–132.

Kilcullen, D. (2006a) 'Counter-Insurgency Redux', *Survival*, 48(4): 111–130.

—— (2006b) 'Twenty-Eight Articles: Fundamentals of Company-Level Counterinsurgency', *Military Review*, May–June 2006, 103–108.

King, G., Keohane, R.O. and Verba, S. (1994) *Designing Social Inquiry: Scientific Inference in Qualitative Research*, Princeton, NJ: Princeton University Press.

Kitson, F. (1971) *Low Intensity Operations: Subversion, Insurgency, Peace-Keeping*, London: Frank Cass.

Klep, C. and Winslow, D. (2000) 'Learning Lessons the Hard Way – Somalia and Srebrenica Compared', in E.A. Schmidl (ed.), *Peace Operations Between War and Peace*, London: Frank Cass.

Kohn, R.H. (1991) 'The Constitution and National Security: The Intent of the Framers', in R.H. Kohn (ed.), *The United States Military Under the Constitution of the United States, 1789–1989*, New York: New York University Press.

Krulak, C.C. (1999) 'The Strategic Corporal: Leadership in the Three Block War', *Marines Magazine*, 28(1): 28–34.

Kümmel, G. (2003) 'The Democratic Control of Multinational Military Missions: Theorizing on an Under-Researched Area of Civil–Military Relations', in G. Kümmel and S. Collmer (eds), *Soldat – Militär – Politik – Gesellschaft: Facetten militärbezogener sozialwissenschaftlicher Forschung*, Liber amicorum für Paul Klein, Baden-Baden: Nomos.

Larson, A.D. (1974) 'Military Professionalism and Civil Control: A Comparative Analysis of Two Interpretations', *Journal of Political and Military Sociology*, 2 (Spring): 57–72.

Libby, L. (1993) 'American Perspectives on Civil–Military Relations and Democracy', Heritage Lecture No. 433. Available online at www.heritage.org/Research/National Security/HL433.cfm (accessed 17 February 2005).

Lijphart, A. (1999) *Patterns of Democracy: Government Forms and Performance in Thirty-Six Countries*, New Haven, CT: Yale University Press.

Lind, W.S. (2006) 'The Long War', *Defense and the National Interest*. Available online at www.d-n-i.net/lind/lind_2_08_06.htm (accessed 21 February 2007).

Lind, W.S., Nightengale, K.M., Schmitt, J., Sutton, J.W. and Wilson, G.I. (1989) 'The Changing Face of War: Into the Fourth Generation', *Marine Corps Gazette*, October 1989, 22–26.

Linn, B.M. (2002) 'The American Way of War Revisited', *Journal of Military History*, 66(2): 501–533.

Longhurst, K. (2000) 'The Concept of Strategic Culture', in G. Kümmel and A.D. Prufert (eds), *Military Sociology*, Baden-Baden: Nomos Verlagsgesellschaft.

Lord, C. (1985) 'American Strategic Culture', *Comparative Strategy*, 5(3): 269–293.

—— (1998), *The Presidency and the Management of National Security*, New York: The Free Press.

Lovelock, R. (2002) 'The Evolution of Peace Operations Doctrine', *Joint Force Quarterly*, Summer 2002, 67–73.

Luttwak, E.N. (1999) 'From Vietnam to Desert Fox: Civil–Military Relations in Modern Democracies', *Survival*, 41(1): 99–112.

McCann, C. and Pigeau, R. (1999) 'Clarifying the Concepts of Control and of Command', Command and Control Research and Technical Symposium, Newport, RI, 29 June–1 July.

Macdonald, K. (1988) '"Vitai Lampada": Preserving the Elite', *Armed Forces and Society*, 14(2): 233–245.

—— (2004) 'Black Mafia, Loggies and Going for the Stars: The Military Elite Revisited', *The Sociological Review*, 52(1): 106–135.

McInnes, C. (1996) *Hot War, Cold War: The British Army's Way in Warfare 1945–1995*, Washington, DC: Brassey's.

—— (2001) 'So who needs doctrine anyway?', unpublished paper presented at the BISA Annual Conference, Edinburgh.

Mack, A.J.R. (1975) 'Why Big Nations Lose Small Wars: The Politics of Asymmetric Conflict', *World Politics*, 27(2): 175–200.

Mackie, T. and March, D. (1995) 'The Comparative Method', in D. March and G. Stoker (eds), *Theory and Methods in Political Science*, London: Macmillan Press Ltd.

Mackinlay, J. (1999) 'Beyond the Logjam: A Doctrine for Complex Emergencies', *Small Wars and Insurgencies*, 9(1): 114–131.

—— (2004) 'Casualties of the US–UK Military Alliance', *World Today*, December 2004.

Mackinlay, J. and Kent, R. (1997) 'A New Approach to Complex Emergencies', *International Peacekeeping*, 4(4): 31–49.

McMaster, H.R. (1997) *Dereliction of Duty: Lyndon Johnson, Robert McNamara, The Joint Chiefs of Staff, and the Lies that Led to Vietnam*, New York: HarperCollins.

Mäder, M. (2004). *In Pursuit of Conceptual Excellence: The Evolution of British Military-Strategic Doctrine in the Post-Cold War Era, 1989–2002*, Bern: Peter Lang.

Mahnken, T.G. (2003) 'The American Way of War in the Twenty-First Century', in Efraim Inbar (ed.), *Democracies and Small Wars*, Portland, OR: Frank Cass.

Marcella, G. (2000) 'National Security and the Interagency Process: Forward into the 21st Century', in D.T. Stuart (ed.), *Organizing for National Security*, Carlisle, PA: Strategic Studies Institute.

Marsh, D. and Stoker, G. (1995) *Theory and Methods in Political Science*, London: Macmillan Press Ltd.

Mattis, J. (2008) 'Assessment of Effects Based Operations'. Memorandum for U.S. Joint Forces Command, 14 August. Available online at http://smallwarsjournal.com/documents/usjfcomebomemo.pdf (accessed 25 October 2008).

Merom, G. (2003) *How Democracies Lose Small Wars: State, Society, and the Failures of France in Algeria, Israel in Lebanon, and the United States in Vietnam*, New York: Cambridge University Press.

Metz, S. (2003) 'Insurgency and Counterinsurgency in Iraq', *The Washington Quarterly*, 27(1): 25–36.

Michael, K. (2007a) 'The Israeli Defence Forces as an Epistemic Authority: An Intellectual Challenge in the Reality of the Israel–Palestinian Conflict', *Journal of Strategic Studies*, 30(3): 443–445.

—— (2007b) 'The Dilemma Behind the Classical Dilemma of Civil–Military Relations: The "Discourse Space" Model and the Israeli Case During the Oslo Process', *Armed Forces and Society*, 33(4): 518–546.

Millet, A. (1979) *The American Political System and Civilian Control of the Military: A Historical Perspective*, Columbus, OH: Mershon Center, Ohio State University.

Millett, A.R., Murray, W. and Watman, K.H. (1986) 'The Effectiveness of Military Organizations', *International Security*, 11(1): 37–71.

Mockaitis, T.R. (1990) *British Counter-Insurgency, 1919–1960*, London: Macmillan.

—— (1999) *Peace Operations and Intrastate Conflict: The Sword or the Olive Branch*, Westport, CT: Praeger.

—— (2000) 'From Counterinsurgency to Peace Enforcement: New Names for Old Games?', in E.A. Schmidl (ed.), *Peace Operations Between War and Peace*, London: Frank Cass.

—— (2004) 'Civil–Military Cooperation in Peace Operation: The Case of Kosovo', Strategic Studies Institute Report. Available online at www.carlisle.army.mil/ssi/pubs/display.cfm/hurl/PubID=583 (accessed 15 January 2005).

Morris, J. (1976) 'The War That Broke the Imperial Spirit', *Horizon*, 18: 49–63.

Moskos, C.C. (1983) 'The All-Volunteer Force', in M. Janowitz and S.D. Wesbrook (eds), *The Political Education of Soldiers*, Beverly Hills, CA: SAGE Publications.

—— (2000) 'Towards a Postmodern Military: The United States as a Paradigm', in C.C. Moskos, J.A. Williams and D.R. Segal (eds), *The Postmodern Military: Armed Forces After the Cold War*, New York: Oxford University Press.

Moskos, C.C., Williams, J.A. and Segal, D.R. (2000) *The Postmodern Military: Armed Forces After the Cold War*, Oxford: Oxford University Press.

Murdock, C.A. (ed.) (2004) *Beyond Goldwater–Nichols: Defense Reform for a New Strategic Era, Phase 1 Report*, Washington, DC: CSIS.

Murray, W. (1997) 'Thinking About Revolutions in Warfare', *Joint Force Quarterly*, 16: 69–76.

Murray, W. and Knox, M. (2001a) 'Thinking About Revolutions in Warfare', in W. Murray and M. Knox (eds), *The Dynamics of Military Revolution, 1300–2050*, Cambridge: Cambridge University Press.

—— (2001b) 'The Future Behind Us', in W. Murray and M. Knox (eds), *The Dynamics of Military Revolution, 1300–2050*, Cambridge: Cambridge University Press.

Murray, W. and Scales, R.H. (2003) *The Iraq War: A Military History*, London: Belknap Press.

Münkler, H. (2002) *Die Neuen Kriege*, Reinbeck: Rowohlt Verlag.

Nagl, J.A. (1999) 'Learning to Eat Soup with a Knife – Military Policy', *World Affairs*, Spring. Available online at www.findarticles.com/p/-articles/mi_m0PBZ/is_2004_May-June/ai_n6123976 (accessed 23 January 2005).

—— (2002) *Counterinsurgency Lessons from Malaya and Vietnam: Learning to Eat Soup with a Knife*, Westport, CT: Praeger.

Nash, W.L. (Chair) (2005) 'In the Wake of War: Improving U.S. Post-Conflict Capabilities', Report of an Independent Task Force Sponsored by the Council on Foreign Relations, 15. Available online at www.cfr.org/content/publications/attachments/Post-Conflict_Capabilities.pdf (accessed 15 September 2005).

Nielsen, S.C. (2005) 'Civil–Military Relations Theory and Military Effectiveness', *Public Administration and Management*, 10(2): 61–84.

Norton, P. (2003) 'The Presidentialisation of British Politics', *Government and Opposition*, 38(2): 274–278.

Odierno, R.T. (2008) 'The Surge in Iraq: One Year Later', *Heritage Lectures*, The Heritage Foundation, 13 March.

O'Hanlon, M.E. (1998) 'Beware the "RMA'nia!"', paper presented at the National Defense University, 9 September. Available online at www.brookings.edu/dybdocroot/views/articles/ohanlon/1998ndu.htm (accessed 2 February 2002).

—— (2004) 'Iraq Without a Plan', *Policy Review*, No. 128. Available online at www.policyreview.org/dec04/ohanlon.html>(accessed 22 January 2005).

Oliviero, C.S. (1998) 'Trust, Manoeuvre Warfare, Mission Command and Canada's Army', *The Army Doctrine and Training Bulletin*, August. Available online at http://armyapp.dnd.ca/ael/ADTB/Vol_1/August_98/english/Trust_maoeuvre.htm (accessed 14 April 2007).

Ollivant, D.A. and Chewning, E.D. (2006) 'Producing Victory: Rethinking Conventional Forces in COIN Operations', *Military Review*, July–August 2006, 50–59.

Otley, C.B. (1973) 'Educational Background of British Army Officers', *Sociology*, 7(2): 191–209.

Perito, R.M. (2004) 'Nation Building: Biting the Bullet in Afghanistan and Iraq', in R.M. Perito, *Where is the Lone Ranger When We Need Him: America's Search for a Postconflict Stability Force*, Washington, DC: US Institute of Peace Press.

Pimlott, J. (1985) 'The British Army: The Dhofar Campaign, 1970–1975', in Ian F.W. Beckett and John Pimlott (eds), *Armed Forces and Modern Counter-Insurgency*, New York: St Martin's Press, Inc.

Porter, A. (2000) 'The South African War and Its Historians', *African Affairs*, 99: 633–648.

Posen, B.R. (1984) *The Sources of Military Doctrine: France, Britain, and Germany Between the World Wars*, New York: Cornell University Press.

Powell, C. (1992) 'US Forces: Challenges Ahead', *Foreign Affairs*, 71(5): 32–45.

Prins, G. (2002) *The Heart of War: On Power, Conflict and Obligation in the Twenty-First Century*, London: Routledge.

Pugh, M. (2001) 'The Challenges of Civil–Military Relations in International Peace Operations', *Disasters*, 25(4): 345–357.

Ricks, T.E. (2006a) *Fiasco: The American Military Adventure in Iraq*, London: Allen Lane.

Robinson, L. (2008) *Tell Me How This Ends: General David Petraeus and the Search for a Way Out of Iraq*, New York: PublicAffairs.

Robinson, P. (1999) 'The CNN Effect: Can the News Media Drive Foreign Policy?', *Review of International Studies*, 25(2): 301–309.

Rose, M. (1999) *Fighting for Peace: Lessons from Bosnia*, London: Warner Books.

Schein, E. (1990) 'Organizational Culture', *American Psychologist*, (45): 109–119.

Schiff, R. (1995) 'Civil–Military Relations Reconsidered: A Theory of Concordance', *Armed Forces and Society*, 22(1): 7–24.

Scruton, R. (2000) *England: An Elegy*, London: Chatto.

Shaw, M. (2005) *The New Western Way of War: Risk Transfer War and Its Crisis in Iraq*, Cambridge: Polity.

Short, A. (1975) *The Communist Insurrection in Malaya, 1948–1960*, Plymouth: Frederick Muller.

Smith, R. (2005) *The Utility of Force: The Art of War in the Modern World*, London: Allen Lane.

Snider, D.M. (2002) 'An Uninformed Debate on Military Culture', in J.F. Lehman and H. Sicherman (eds), *America the Vulnerable: Our Military Problems and How to Fix Them*, Philadelphia, PA: Foreign Policy Research Institute.

Snider, D.M. and Watkins, G.L. (2002) 'Introduction', in L.J. Matthews (ed.), *The Future of the Army Profession*, Boston, MA: McGraw-Hill.

Steele, C.E. (2004) 'Zero-Defect Leaders: No Second Chance?', *Military Review*, September–October 2004, 66–70.

Steele, R.D. (2000) 'Presidential Leadership and National Security Policy Making', in D.T. Stuart (ed.), *Organizing for National Security*, Carlisle, PA: SSI.

Storr, J. (2003) 'A Command Philosophy for the Information Age: The Continuing Relevance of Mission Command', *Defence Studies*, 3(3): 119–129.

Strachan, H. (1997) *The Politics of the British Army*, Oxford: Clarendon Press.

—— (2003) 'The British Way in Warfare', in D. Chandler and I. Beckett (eds), *The Oxford History of the British Army*, Oxford: Oxford University Press.

—— (2006) 'Making Strategy: Civil–Military Relations After Iraq', *Survival*, 48(3): 59–82.

Strawson, J. (2003) 'The Thirty Years Peace', in D. Chandler and I. Beckett (eds), *The Oxford History of the British Army*, Oxford: Oxford University Press.

Stuart, D.T. (2000) *Organising for National Security*, Carlisle, PA: Strategic Studies Institute.

Summers, H.G. (1982) *On Strategy: A Critical Analysis of the Vietnam War*, Novato, CA: Presidio Press.

Thompson, R. (1966) *Defeating Communist Insurgency: The Lessons of Malaya and Vietnam*, New York: Praeger.

Thornton, R. (2000) 'The Role of Peace Support Operations Doctrine in the British Army', *International Peacekeeping*, 7(2): 41–62.

—— (2003). 'A Welcome "Revolution"? The British Army and the Changes of the Strategic Defence Review', *Defence Studies*, 3(3): 38–62.

—— (2004a) 'The British Army and the Origins of Its Minimum Force Philosophy', *Small Wars and Insurgencies*, 15(1): 83–106.

—— (2004b) 'Historical Origins of the British Army's Counter-Insurgency and Counter-Terrorist Techniques', Geneva Centre for the Democratic Control of the Armed Forces Conference paper. Available online at www.dcaf.ch/news/PfP_7thConf_Bucharest/Baxter.pdf (accessed 14 November 2004).

Trompenaars, F. and Hampden-Turner, C. (1997) *Riding the Waves of Culture: Understanding Cultural Diversity in Business*, London: Nicholas Brealey.

Ucko, D. (2008) 'Innovation or Inertia: The U.S. Military and the Learning of Counterinsurgency', *Orbis*, 52(2): 290–310.

Varhola, C.H. (2004) 'American Challenges in Postwar Iraq', FPRI E-Notes. Available online at www.fpri.org/enotes/20040527.americawar.varhola.iraqchallenges.html (accessed 24 March 2007).

Walker, M. (2005) 'The Heart of Defence: Men and Women of the UK Armed Forces', *RUSI Journal*, 150(6): 24–29.

Weaver, W. (1948) 'Science and Complexity', *American Scientist*, 36: 536.

Weigley, R.F. (1973) *The American Way of War: A History of United States Military Strategy and Policy*, Bloomington, IN: Indiana University Press.

—— (2000) 'The American Civil–Military Cultural Gap: A Historical Perspective, Colonial Times to the Present', in P. Feaver and R. Kohn (eds), *Soldiers and Civilians: The Civil–Military Gap and American National Security*, Cambridge, MA: MIT Press.

Weinberger, C.W. (1990) *Fighting for Peace: Seven Critical Years in the Pentagon*, New York: Warner Books.

Wesbrook, S.D. (1983) 'Sociopolitical Training in the Military: A Framework for Analysis', in M. Janowitz and S.D. Wesbrook (eds), *The Political Education of Soldiers*, Beverly Hills, CA: SAGE Publications.

Williams, M.C. (1998) *Civil–Military Relations and Peacekeeping*, London: Oxford University Press.

Winton, H. (1988) *To Change an Army*, Lawrence, KS: University Press of Kansas.

Woodward, B. (2004) *Plan of Attack*, New York: Simon & Schuster.

Younez, K. and Rosen, N. (2008). *Uprooted and Unstable: Meeting Urgent Humanitarian Needs in Iraq*, Refugees International, April 2008.

Zucker, L.G. (1986) 'Production of Trust: Institutional Sources of Economic Structure', in B.M. Staw and L.L. Cummings (eds), *Research in Organizational Behavior*, Vol. 8, Greenwich, CT: JAI Press.

Newspaper articles

ABCNews (2003) 'American Flag Flap: Stars and Stripes on Saddam's Doomed Statue Strikes a Sensitive Chord' 10 April. Available online at http://abcnews.go.com/sections/ GMA/Primetime/Iraq030410USFlagStatue.html (accessed 24 May 2004).

Abdul-Ahad, G. (2007) '"Welcome to Tehran" – How Iran Took Control of Basra', *Guardian*, 19 May.

BBC News (2004) 'Analysts Warn of Army Reform Risk', 16 December. Available online at http://news.bbc.co.uk/2/hi/uk_news/4102481.stm (accessed 25 June 2006).

—— (2006a) 'Former Army Chief Criticises MoD', 7 December. Available online at http://news.bbc.co.uk/2/hi/uk_news/6215296.stm (accessed 24 February 2008).

—— (2006b) 'Iraq Abuse Case Soldiers Jailed', 25 February. Available online at http:// news.bbc.co.uk/2/hi/uk_news/4296511.stm (accessed 15 April 2006).

Beaumont, P. (2007). 'Handover in Basra as Killings Go On', *Observer*, 16 December. Available online at www.guardian.co.uk/world/2007/dec/16/uk.iraq.

Bunting, M. (2004) 'Screams Will not be Heard', *Guardian*, 8 April. Available online at www.guardian.co.uk/comment/story/0,3604,1345833,00.html (accessed 30 June 2006).

Clarke, V. (2003) 'DoD News Briefing – ASD PA Clarke and Maj. Gen. McChrystal', 14 April. Available online at www.defenselink.mil/transcripts/2003/tr20030414–0105.html (accessed 30 August 2005).

Dagher S. (2007). 'As British Troops Exit Basra, Shiites Vie to Fill Power Vacuum', *Christian Science Monitor*, 17 September.

Devenny, P. and McLean, R. (2005) 'The Battle for Basra', *American Spectator*, 1

November. Available online at www.spectator.org/dsp_article.asp?art_id=8953 (accessed 04 September 2006)

Duffy, M. (2006) 'The Shame of Kilo Company', *Time*, 167:23.

Economist, The (2002) 'A Model of Nation-Building?', 17 April. Available online at www.economist.com/agenda/displayStory.cfm?story_id=1086568 (accessed 14 February 2005).

—— (2007) 'Beating the Retreat', 19 December.

—— (2008) 'The Forgotten War', 19 March.

Finer, J. (2006) 'Troops Facing Murder Probe', *Washington Post*, 1 July, A01.

Fukuyama, F. (2005) 'Invasion of the Isolationists', *New York Times*, 31 August.

Garamone, J. (2004) 'Myers: Changing Military Culture Key to Transformation', *American Forces Press Service*, 10 July. Available online at www.au.af.mil/au/awc/awcgate/af/myers_chg_culture.htm (accessed 15 February 2005).

Harding, T. (2004) 'Iraqis Urge the Army to Reclaim the Streets from Shia Rebels', *Daily Telegraph*, 30 August. Available online at www.telegraph.co.uk/core/Content/display-Printable.jhtml?xml=/news/2004/08/30/wirq130.xml&site=5 (accessed 3 August 2006).

Harrison, D. (2004) '"Payback Time" for Black Watch', *The Times*, 26 November. Available online at www.timesonline.co.uk/article/0,,7374–1375087,00.html (accessed 25 January 2007).

Hider, J. (2006) 'Hardliners Exploiting Britain's Softly-Softly Approach', *The Times*, 1 February. Available online at www.timesonline.co.uk/article/0,,7374–2019096,00.html (accessed 3 June 2007).

Hirsh, M. (2003) 'Our New Civil War: Freeing a Nation Is One Thing; Resurrecting It Another', *Newsweek*, 12 May. Available online at http://msnbc.msn.com/id/3068556/ (accessed 15 February 2005).

Holt, D. (2003) 'Army Institute to be Shut Down: Critics Hit Loss of Training Center for Peacekeeping', *Chicago Tribune*, 15 April. Available online at www.chicagotribune.com/news/nationworld/chi0304150249apr-15,1,533388.story?ctrack=2&cset=true (accessed 14 February 2005).

Independent (2006) 'Operation Sinbad: Mission Failure Casts Doubt on Entire British Presence in Iraq', 8 October. Available online at http://news.independent.co.uk/world/middle_east/article1819651.ece (accessed 4 March 2007).

Jordan, M. (2005) 'Blair Failed in Dealing With Bush, Book Says', *Washington Post*, 8 November. Available online at www.washingtonpost.com/wp-dyn/content/article/2005/11/07/AR2005110701569.html (accessed 4 March 2007).

Judd, T. (2007) 'Serving British Soldier Exposes Horror of War in "Crazy" Basra', *Independent*, 27 April. Available online at http://news.independent.co.uk/world/middle_east/article2488848.ece (accessed 13 May 2007).

Kaplan, F. 'Challenging the Generals', *New York Magazine*, 26 August.

Kite, M. and Thomson, A. (2004) 'Violence in Iraq Will Get Even Worse, Says Blair', *Daily Telegraph*, 18 April. Available online at www.telegraph.co.uk/news/main.jhtml?xml=/news/2004/04/18/wirq18.xml (accessed 15 January 2007).

Knickmeyer, E. and Finer, J. (2005) 'British Smash into Iraqi Jail to Free 2 Detained Soldiers', *Washington Post*, 20 September, A01.

Knickmeyer, E. and Hernandez, N. (2006) 'Iraq Plans Probes: Ethics Training Set for Troops', *Washington Post*, 2 June, A16.

Kwiatkovski, K. (2004) 'The New Pentagon Papers', *Salon.com*, 10 March. Available online at http://dir.salon.com/story/opinion/feature/2004/03/10/osp_moveon/index.html (accessed 15 September 2005).

Lloyd Parry, R. (2005) 'No Turning Back in the Battle to Win Over Hearts and Minds', *Daily Telegraph*, 8 November. Available online at www.telegraph.co.uk/news/main. jhtml;jsessionid=0CXATDY0FA-CWRQFIQMFSFF4AVCBQ0IV0?xml=/news/2004/11/06/wirq306.xml (accessed 17 March 2007).

Lumpkin, J.J. and Linzer, D. (2003) 'Army Says Policy Choice Led to Chaos in Iraq', *Philadelphia Inquirer*, 28 November 2003.

Lynch, C. and Partlow, J. (2007) 'Civilian Toll in Iraq at "Higher Levels"', *Washington Post*, 12 June. Available online at www.washingtonpost.com/wp-dyn/content/article/2007/06/11/AR2007061100336.html?referrer=email (accessed 3 June 2007).

North, A. (2006) 'Fatal Basra Crash Sparks Unrest', *BBC News*, 6 May. Available online at http://news.bbc.co.uk/2/hi/middle_east/4981148.stm (accessed 13 June 2007).

O'Hanlon, M.E. (2005) 'Civil–Military Relations: Our Dangerous, Growing Divide', *Washington Post*, 28 November. Available online at www.brookings.edu/views/op-ed/ohanlon/20051128.htm (accessed 29 June 2006).

—— (2006) 'Taking It to the Streets: In Fiasco, Thomas Ricks Criticizes the Military's Performance in Iraq', *Slate*, 28 July. Available online at www.brookings.edu/views/articles/ohanlon/20060728.htm (accessed 13 May 2007).

Partlow, J. (2007) 'Attacks Kill 17 U.S. Soldiers in Iraq', *Washington Post*, 4 June. Available online at www.washingtonpost.com/wp-dyn/content/article/2007/06/04/AR2007060400360.html (accessed 06 June 2007).

Philps, A. (2003) 'Aid Officials Overwhelmed by Chaos and Violence', *Daily Telegraph*, 12 May. Available online at www.commondreams.org/headlines03/0512–06.htm (accessed 30 August 2005).

Pincus, W. (2005) 'Memo: U.S. Lacked Full Postwar Iraq Plan', *Washington Post*, 12 June.

Poole, O. (2006) 'Worst War Crime Committed by US in Iraq', *Daily Telegraph*, 27 May. Available online at www.telegraph.co.uk/news/main.jhtml?xml=/news/2006/05/27/-wus27.xml&sSheet-=/news/2006/05/27/ixnews.html (accessed 12 June 2006).

Rees-Mogg, W. (2007) 'Blood on a Budget: Our Soldiers Betrayed', *The Times*, 27 August.

Ricks, T.E. (2006b) 'In Iraq, Military Forgot Lessons of Vietnam', *Washington Post*, 23 July.

—— (2006c) 'The Lessons of Counterinsurgency: U.S. Unit Praised for Tactics Against Iraqi Fighters, Treatment of Detainees', *Washington Post*, 16 February, A14.

Royle, T. (2005) 'Basrah Burns: The British Army's Softly-Softly Approach in Iraq', *Sunday Herald*, 25 September. Available online at www.findarticles.com/p/articles/mi_qn4156/is_20050925/ai_n15618155 (accessed 3 November 2006).

RUSI Journal (2007) 'RUSI Interview with General David Richards', 152(2) April.

Sands, S. (2006) 'Sir Richard Dannatt: A Very Honest General', *Daily Mail*, 12 October. Available online at www.dailymail.co.uk/pages/live/articles/news/news.html?in_article_id=410175&in_page_id=1770 (accessed 1 March 2007).

Scott Tyson, A. (2004) 'A General of Nuance and Candor: Abizaid Brings New Tenor to Mideast Post', *Christian Science Monitor*, 5 March. Available online at www.csmonitor.com/2004/0305/p01s02-usmi.html (accessed 13 January 2005).

Smith, M. (2004) 'Black Watch Will Operate by Army Rules', *Daily Telegraph*, 22 October. Available online at www.telegraph.co.uk/news/main.jhtml?xml=/news/2004/10/22/wirq122.xml&sSheet=/news/2004/10/22/ixhome.html> (accessed 4 March 2007, 23 June 2007).

—— (2007) 'Army Officers Set Up Union to Vent War Anger', *Sunday Times*, 21 May.

Stannard, M.B. (2004) 'Fallujah on Verge of Falling – Fighting Flares Across Iraq, Guns and Money: Insurgency Can't Be Eliminated With Purely Military Means', *San Francisco Chronicle*, 14 November. Available online at www.sfgate.com/cgibin/article. cgi?f=/c/a/2004/11/14/MNGF69RDSN1.DTL (accessed 1 December 2004).

Times Online (2005) 'British Forces Break Soldiers Out of Basra Jail', 19 September. Available online at www.timesonline.co.uk/article/0,,7374–1788054,00.html (accessed 14 August 2006).

White, J., Lane, C. and Tate, J. (2006) 'Homicide Charges Rare in Iraq War', *Washington Post*, 28 August, A01.

Wood, P. (2006) 'Taking the Pulse of Life in Basrah', *BBC News*, 8 May. Available online at http://news.bbc.co.uk/1/hi/uk/4752709.stm (accessed 15 March 2007).

Interviews

UK

Codner, M. (2004) Director of Military Sciences, Royal United Services Institute, London, interview by author, 22 November.

Connal, J. (2005) Special Adviser to the Secretary of State for Defence, Ministry of Defence, London, 23 March.

Heywood, Captain L. (2007) CIMIC officer in Iraq, interview by author at RUSI, 26 January.

Lowe, Lieutenant Colonel M. (2004) Commanding Officer of 3rd Battalion, The Parachute Regiment, Colchester, 10 May.

Mayall, Brigadier S. (2004) Director, Resources and Plans, Former Commander Multi-National Brigade (Centre) KFOR, Former Commander 1st Mechanised Brigade, MoD, 18 November.

Palmer, B. (2005) Deputy Director, Resources and Plans, Ministry of Defence, London, 23 March.

Presentation on the 'Comprehensive Approach', by Edwin Samuels, Foreign and Commonwealth Office and Lieutenant Colonel Tim Russell, MoD, Swedish Ministry of Defence, 24 May 2006.

Russell, Lieutenant Colonel T. (2005) Directorate of Strategic Plans, Ministry of Defence, London, 23 March.

Thornton, Dr R. (2005) King's College London, 24 March.

Trott, C. (2005) Head of Policy and Strategy, Post Conflict Reconstruction Unit, DFID, London, 22 March.

US

Cordesman, A. (2005) Center for Strategic and International Studies, Washington, DC, 15 March.

Grissom, A. (2005) RAND Corporation, email to the author, 2 March.

Harris, Colonel J. (2005) US National War College, Washington, DC, 10 March.

Louis, Colonel R.G. (2005) US National War College, Washington, DC, Special Forces expert, 10 March.

McMaster, Colonel H.R. (2007) International Institute for Strategic Studies, London, 23 January.

Moisan, Colonel A. (2005) US National Defense University, Washington, DC, 11 March.
Murdock, C. (2005) Center for Strategic and International Studies, Washington, DC, 15 March.
Nagl, Lieutenant Colonel J. (2005) Military Advisor to Deputy Defense Secretary Paul Wolfowitz, Department of Defense, 9 March.
Parmly, M. (2005) US National War College, Washington, DC, 11 March.
Roundtable discussion at the RAND Corporation, chaired by Dr Adam Grissom, Washington, DC, 8 March 2005.
Roundtable discussion at US Department of State, chaired by David Armitage, Washington DC, 14 March 2005.
Stevenson, Dr C. (2005) US National War College, Washington, DC, 10 March.
White, Colonel G. (2004) US National War College, Washington, DC, 10 March.

Official documents, speeches and press releases

Baker, J.A. III, and Hamilton, L.H. (2006) *The Iraq Study Group Report: The Way Forward – A New Approach*, United States Institute of Peace.
Bush, G.W. (2003) 'Address to the American Enterprise Institute', 26 February. Available online at www.whitehouse.gov/news/releases/2003/02/iraq/20030226–11.html (accessed 24 August 2005).
—— (2004) 'President Outlines Steps to Help Iraq Achieve Democracy and Freedom', Remarks by the President on Iraq and the War on Terror, US Army War College, 24 May. Available online at www.whitehouse.gov/news/releases/2004/05/20040524–10.html (accessed 30 August 2005).
Center for Army Lessons Learned (2004) 'On Point: The United States Army in Operation Iraqi Freedom'. Available online at www.globalsecurity.org/military/library/report/2004/onpoint/intro.htm (accessed 24 August 2005).
Dannatt, R. (2007) 'Address at the RUSI Future Land Warfare Conference on the subject of "Tomorrow's Army; Today's Challenges"', 5 June. Available online at www.mod.uk/DefenceInternet/DefenceNews/DefencePolicyAndBusiness/ (accessed 2 September 2007).
Feith, D.J. (2003) 'Post-War Planning', Hearing of the Senate Foreign Relations Committee, 11 February. Available online at www.iraqwatch.org/government/US/HearingsPreparedstatements/sfrc-feith-021103.htm (accessed 8 August 2005).
Gates, R. (2007) 'Report to Congress on the Implementation of DoD Directive 3000.05, *Military Support for Stability, Security, Transition and Reconstruction (SSTR) Operations*', 1 April.
Grossman, M.I. (2003) 'The Future of Iraq', Hearing of the Senate Foreign Relations Committee, 11 February. Available online at www.iraqwatch.org/government/US/HearingsPreparedstatements/sfrc-grossman-021103.htm (accessed 8 August 2005).
House of Commons Defence Committee (2005) *Iraq: An Initial Assessment of Post Conflict Operations: Government Response to the Committee's Sixth Report of Session 2004–05*, HC 436, London: The House of Commons.
Joint Doctrine and Concepts Centre (JDCC) (2001) JWP 0–01, *British Defence Doctrine*.
—— (2004a) JWP 5–00 *Joint Operations Planning*.
—— (2004b) JWP 3–00 *Joint Operations Execution*.
Lugar, R. and Biden, J. (2003) 'The Future of Iraq', Congress, Senate, Committee on Foreign Relations, 108th Congress, 1st session.
Nash, W.L. (Chair) (2005) 'In the Wake of War: Improving U.S. Post-Conflict Capabil-

ities', report of an Independent Task Force Sponsored by the Council on Foreign Relations, 15. Available online at www.cfr.org/content/publications/attachments/Post-Conflict_Capabilities.pdf (accessed 15 September 2005).

Review of Intelligence on Weapons of Mass Destruction: Report of a Committee of Privy Counsellors (2004) HC 898, HMSO, 14 July.

Rumsfeld, D. (2003) 'DoD News Briefing – Secretary Rumsfeld and Gen. Myers', 3 March. Available online at www.defenselink.mil/transcripts/2003/t03212003_t0321sd1.html (accessed 3 February 2005).

Straw, J. (2003) 'Written Ministerial Statement by the Foreign Secretary, Jack Straw', House of Commons, Tuesday, 7 January. Available online at http://sv.uknow.or.jp/be_e/ukview/speeches/speeches/SP000178_1__e.htm (accessed 6 August 2008).

Thornton, R. (2005) 'British Counter-Insurgency Operations in Iraq', in House of Commons Defence Committee, *Iraq: An Initial Assessment of Post Conflict Operations: Sixth Report of Session 2004–05, Volume II, HC 65-I*, London: The House of Commons.

UK Army Doctrine Publication (1995) Vol. 2, *Command*, Army Code 71564.

—— (2000) 'Soldiering, the Military Covenant', GD&D/18/34/71 Army Code 71642. Available online at www.army.mod.uk/servingsoldier/usefulinfo/valuesgeneral/adp-5milcov/ss_hrpers_values_adp5_1_w.html#milcov (accessed 20 June 2006).

—— (2005) *Land Operations.*

UK Army Doctrine Publication 3000 (n.d.) *The Nature of Doctrine.*

UK Army Field Manual (2001) Vol. 1, Part 10, *Counter Insurgency Operations.*

UK Ministry of Defence (UK MoD) (2002) *The Strategic Defence Review: A New Chapter*. Available online at www.mod.uk/issues/sdr/newchapter.htm (accessed 24 July 2004).

—— (2003a) 'Operations in Iraq: Lessons for the Future'. Available online at www.mod.uk/linked_files/publications/iraq/opsiniraq.pdf (accessed 25 October 2004).

—— (2003b) 'NEC Outline Concept: Part 1 – Background and Programme of Work'. Available online at www.mod.uk/issues/nec/concept_papers.htm (accessed 23 July 2004).

—— (2003c) *Iraq: Military Campaign Objectives*. Available online at www.operations.mod.uk/telic/objectives.pdf (accessed 15 April 2005).

—— (2003d) *Operations in Iraq, First Reflections.*

—— (2003e) 'Defence Secretary and Chief of the Defence Staff: Press Conference at the Ministry of Defence', London, 21 March. Available online at www.operations.mod.uk/telic/press_21march.htm (accessed 23 November 2005).

—— (2005) 'Defence Framework: How Defence Works', London: Ministry of Defence.

—— (2006) *The Comprehensive Approach*, Joint Discussion Note, 4/05.

—— (2008) 'Basra is "secure" says UK's military chief in southern Iraq', *Defence News*, 13 October. Available Online at www.mod.uk/DefenceInternet/DefenceNews/Military-Operations/BasraIssecureSaysUksMilitaryChiefInSouthernIraq.htm (accessed 25 October 2008).

—— (n.d.a) *Departmental Framework*. Available online at www.mod.uk (accessed 09 June 2006).

—— (n.d.b) 'About the MoD', MoD website. Available online at www.mod.uk/aboutus/modorg/index.html (accessed 17 February 2005).

—— (n.d.c) 'Key Facts about Defence', MoD Website. Available online at www.mod.uk/DefenceInternet/AboutDefence/Organisation/-KeyFactsAboutDefence/ (accessed 5 March 2007).

—— (n.d.d), 'UK Operations in Iraq: Key Facts and Figures', Defence Factsheet. Available online at www.mod.uk/DefenceInternet/FactSheets/OperationsFactsheets/Operations InIraqKeyFactsFigures.htm (accessed 13 August 2006).

US Department of Defense (US DoD) (1995) *Joint Doctrine for Military Operations Other Than War*. Joint Publication 3-07. Washington DC: Department of Defense.

—— (1996) *Interagency Coordination During Joint Operations Vol. 1*, Joint Publication 3-08, Washington, DC: Department of Defense.

—— (1997) *National Military Strategy*, Executive Summary.

—— (2000), *Joint Vision 2020*. Available online at www.dtic.mil/jointvision/jvpub2.htm (accessed 25 January 2009).

—— (2001) *Doctrine for Joint Operations*, Joint Publication 3-0.

—— (2003) *Stability Operations and Support Operations 3-07*.

—— (2006) *Quadrennial Defense Review Report*, Washington, DC: Department of Defense.

—— (2007) 'Network centric operations (NCO) case study: The British Approach to Low-Intensity Operations Part I'. Available online at www.stormingmedia.us/10/1040/A104074.html (accessed 8 October 2008).

US Department of the Army (2001) *Tactics*, FM 3-90. Washington DC: Department of Defense.

—— (2003) FM 6–0, *Mission Command: Command and Control of Army Forces*. Available online at www.globalsecurity.org/military/library/policy/army/fm/6–0/ (accessed 6 March 2005).

—— (2004) 'FMI 3–07.22 Counterinsurgency Operations'. Available online at www.fas.org/irp/doddir/army/fmi3–07–22.pdf (accessed 15 January 2005).

—— (2006) FM 3–24, *Counterinsurgency*.

US Department of the Navy (2006) 'MCDP 6 Command and Control', Washington, DC: Headquarters United States Marine Corps.

US Department of State (2003) 'Humanitarian Relief Planning for Iraq', 28 February. Available online at http://fpc.state.gov/fpc/18150.htm (accessed 3 February 2005).

US JCS (1995) 'JP3.07 Joint Doctrine for Military Operations Other than War'. Available online at www.dtic.mil/doctrine/jel/new_pubs/jp3_07.pdf (accessed 12 December 2004).

—— (1999) 'JP3–07.3 Joint Tactics, Techniques, and Procedures for Peace Operations'. Available online at www.dtic.mil/doctrine/jel/new_pubs/jp3_07_3.pdf (accessed 12 December 2004).

US Joint Forces Command (2001) 'Effects-Based Operations White Paper Version 1.0', Norfolk, VA: Concepts Department J9.

—— (2007) 'Effects-Based Approach to Operations'. Available online at www.jfcom.mil/about/fact_ebo.htm (accessed 12 March 2007).

US White House (2002) *The National Security Strategy of the United States of America*. Available online at www.whitehouse.gov/nsc/nss.html (accessed 3 February 2006).

—— (2005) *National Strategy for Victory in Iraq*. Available online at www.whitehouse.gov/infocus/iraq/iraq_strategy_nov2005.html (accessed 6 December 2005).

Wolfowitz, P. (2003) 'Testimony on Iraq Reconstruction', Deputy Secretary of Defense Testimony for the Senate Foreign Relations Committee, 22 May.

Zinni, A. (2003) 'The Future of Iraq', Hearing of the Senate Foreign Relations Committee, 11 February.

Index

Lightning Source UK Ltd.
Milton Keynes UK
UKOW04f0640100914

238310UK00001B/47/P